ROUTLEDGE LIBRARY EDITIONS: LINGUISTICS

Volume 7

THE LINGUISTIC DESCRIPTION OF OPAQUE CONTEXTS

THE LINGUISTIC DESCRIPTION OF OPAQUE CONTEXTS

JANET DEAN FODOR

LONDON AND NEW YORK

First published in 1979

This edition first published in 2014
by Routledge
2 Park Square, Milton Park, Abingdon, Oxon, OX14 4RN

Simultaneously published in the USA and Canada
by Routledge
711 Third Avenue, New York, NY 10017

Routledge is an imprint of the Taylor & Francis Group, an informa business

© 1979 Janet Dean Fodor

All rights reserved. No part of this book may be reprinted or reproduced or
utilised in any form or by any electronic, mechanical, or other means, now
known or hereafter invented, including photocopying and recording, or in any
information storage or retrieval system, without permission in writing from the
publishers.

Trademark notice: Product or corporate names may be trademarks or registered
trademarks, and are used only for identification and explanation without intent
to infringe.

British Library Cataloguing in Publication Data
A catalogue record for this book is available from the British Library

ISBN: 978-0-415-64438-9 (Set)
eISBN: 978-0-203-07902-7 (Set)
ISBN: 978-0-415-71582-9 (Volume 7)
eISBN: 978-1-315-88030-3 (Volume 7)

Publisher's Note
The publisher has gone to great lengths to ensure the quality of this book but
points out that some imperfections in the original copies may be apparent.

Disclaimer
The publisher has made every effort to trace copyright holders and would
welcome correspondence from those they have been unable to trace.

The Linguistic Description of Opaque Contexts

Janet Dean Fodor

Garland Publishing, Inc. ■ New York & London
1979

Library of Congress Cataloging in Publication Data

Fodor, Janet Dean.
  The linguistic description of opaque contexts.

  (Outstanding dissertations in linguistics ; 13)
  Originally presented as the author's thesis, MIT, 1970.
  1. Semantics.   2. Generative grammar.
I. Title.   II. Series.
P325.F58   1979   415   78-66537
ISBN 0-8240-9686-X

© 1979 Janet Dean Fodor
All rights reserved

All volumes in this series are printed on acid-free,
250-year-life paper.
Printed in the United States of America

PREFACE

The study of referential opacity, in one form or another, goes back to the Scholastic philosophers of the middle ages. In modern philosophy, the problem of opacity rears its head almost wherever one looks. For logicians it puts special demands on systems for representing the logical forms of sentences and the inference rules which apply to them. In the philosophy of language it bears on questions about the nature of meaning, by undermining the simple identification of meaning with reference. In ontology it threatens a clutter of strange imaginary entities which must either be made sense of or else be analyzed away. And in the philosophy of mind, opacity is central to questions about the language of thought, and how thoughts are related to what they are thoughts about.

The cumbersomely modest title of this dissertation was intended to make it quite clear that I wasn't even attempting to address these deep and difficult philosophical problems. Instead, I approached opaque constructions simply as sentences of a natural language whose grammar we wish to determine. The study of opacity thus falls under the general program of showing how the meaning of any complex sentence is composed from the meanings of its constituent clauses, phrases and words. Opaque constructions are special from this point of view only because

the compositional principles that determine their meaning are
so intricate. In the simplest possible case, we might expect
that what a clause contributes to the meaning of a sentence
in which it appears is just the meaning that it would have had
if it occurred alone as an independent sentence. But this is
notoriously not the case for clauses embedded as complements
to opaque predicates like <u>is necessary</u> or <u>John believes</u>.

This approach to opacity is closest to that of the logician, for it involves as a first step deciding what these sentences mean, and we can often do this by deciding what inferences
we are prepared to draw from them. It also involves a similar
project of devising a formal system for representing these
sentence meanings. The main difference is one of emphasis.
Where linguists are concerned primarily with discovering the
rules which relate meaning representations with the surface
forms of sentences, logicians concentrate on formalizing the
rules of inference which apply to the meaning representations
to specify what sentences entail. Putting these together, it
would seem that we have a splendid joint research program. But
it is a program which is bedevilled at the outset by the fact
that nobody can agree about what opaque constructions mean,
and so that is what my dissertation turned out mostly to be
about. With some hindsight, I would now add two further points
which help to explain the uncertainty and disagreement about
the data.

The main argument of the dissertation is that the

systematic ambiguity of opaque constructions has generally been underestimated. The characteristic manifestation of opacity is the variable validity of two inference rules--Existential Generalization and Substitutivity of Identicals. Traditionally it has been assumed that these two inference rules go hand in hand; an opaque construction has one interpretation to which both rules apply, and another interpretation to which neither does. What I tried to establish was that this is false. It is possible to find some relatively clear examples for which there are four distinct interpretations--the two which are usually acknowledged, and two more for which one of the inference rules is valid but the other is not. (Though I left this as a purely descriptive linguistic claim in the dissertation, I think it has some bearing on deeper questions about the source of opacity. That is, I believe the independence of the two kinds of opacity reflects the existence of two distinct peculiarities about mental states and their relation to the world. We can believe something without there having to be anything that we believe it _of_. And this is related to, but is not the same as, the fact that we can believe something if it is described in one way without necessarily believing it if it is described in another.)

A second sort of complication, which emerges here and there in the dissertation but which I now think deserves considerably more attention, is that different opaque predicates seem to have a somewhat different logic. I have in mind here iv

not only the difference between the modal operators (<u>necessarily</u>, <u>possibly</u>) and the psychological verbs (<u>believes</u>, <u>realizes</u>, <u>hopes</u>, <u>wants</u>, etc.), but also subtle differences among the psychological verbs. One rather rough and ready illustration may serve to suggest the point. Let us imagine that John wants <u>x</u>, and that he knows that <u>x</u> entails <u>y</u>. It is a sad fact about wants that in these circumstances John may very much <u>not</u> want <u>y</u>. But suppose instead that John believes <u>x</u> and knows that <u>x</u> entails <u>y</u>. Then it is at least empirically plausible, and might even be held to be logically necessary, that John also believes <u>y</u>.

I suspect that this second reason for the confusions about what opaque constructions mean is related to the third, which is much easier to appreciate now than it was in 1970. In the last few years, Hilary Putnam and others have argued that many of the inferences drawn from sentences have been miscategorized as logical entailments; in fact they are consequences of the informal (and no doubt often incorrect) empirical theories about the nature of things in the world which guide our use of the language. This thesis has been developed primarily for nouns that name 'natural kinds'. But there seems no reason why it shouldn't be equally true of verbs, including the psychological verbs which create opaque contexts. If so, then there might very well be no precise and general logic which characterizes all of these verbs. One person's notion of what believing is may be slightly different from another's, and at best they may both be a little fuzzy around the edges. Also,

v

our ideas about what believing is may not mesh perfectly with
our ideas about what wanting is.

This approach strikes me as well worth pursuing, even
though it can make one feel a little weary. How much easier it
would be to come up with a convincing theory of opacity if the
facts were tidy and inferences were either clearly valid or
clearly invalid. But it does have the interesting effect of
forcing attention onto the opposite question, viz. what is there
in common between all of the various opaque predicates which
accounts for the logical similarities that they do show? An
answer to this would be a contribution to an explanatory theory
in semantics, which we have all too little of at present. At
one further remove we might even ask what it is about certain
constituents of sentences which allows them to vary in scope
relative to other constituents. What, for example, do noun
phrases and opaque predicates have in common with negation and
adverbial modifiers? Though my dissertation documents some
anomalies in the standard representations of scope relations
in opaque constructions, it also supports the general assumption
that scope variation is what lies at the heart of it all. I
must admit, though, that I've pondered this question on and
off for years and still have no glimmer of what the answer is.

Some of these issues about opacity, and many others as
well, are addressed in more recent publications. I cannot review or even mention them all here, so I will simply list a
handful and let their bibliographies point the way to the

others. In linguistics there have been recent Ph.D. dissertations by Barbara Abbott (A Study of Referential Opacity , University of California at Berkeley, 1976) and by James Gee (Perception, Intentionality and Naked Infinitives: A Study in Linguistics and Philosophy, Stanford University, 1975), and articles by Peter Cole ("On the origins of referential opacity," in Syntax and Semantics Volume 9, Peter Cole (ed.), Academic Press, 1978), by William Greenberg ("De dicto and de re without relative scope," in Papers from the Twelfth Regional Meeting of the Chicago Linguistic Society, 1976), by Georgette Ioup ("Specificity and the interpretation of quantifiers," Linguistics and Philosophy Volume 1, 1977), by Ray Jackendoff ("On belief contexts," Linguistic Inquiry Volume 6, 1975), and by Tania Reinhart ("On certain ambiguities and uncertain scope," in Papers from the Eleventh Regional Meeting of the Chicago Linguistic Society, 1975). In philosophy there has been far more, including Jaakko Hintikka's book (The Intentions of Intentionality and Other New Models for Modalities, Reidel, 1975), and articles by Roderick Chisholm ("Knowledge and belief: 'de dicto' and 'de re'," Philosophical Studies Volume 29, 1976; "Thought and its reference," American Philosophical Quarterly Volume 14, 1977), by Keith Donnellan ("The contingent a priori and rigid designators," in Midwest Studies in Philosophy Volume II, Peter A. French, Theodore W. Uehling, Jr. and Howard K. Wettstein (eds.), The University of Minnesota, 1977), by Brian Loar ("Reference and propositional attitudes," Philosophical Review Volume 81,

1972), by Richard Sharvy ("Three types of referential opacity," Philosophy of Science Volume 39, 1972), and by W.V.O. Quine ("Intensions revisited," in Midwest Studies in Philosophy, reference as above).

Surprisingly, I still believe that most of what I wrote **nine** years ago is true. Only the last chapter, dealing with the relation between semantics and syntax, is noticeably dated. Some of its morals (e.g. that semantic representations differ in structure as well as vocabulary from syntactic representations) are now old hat. And some of the burning issues (e.g. generative versus interpretive semantics) have given way to others (interpretation of deep structure versus interpretation of surface structure, trace theory). But even if it were all true, it would still be only a very small bite out of a very large problem. I hope that the publication of this volume will be useful, even if only to save others the trouble of taking the same bite again.

THE LINGUISTIC DESCRIPTION OF OPAQUE CONTEXTS

by

JANET DEAN FODOR

B.A.(Hons.) Oxford University

(1964)

SUBMITTED IN PARTIAL FULFILLMENT

OF THE REQUIREMENTS FOR THE

DEGREE OF DOCTOR OF

PHILOSOPHY

at the

MASSACHUSETTS INSTITUTE OF

TECHNOLOGY

June, 1970

CONTENTS

CHAPTER I.   INTRODUCTION.
             Section 1.   The definition of opacity........ 1
             Section 2.   Opacity and linguistic
                          description...................... 13
             Section 3.   Linguistics and formal logic...... 18
             Section 4.   Organisation of the work......... 24

CHAPTER II. OPACITY AND INDEFINITE NOUN PHRASES.
             Section 1.   Opacity and scope................ 27
             Section 2.   Specificity and the existential
                          quantifier...................... 38
             Section 3.   Non-specific noun phrases and
                          existence....................... 48
             Section 4.   The conjunctive analysis of noun
                          phrases......................... 65
             Section 5.   Specific noun phrases and
                          existence....................... 90
             Section 6.   Logical relationships between
                          the readings....................113

CHAPTER III. OPACITY AND DEFINITE NOUN PHRASES.
             Section 1.   The referential/attributive
                          ambiguity.......................130
             Section 2.   The referential/attributive
                          distinction as a scope phenomenon.136
             Section 3.   Definite noun phrases and the
                          universal quantifier.............143
             Section 4.   All, every, each and opaque
                          contexts........................153
             Section 5.   Referential and attributive noun
                          phrases and existence............168
             Section 6.   On knowing who...................184
             Section 7.   Predicate nominals and attributive
                          noun phrases....................202
             Section 8.   Logical relationships between
                          definite and indefinite noun
                          phrases.........................215

CHAPTER IV. OPACITY AND DESCRIPTIONS.
             Section 1.   The ambiguity of the descriptive
                          content of noun phrases..........224
             Section 2.   The formal representation of the
                          ambiguity.......................232
             Section 3.   Paradoxes of scope...............239
             Section 4.   Simplification of conjunctions
                          and the opaque reading...........243

Section 5.	The speaker's responsibility for the description	247
Section 6.	Peculiarities of the scope of the description operator	276
Section 7.	The substitutivity of non-nominal constituents	282
Section 8.	Descriptive content and surface structure	290
Section 9.	Implications for semantic representation	296
Section 10.	The meaning of 'under the description...'	299
Section 11.	Some further logical relationships between noun phrases	306

CHAPTER V. THE SYNTAX OF OPAQUE CONSTRUCTIONS.

Section 1.	Introduction	313
Section 2.	Surface structures and semantic interpretation	315
Section 3.	Opacity and the level of deep structure	319
Section 4.	Specificity and deep structures. 'There is...' constructions	338

For Katherine, who once was Ffitzwilliam.

ACKNOWLEDGEMENTS.

I wish to thank Professors Noam Chomsky, James Thomson and John Ross for reading this thesis and providing, in the very short time I allowed them, a great many helpful comments and criticisms. I am also grateful to Michael Harnish for his observations and his encouragement. I regret that I have not been able to incorporate all of the suggestions that I have received; none of those who have advised me should be held responsible for my errors and confusions.

My husband, Jerry Fodor, was tolerant of my tantrums in the early stages of this work and of my neglect of him in the later stages. He also suffered through long and tortuous discussions at all hours of the day and night, and thereby saved me from many of my most embarrassing mistakes. I doubt whether, without his support, I would have completed this thesis.

My dog, Humphrey, kept me company through long hours at the typewriter and took me for walks three times a day.

And then there is Ffitzwilliam, whom I wish a happy birthday.

```
    O   O     O   O
    O   O     O   O   O
    O   O     O   O   O
   FISH FISH  FISH FISH  O
        I WANT TO CATCH A FISH
      O   O     O   O   O
      O   O     O   O   O
      O   O     O   O   O
     FISH FISH    FISH FISH FISH
```

(Mel's thoughts)

_____

```
    o     o     o   o
    o     o     o   o  o
    o     o     o   o  o
   fish  fish  fish fish o
         I want to catch a fish
       o   o   o   o   o
       o   o   o   o   o
       o   o   o   o   o
      fish  fish  fish fish fish
                  o
                  o
                  o
   I want to catch a fish
   I want to I want to I want to
                  o
                  o
                  o
     want to catch a fish
                o   o
                o   o
                o   o
       catch a fish fish   want to
   want to want to want to
      want want  want
         o          o
         o          o
         o          o
      a fish to catch a fish to catch
     catch  catch  catch a  catch a  catch
         o        o   o
         o        o   o
         o        o   o
   catch a fish  catch a fish fish
                         o
                         o
                         o
     and then I want to catch another one
```

This poem by Keith Gunderson is from his collection <u>A Continual Interest in the Sun and Sea, & Inland Missing the Sea</u>, Nodin Press 1977. Gunderson explains that Mel is an excellent potter but unskilled fisherperson. The poem is a record of his fantasy life wherein he dreams of emulating the poet's fishing prowess.

CHAPTER I. INTRODUCTION.

Section 1. The definition of opacity.

The terms 'opaque context' or 'opaque construction' are used of a certain general class of sentence forms with characteristic logical properties. Two inference rules, existential generalization and substitutivity of identicals, which are otherwise valid, give rise to invalid arguments when applied to opaque contexts.

A simple case of existential generalization is the inference, obviously valid, from (1) to (2) or (3).

(1) My brother is a busdriver.

(2) Someone is a busdriver.

(3) There is someone (at least one person) who is a busdriver. As a formal inference rule, existential generalization consists of replacing a constant term in a formula by a variable not already present in the formula, and prefacing the whole with an existential quantifier binding that variable.

Now suppose we consider the sentence:

(4) Mary doesn't realise that my brother is a busdriver. and formalize it partially as:

(5) Mary doesn't realise Fa.

Existential generalization of (5) yields:

(6) ($\exists$x) Mary doesn't realise Fx.

which corresponds to the English sentence:

(7) There is someone whom Mary doesn't realise is a busdriver.

This, however, does not constitute a valid inference from (4), though at first sight it may seem to. Sentence (4) can be construed in such a way that it is quite compatible with Mary's knowing of my brother that he is a busdriver -- what she fails to realise may be merely that the person whom she knows to be a busdriver is my brother. If (4) is construed in this way it does not entail that my brother is someone such that Mary doesn't realise that he is a busdriver. And though (4), on this interpretation, is compatible with (7), since there may of course be someone else whom Mary doesn't realise is a busdriver, it certainly does not entail (7).

There is an alternative way of construing (4), for which (4) is true only if my brother is such that Mary doesn't realise of him, under any description, that he is a busdriver. On this interpretation, the inference from (4) to (7) is valid. This does not alter the fact that the rule of existential generalization must not be allowed to apply freely to sentences like (4). What it does show is that the problem posed by opaque contexts is to find a way of capturing valid inferences like this one without simultaneously generating any invalid arguments. We obviously cannot do this if the logical inference rules are applied to the surface forms of sentences, for the two readings of (4) that we have observed, which differ with respect to the validity of existential generalization, can both be expressed by one and the same surface structure. What we must do, therefore, is to provide two formally distinct

3

representations of the sentence, one for each of these two readings. The applicability of the rule of existential generalization can then be made conditional upon some formal property of representations of this kind, a property common to the representation of one of the two readings of (4), and the representations of other sentences, like (1) above, for which existential generalization is generally valid.

Another problem about existence and opaque contexts arises in connection with sentences where existential generalization itself is not strictly at issue. Sentence (8) is ambiguous.

(8) Mary believes that a friend of mine is a busdriver.

It contains no proper name or definite description, and it would not be formalised with a constant, as in (5). There is therefore no question here of whether or not it is valid to substitute a bound variable for a constant. Instead sentence (8) would be formalised directly by means of a bound variable, and the question that arises is where to position the binding quantifier. Is it proper to represent (8) as:

(9) ($\exists$x) (x is a friend of mine and Mary believes x is a
busdriver).

Once again, the answer is that the sentence is ambiguous, and what we should say about its logical form depends upon which of its readings we are considering. Certainly sentence (8) can be construed in such a way that (9), or the corresponding

English sentence:

(10)   There is a friend of mine whom Mary believes to be a
busdriver.

captures its meaning correctly. But (8) is also, on another
reading, compatible with the falsity of (9) or (10), since Mary
might believe that there is a friend of mine who is a busdriver
without there being anyone in particular of whom it would be
true to say that Mary believes that he is a friend of mine and
a busdriver. This reading of (8) can apparently be paraphrased
as:

(11)   Mary believes that there is a friend of mine who is a
busdriver.

which suggests formalizing it as:

(12)   Mary believes ($\exists$x) (x is a friend of mine and x is a
busdriver).

in contrast to (9).

As with the earlier examples, we cannot afford to ignore
the ambiguity of sentences like (8), for certain kinds of
argument are valid or invalid depending on which reading is
concerned. A simple example is the inference from (8) to the
conclusion that there is a friend of mine, that is, that I
have at least one friend. This is a legitimate inference
from (8) on the first of the two readings that we considered, but
it is illegitimate on the second one. The problem once again
is therefore to provide distinct representations for each

reading of an ambiguous sentence so that the inference rules can apply differentially to the different readings.

Notice that in cases like (8) the ambiguous sentence has two distinct natural language paraphrases, whose form suggests one quite natural way of extending the standard system of predicate calculus to provide the kind of formal representations that we need; the difference in position of the words there is in the informal paraphrases (10) and (11) suggests using difference of position of the existential quantifier, as in (9) and (12), to mark the distinction in formal logical representations of (8). There are undoubtedly other ways, however, in which this distinction could be marked, and it is with the consequences for the logical system in general of. adopting one way rather than another of marking it that much of the philosophical literature on opacity is concerned. The following chapters will be largely concerned with the analogous question with respect to systems of linguistic description.

In addition to problems concerning existence, opaque contexts pose a problem in connection with the substitution of one name or description of an object for another. This can be illustrated by means of sentence (4) again. The argument from (13) and (14) to (15) is valid.

(13) My (only) brother is a busdriver.

(14) Tom is my (only) brother.

(15) Tom is a busdriver.

Within an opaque context, however, this kind of inference is
not valid. Thus (18) does not follow from (16) and (17).

(16) Mary doesn't realise that my (only) brother is a busdriver.

(17) Tom is my (only) brother.

(18) Mary doesn't realise that Tom is a busdriver.

In the light of the earlier discussion of sentence (4), the
reason why this argument is not valid should be obvious.
Sentence (16) can be construed in such a way that it is
compatible with Mary's knowing of someone that he is a busdriver, and even with her knowing of the person who is, in
fact, my brother, that he is a busdriver. For it may be that
what she fails to realise is just that this person whom she
knows to be a busdriver is my brother. But since it is quite
possible that Mary should realise that one person she knows to
be a busdriver is Tom, it follows that (18) might well be
false even though (16) and (17) were true. It is clear,
therefore, that (18) is not entailed by (16) and (17).

But sentence (16) is ambiguous and can be read as saying
that Mary does not realise of my brother Tom, under any
description at all, that he is a busdriver. On this reading
the argument from (16) and (17) to (18) is valid. Therefore,
just as for the inference rules governing existential inferences,
the proper move is not to block the substitutivity of identicals
in general, or even to block it for a sentence like (16). It
is rather to devise some way of distinguishing formally between

the different readings of such sentences so that the inference
rule can be set up so as to apply to the sentence on one
reading but not on another.

The examples that I have used to illustrate the nature
of opacity have all been ambiguous. Each can be read in such
a way that existential generalization and the substitutivity
of identicals give rise to invalid arguments, but each has, in
addition, a reading for which these inference rules are valid.
This appears, in fact, to be a general truth about opaque
contexts. Although there are a great many sentences, for
example (1) above, which have no opaque reading at all, it
seems that any sentence which does have an opaque reading also
has a non-opaque ('transparent') reading, for which the usual
inference rules hold. The only obvious exception to this is
the case of quotation. Quine (Word and Object, p. 142) gives
the example:

(19)   'Tully was a Roman' is trochaic.

and there is surely no way of reading this sentence which
would permit one either to infer:

(2)   There is someone such that 'he is a Roman' is trochaic.

or, given the extra premise:

(21)   Tully is (was) Cicero.

to infer:

(22)   'Cicero was a Roman' is trochaic.

Examples involving the direct quotation of speech are similar, for example:

(23)   John said 'Tully was a Roman'.

Quine also gives the example (p. 153):

(24)   Giorgione was so-called because of his size.

from which we cannot infer:

(25)   There is someone who was so-called because of his size.

nor, even given the extra premise:

(26)   Giorgione is (was) Barbarelli.

can we infer:

(27)   Barbarelli was so-called because of his size.

since (27) is false though (24) is true. However, the absence of any transparent reading of (24) for which such arguments are valid probably should not be regarded as violating the general rule that all opaque contexts other than quotational ones also have transparent readings. As Quine points out, (24) can be paraphrased as:

(28)   Giorgione was called 'Giorgione' because of his size.

and, if this paraphrase is taken as the proper analysis of the sentence, then what we have is simply another example of quotation.

An assumption which is at least implicit in almost all discussions of opacity is that the two inference rules, existential generalization and the substitutivity of identicals, stand or fall together; that these two criteria pick out exactly the same set of sentences. Indeed, in many cases it seems that the implicit claim is that it is <u>because</u> of the failure of one of these rules in certain contexts that the other rule is also invalid. There are, however, examples which suggest that this cannot be the case. Thus the sentence:

(29) He recognised his long lost daughter.

appears to have no reading which does not permit existential generalization, i.e. the inference of:

(30) There is someone that he recognised.

Yet with respect to the substitutivity of identicals (29) is ambiguous. We can take it to mean that he recognised his daughter <u>as</u> his daughter, that is, that he realised that she was his daughter. In this case (29) is not logically equivalent for example to (30):

(30) He recognised his usual waitress.

even if, in fact, his usual waitress was his long lost daughter. On the other hand, if we take (29) to mean simply that he recognised a certain person (a person who happened, as a matter of fact, to be his long lost daughter) as someone familiar to him in some way, with no implication that he realised that this person was his daughter, then the substitutivity of identicals <u>is</u> valid. Thus the context:

(31) He recognised.....

is apparently transparent by the criterion of existential generalization but opaque by the criterion of substitutivity

of identicals, and the two criteria therefore cannot be held
to be co-extensive. It should be admitted, however, that
examples of this kind are not common. Furthermore it is
arguable whether there are any examples which are opaque by
the criterion of existential generalization but transparent by
the criterion of substitutivity of identicals. If, therefore,
we deny that there is some necessary connection between the
validity of these two rules, we do at least owe some account
of the very extensive correlation between them.

It appears, however, that an even stronger version of
this claim is generally held to be true, that is, that any
reading of a sentence for which one of these two inference
rules is valid is a reading for which the other rule is also
valid. Thus if we interpret a sentence in such a way that we
are prepared to accept existential generalization of it, then,
it is claimed, we must also accept the substitution of co-
extensive descriptive phrases, and vice versa. It is this
point which Quine seems to be making in the following passage
(Word and Object, p. 148).

> ...see what urgent information the sentence 'There
> is someone whom I believe to be a spy' imparts, in
> contrast to 'I believe that someone is a spy' (in
> the weak sense of 'I believe there are spies'). The
> one corresponds to (2) [i.e. Someone is such that Tom
> believes that he denounced Catiline], the other to
> (1) [i.e. Tom believes that someone (is such that he)
> denounced Catiline]. Surely, therefore, the transparent
> sense of belief is not to be lightly dismissed. Yet
> let its urgency not blind us to its oddity. "Tully,"
> Tom insists, "did not denounce Catiline. Cicero did."
> Surely Tom must be acknowledged to believe, in every

> sense, that Tully did denounce Catiline. The oddity
> of the transparent sense of belief is that it has Tom
> believing that Tully did and that he did not denounce
> Catiline. This is not yet a contradiction on our part
> or even on Tom's, for a distinction can be reserved
> between (a) Tom's believing that Tully did and that
> Tully did not denounce Catiline, and (b) Tom's believing
> that Tully did and did not denounce Catiline. But the
> oddity is there, and we have to accept it as the price
> of saying such things as (2) or that there is someone
> whom one believes to be a spy.

Quine talks of the transparent sense of belief, and it is clear

from this, and from the passage in general, that he does not

recognise the possibility of reading his examples in such a

way that they are transparent with respect to existential

generalization but opaque with respect to the substitutivity of

identicals or vice versa. The last sentence of this passage in

fact strongly suggests that he regards this as impossible.

Sentence (29) is sufficient to falsify the claim that a

reading of a sentence which is opaque by one of the two criteria

is necessarily a reading which is opaque by the other. But I

shall also argue, in Chapter IV, that this claim is in general

quite false and that the two criteria are in this sense

completely independent. And I hope to make it clear in the

course of this work that the failure to realise this has led to

considerable confusion about the nature of opacity, and,

inevitably, to confusion about how opaque readings of sentences

can be represented in a formal system of logic or linguistic

description.

In the light of these remarks, some comments on

terminology are probably in order at this point. Opaque

contexts are customarily defined as those for which the rules
of existential generalization and substitutivity of identicals
do not hold. We have already had occasion, however, to use
the term 'opaque' and the complementary term 'transparent' in
two quite distinct ways. A context may be called opaque if
it is open to at least one reading for which these rules of
inference do not hold, on the grounds that this one reading
is sufficient to invalidate the application of the inference
rules to that context. On the other hand, the systematic
ambiguity of the examples means that we shall be concerned
largely with distinguishing between the various readings of a
context which is opaque in this sense. Thus we shall want to
be able to refer to an opaque reading of a context, a reading
for which the inference rules are invalid, and to a transparent
reading of it, a reading for which the inference rules are
valid. I shall try always to make it clear whether I am
referring to an opaque context, where 'context' means something
that can be ambiguous, and where I am referring to an opaque
reading of a context. The latter will much more commonly be
the case.

In view of my claim that the two criteria for opacity
are logically independent, I shall also distinguish between a
reading of a sentence which is opaque or transparent with
respect to existential generalization, and a reading which
is opaque or transparent with respect to the substitutivity of

identicals. The former kind of opacity is often referred to in the linguistic literature as 'non-specificity', and the latter kind as the opacity of descriptive content, and I shall make use of these terms too. I shall also use the terms 'opaque' and 'transparent' somewhat indiscriminately to characterise contexts in which noun phrases may occur, such as Mary believes...is a busdriver, and also to characterise complete sentences, such as Mary believes Tom is a busdriver, though in this case it will usually be necessary to specify which noun phrase in the sentence is under consideration. I shall even, on occasion, characterise an instance of a noun phrase as either opaque or transparent, for example the noun phrase Tom in the sentence above. This usage is sloppy but it is extremely convenient and not, as far as I can see, in any dangerous way misleading. In all of these ways of talking, a certain noun phrase in a sentence is singled out and is said either to be subject to, or not to be subject to, either existential generalization or substitutivity.

Section 2. Opacity and linguistic descriptions.

Any sentences of any natural language are of course legitimate data for the linguist, but it should be clear from the preceding section that opaque constructions are a class of sentences of special interest. Their characteristic behavior in connection with certain logical inference rules is simply an indication that they have certain special semantic characteristics, and a complete description of a language must contain some account of these. It must also state <u>which</u> sentences of a language have these characteristics. The criteria for opacity given in the previous section were logical (i.e. semantic) criteria, not syntactic ones, and in fact it appears that there are no syntactic characteristics (at least no superficial ones) which correlate exactly with the existence of an opaque reading of a sentence and which could therefore be used as a criterion for opacity. A rather striking partial correlation between syntactic form and opacity does exist, however, at least in English. With some exceptions on either side, it is just those sentences which exhibit complement structure that have opaque. readings. Exceptions to this are sentences containing modal verbs, for example:

(32) John should buy a raincoat.

(33) We may see an elephant.

and sentences containing certain verbs such as <u>recognise</u>, <u>look for</u>, thus:

(34) He recognised his long lost daughter.

(35) I am looking for a telephone directory.

Each of these sentences has a reading which is opaque by at least one of the two logical criteria. An exception of the opposite kind is a complement construction where the main verb is <u>true</u>:

(36) It is true that Bill trod on a snail.

(37) It is true that my brother is a busdriver.

Such sentences apparently have no opaque reading.

If we ignore these exceptional cases for the moment, what we are dealing with when we study opaque contexts is one case of what Katz and Fodor (The Structure of a Semantic Theory, Language 1963) call 'the projection problem'. The meaning of a sentence is a function of the particular lexical items that it contains and the grammatical relations which hold between these items. The grammar must contain rules which state how the grammatical relations between the constituents of any given sentence determine how the meanings of these constituents interact to determine the meaning of the sentence as a whole. In the case of opaque contexts, it appears that we are dealing with the projection problem for sentoids subordinated as complements to higher verbs. What we need is a general set of rules which show how the meanings of the constituents of a sentoid are affected by the presence of a higher verb to which that sentoid is subordinated; in particular how and why the semantic properties of noun phrases in such a sentoid differ from those which they exhibit when the sentoid stands alone as an independent sentence. Thus the task is to give a general semantic description of complement constructions, and to state the rules which map formal representations of the meanings of these constructions onto representations of their superficial syntactic form.

A complete account of opacity would, ideally, also provide an explanation, rather than a mere statement, of the fact that every sentence which has an opaque reading also has a transparent reading and of the fact that the converse does not hold. It would also explain why just those sentences which have an opaque interpretation have one, and why those which do not do not. As far as I know, no explicit answer to this latter question has been given, but there is a very widespread implicit assumption in the literature on opacity that the correlation between opacity and complement structure is no accident. This assumption comes out in decisions as to how the logical form of opaque contexts should be represented. It is generally assumed that the natural state of affairs, the 'unmarked case', is that a noun phrase within a complement clause should be interpreted opaquely and a noun phrase not in such a clause should be interpreted transparently. Thus in order to represent a reading of a sentence for which a noun phrase within a complement clause is interpreted as transparent, it is usual to position this noun phrase, (or some representative of it such as a quantifier binding it) in the main clause. To represent the opaque interpretation of such a noun phrase, it and any quantifier or other element related to it, is simply left within the complement clause. We have in fact already seen an example of this in the contrast between (9) and (12)

17

above. Furthermore, it is often suggested that sentences which have an opaque reading but which do not contain overt complement structure should be represented by means of formal structures which do. Thus Quine (J. of Phil. 1956) suggests representing the two readings of the sentence:

(38) I want a sloop.

in the following way:

(39) ($\exists$x) (x is a sloop and I wish that I have x).

(40) I wish that ($\exists$x) (x is a sloop and I have x).

where the verb want is replaced by the overt complement construction wish that I have. Thus a whole system of formal representation for opaque contexts has been considered which is essentially tied to the concept of complement structure.

Some justification for this approach will be found in the following chapters. It is worth pointing out here, however, that if there is indeed something in the idea that there is an inherent connection between opacity and complement structure, then there is a very simple answer to our other question, viz. why every sentence that has an opaque interpretation should also have a transparent one though not vice versa. In a sentence containing a complement clause, every constituent of the complement clause is, ipso facto, a constituent of the sentence as a whole. But not all constituents of a sentence are constituents of a complement clause. Thus if being a constituent of a complement clause is what is required for

having an opaque interpretation, and being a constituent of
something other than a complement clause is what is required
for having a transparent interpretation, then our observation
is explained.

Section 3. Linguistics and formal logic.

The syntactic properties of complement constructions in
English are, if not fully determined, at least as well understood as those of most other aspects of English syntax. If
we were also in possession of an adequate semantic description
of these constructions, we would be able to concentrate on an
examination of the rules needed to define a mapping between
the syntactic and the semantic structures. The mapping would
be constrained at both ends, and it would thus be reasonable
to hope that conclusions about its formal properties would be
somewhat more secure than is often the case.

A great deal of attention has been directed recently to
the formal nature of this mapping, and it has become clear
that the problem is not so much that of devising a formal
system which will do the job, as of evaluating the many types
of system which are available in principle and of selecting
between them in some motivated way. The desire to impose
strong semantic constraints as well as surface syntactic ones
in order to limit this choice is surely much of the reason for
the growing trend amongst linguists to concentrate on those
semantic phenomena which have already been studied in detail

by logicians. The idea, very roughly, seems to be that the work of the logician will provide us with a precise and detailed account of the semantic phenomena in question, embodied in a system of formal representations of sentences, and that these representations can be adopted as a model for semantic representations in a linguistic description of the language. With the semantic representations fixed, it should be possible to draw some conclusions about the nature of the system required to map them onto surface syntactic structures. Even if this is in fact an exaggeration of the attitude of many linguists to logic, it is worth considering briefly the nature of the relationship between the two fields, so that when we do refer to the work done in logic, we are aware of the status of any claims we make on the basis of it. In particular, the present study of opacity is heavily indebted to the work of logicians and philosophers. Although it will become clear to some extent in later chapters, I should give some account of my own approach to this work and of why I have not, in fact, been able to take over its conclusions, unrevised, as the foundation for a grammar of this area of English.

There are two reasons for this. One is that the logic of opaque contexts is not at present in any state to be taken as the foundation for anything except further work. This is not intended as criticism, for the problems in this area are enormous. One is dealing almost entirely with ambiguous

sentences, sentences whose possible readings often differ in
such subtle ways that one is in doubt even as to how many
readings a given sentence should be assigned. A great deal
turns on whether certain sentences are or are not ambiguous in
certain ways, but independent corroboration of one's intuitions
is hard to come by, since the suspected ambiguities are often
apparent only upon very careful consideration and are overlooked
or misconstrued by the naive native speaker. Furthermore,
although there are certain logical-semantic characteristics
which are shared by the whole class of opaque constructions,
these tend to interact in complex ways with the semantic
properties of particular lexical items or classes of lexical
items. Certain very limited classes of opaque constructions,
such as those connected with the concepts of necessity and
possibility (cf. Hughes and Cresswell, 1968, for example), or
with belief and knowledge (cf. Hintikka, 1962), have been
studied in detail and at least a partial system of formal
representations and inference rules has been developed for
them. Even in these areas, most logicians would, I am sure,
be the first to agree that a great many unsolved problems
still exist. For other classes of opaque contexts there
exists little more than a body of informal remarks about the
properties that a formal system will eventually have to have.
Thus even a linguist who is in principle prepared to accept the
logicians' analyses as the basis for a grammar of opaque contexts will find that nothing like a complete system exists

for him to borrow.

Even if there were such a complete system, however, it is not obvious that it would be suitable for incorporation into a linguistic description. It is true that both the linguist and the logician are interested in providing formal representations of the semantic characteristics of the sentences of a natural language. (There are, of course, whole areas of logic which are not concerned with this at all, for example the study of the foundations of mathematics.) It cannot simply be assumed, however, that the types of formal representational system they devise will necessarily be identical. The interests of the linguist and the logician in the sentences of a natural language differ in emphasis and priorities, even if not in principle. For the logician the primary task is to formulate a set of inference rules which, when applied to the representations of sentences, determine their entailments and thus the class of valid arguments into which they enter. The job of formulating principles for assigning appropriate formal representations to the sentences of the language is one which the logician tends to acknowledge in principle but disregard in practice, in favour of studying the properties of the formal system itself: its axioms, inference rules, well-formedness conditions, and general properties such as consistency and completeness. It is obvious that, for the linguist, though the set of inference rules is interesting inasmuch as it defines certain semantic relationships between sentences, the primary task is to formulate the rules which relate semantic representations to syntactic (and ultimately phonological) representations.

In a formal system, whether of logic or linguistics, the applicability of the rules of the system to its formulae must be mechanically determinable -- whether or not a given rule applies to a given formula must depend solely on the configurations of symbols in the formula and in the formal statement of the rule. Thus the rules of the system and the nature of its formulae interact very closely and neither can be decided upon independently. A decision about one affects, and is affected by, decisions about the other. Semantic representations will interact both with inference rules and with rules which map them onto surface structures, and it is quite possible that by concentrating on one of these sets of rules rather than the other, we will be led to different conclusions about the optimal form of semantic representations. One might suspect that simplicity considerations, if nothing else, would actually pull in opposite directions in the two cases. The closer the semantic representations to surface structures, the simpler the grammatical system could be, but, in all likelihood, the definition of entailment relationships over these structures would thereby be complicated. A system of logic, developed with little or no reference to the task

of correlating its formal representations with the surface
structures of sentences of a natural language, however adequate
it may be as a system of logic, may be far from optimal from
the point of view of a linguistic description of that language.

A well-developed logical system may be a helpful source
of semantic insights to the linguist, and also a source of
ideas as to how a certain semantic phenomenon could be formally
represented. That it cannot tell us how it should be represented
should be clear simply from the fact that there may well exist
two or more alternative logical systems which describe the
same set of phenomena. Unless these systems can be shown to
be 'mere notational variants' (and this is a concept which it
is not at all easy to define), we must at the very least
select between these alternative systems as models for a
linguistic description. And there is, of course, no guarantee
that some further system might not be developed which would
be preferable to any which is currently available. What we
should ultimately be seeking, obviously, is the optimal overall
system in which the different, and probably conflicting,
demands of syntactic and logical-semantic representation are
both satisfied as simply and generally as possible. Semantic
information will certainly serve to constrain the choice
between different possible types of mapping between syntactic
and semantic representations. But it is misleading to imply
that the semantic representations could be fully determined
independently. Rather they will, in their turn, be constrained

by the requirements of the syntax.

Section 4. Organisation of the work.

It was my intention in beginning this work to use it to illustrate the kind of general remarks of the preceding section by treating it as an exercise in evaluating and modifying a system of formal logic from the point of view of its suitability as a model for linguistic descriptions. I soon found, however, that there exists only a very incomplete and somewhat confused logical analysis of opaque constructions in general, apart from special areas such as modal logic and epistemic logic. Although some broad suggestions have been made, many questions remain concerning the details of both the formal representations and the inference rules which would apply to them. What I have in fact attempted to do, therefore, is to fill in the answers to some of these questions and thus to develop a logic of opacity, simultaneously keeping in mind the need to correlate the semantic representations assigned to sentences with representations of their surface structure.

The discussion is organised roughly around the two criteria for opacity, the failure of existential generalization and the failure of substitutivity of identicals, and other semantic phenomena associated with each. Chapter II deals with indefinite noun phrases in opaque contexts and the validity of existential inferences from such sentences. In Chapter III some analogous phenomena associated with definite noun phrases in opaque contexts are examined. In both cases I have attempted first to determine the general nature of the semantic phenomena under consideration, in order to delineate the minimal formal characteristics of any system of semantic representation adequate for capturing the meanings of opaque sentences. To a large extent my conclusions on this question agree with the assumptions to be found in the philosophical literature. A second question then arises, which is what particular embodiment of such a formal representational system we should adopt; which particular semantic markers or operators with the appropriate formal properties should actually appear in the semantic representations. To answer this requires a detailed examination of the entailments of the various readings of opaque constructions, and of the semantic and logical relationships among them, and between them and other sentences of English. My observations and conclusions on this matter differ in certain respects from those of the philosophical literature.

The failure of the substitutivity of identicals is the topic of Chapter IV. I argue for the claim outlined in Section 1 above, that this phenomenon is independent of those related to existential generalization. I then attempt to show that the general nature of the phenomenon differs in significant ways from that of the phenomena discussed in Chapters II and III, and thus makes different demands on a representational system.

Finally, in Chapter V, I turn from a semantic analysis of opaque constructions to a consideration of their syntactic properties, and the nature of the system of grammatical rules which provides a mapping between the two.

CHAPTER II. OPACITY AND INDEFINITE NOUN PHRASES.

Section 1. Opacity and scope.

It was observed in the previous chapter that the sentence:

(1) Mary believes that a friend of mine is a busdriver.

has at least two possible readings. It has a transparent reading, on which it means that there is some particular friend of mine such that Mary believes he is a busdriver, and it has an opaque reading, on which it means simply that Mary believes that there is a friend of mine who is a busdriver, though she may not know, or may not be concerned with, which particular friend it is. In the linguistic literature, the first reading is usually characterised as one on which the noun phrase a friend of mine is specific, and the second as one on which the noun phrase a friend of mine is non-specific.

Though perhaps not intentionally, these two different kinds of terminology hint at two different approaches to the problem of characterising the nature of the ambiguity of a sentence like (1). Talk of specific and non-specific noun phrases suggests that the ambiguity is located in the noun phrase, thus that in (1) it is the phrase a friend of mine which has two possible readings. Talk of transparent and opaque contexts suggests that it is the rest of the sentence, the context in which the noun phrase appears, which is ambiguous. In particular, since it is apparently the main verb of the sentence which determines whether there is an opaque reading or not, we might suppose that the ambiguity is located in this verb. One does in fact find references in the philosophical literature to 'the transparent sense of belief' (or 'of believes') and 'the opaque sense of belief' (or 'of believes'). What I shall attempt to show is that neither of these accounts of the ambiguity is correct; the ambiguity of (1) consists neither in the ambiguity of believe nor in the ambiguity of a friend of mine. There are, in fact, no constituents in this sentence which are in themselves ambiguous, and we cannot account for the ambiguity by providing two distinct dictionary entries for any lexical item(s). The ambiguity is a relational one, much more like that of the phrase old men and women than like that of light coat or colourful ball.

It can easily be demonstrated that marking the verb as ambiguous is inadequate. A sentence which has two indefinite noun phrases in a complement clause has four possible readings of the relevant kind. Thus the sentence:

(2) Mary believes that a friend of mine swallowed a dime.

can be taken to mean (a) there is a particular friend of mine and a particular dime such that Mary believes that the one swallowed the other, (b) there is a particular friend of mine such that Mary believes that he swallowed some dime or other, (c) there is a particular dime such that Mary believes that some friend or other of mine swallowed it, (d) Mary believes that some friend or other of mine swallowed some dime or other. A similar sentence with three indefinite noun phrases in its complement has eight possible readings, with four indefinite noun phrases there are sixteen possible readings, and so on. In other words, the specificity of any one noun phrase in the complement varies independently of that of any others. The important point is that there are readings on which one noun phrase is specific and another is non-specific. If we locate the ambiguity in the verb, we should have to say, for such a reading, that the verb simultaneously has both of its possible readings, and this is absurd. Notice that what is ruled out is any kind of analysis which ascribes the ambiguity of sentences like (1) and (2) to there being alternative dictionary entries for _believe_. It makes no difference what form these dictionary entries take, whether, for example, they are sets of semantic markers, or whether they are complex semantic markers containing open positions into which semantic material from other designated constituents of the sentence is to be inserted. The latter device does make possible the characterization of certain relational ambiguities, but it cannot, at least without serious modification, cope with examples where the number of possible readings depends upon the number of constituents of a certain kind in the sentence, where the number is in principle unlimited.

The dependence of the number of possible readings on the number of noun phrases in the complement clause shows that

it is not the matrix verb which is the locus of the ambiguity.
We can also show that the noun phrases are not the locus of the
ambiguity by showing that the number of possible readings
depends upon the number of matrix verbs in the sentence, i.e.
upon the degree of embedding. If we add an extra matrix
clause to sentence (1), for example:

(3)   I hope that Mary believes that a friend of mine is a
                                            busdriver.

we find that the resulting sentence has three possible readings
with respect to specificity. Sentence (3) can be taken to
mean (a) there is a certain friend of mine such that I hope
that Mary believes that he is a busdriver, (b) I hope that
there is some friend of mine such that Mary believes that he
is a busdriver, (c) I hope that Mary believes that there is a
friend of mine who is a busdriver. Embedding sentence (3) as
the complement to yet another matrix verb would produce a
sentence with four possible readings. Though the ability to
keep track of the various readings diminishes rapidly beyond
this point, it should be clear that every time we add an
extra matrix clause we increase the number of possible readings
of the sentence by one.

The terms 'specific' and 'non-specific', with their
implicit suggestion that the distinction is a binary one,
are therefore misleading. There are, roughly, as many ways of
reading a sentence as there are clauses in which the noun

phrase in question appears.[FN] This is already sufficient to show that a simple feature system, of the kind that is often used in linguistic descriptions for marking syntactic or semantic distinctions, will not be adequate for distinguishing the possible readings of opaque constructions. Since there is no limit to the number of complement clauses that a sentence may contain, there would be no limit to the number of values that a feature would have to be able to assume in order to represent the full range of possible readings. Even if some upper bound were to be fixed arbitrarily, it is clear that a multi-valued feature would be inappropriate for it would be too rich a representational device for simpler sentences. That is, for many sentences it would predict more degrees of ambiguity than they in fact exhibit. Thus at best we would need a variable-valued feature, with the number of values it

---

FN. Clauses below that in which the noun phrase directly appears, at least in deep structure, do not contribute possible readings. Furthermore, it is in general only unbroken sequences of mutually embedded complement clauses for which this numerical correlation between number of readings and number of clauses holds. Embedding a sentence as a relative clause, or as an adverbial, does not increase its number of readings, though adding an adverbial to the sentence does in some cases do so. See Chapter V for further details of this. Sentences with verbs like look for are also, of course, exceptions to the numerical generalization, since they have a non-specific as well as a specific reading even when they are not embedded as complements to higher clauses. These cases will also be discussed in Chapter V. Meanwhile, I shall restrict my discussion of opacity to those cases in which it is associated with complement structure.

could assume for any given sentence determined somehow by the number of clauses in the sentence. This begins to sound quite bizarre, and in any case it can be seen to be inadequate for another reason.

Although in many cases it is insufficient to designate a noun phrase as simply specific or non-specific, the idea of a scale of specificity values is not appropriate either, in view of the kinds of paraphrase we have to supply to distinguish between the various possible readings. It is not just the number of readings that varies with the number of clauses in the sentence; the nature of these readings is also essentially connected with which clauses are present. The noun phrase a friend of mine in our examples is not in itself ambiguous -- there appears to be no way of paraphrasing just that phrase in order to capture the possible readings of the sentences. (Notice that to paraphrase it as a certain friend of mine as opposed to some friend or other of mine would be insufficient in just the same way as using a binary abstract feature would be insufficient. Neither permits sufficient distinctions to be made.) In order to bring out the different readings, we have to paraphrase not just the noun phrase in question, but the whole sentence. What we have to mark is not a degree of specificity, like a degree of rounding in a vowel. It is with respect to which of the clauses of the sentence the noun phrase is specific or non-specific. Thus what we need is not a variable-valued feature, but a variable number of binary feature specifications. We must mark each noun phrase as either specific or non-specific with respect to each of the clauses in the sentence. (Alternatively we could mark each of the clauses as plus or minus some feature (the inverse of specificity) with respect to each noun phrase that it contains.) This begins to bring out more clearly the relational nature of the ambiguity.

Even this system of representation is inadequate, however, for it predicts too many possible readings for sentences. Assuming that the proposed feature specifications for a given sentence are all independent of each other, there should be $2^{\underline{n}}$ readings for a sentence with one indefinite noun phrase in the lowest of $\underline{n}$ clauses. In considering sentences (1) and (3) earlier, however, we came to the conclusion that there are only $\underline{n}$ possible readings for such a sentence (with the exceptions noted in the footnote to p.31). There must therefore be some correlation among the set of feature specifications for a sentence, which cuts down the number of possible readings. Two restrictions appear to hold in fact. One is that, if we confine ourselves to cases where opacity is associated with complement structure, a noun phrase is always interpreted as specific with respect to the lowest clause in the structure in which it appears. The other is that if a noun phrase is interpreted as specific with respect to a given clause then it must also be interpreted as specific, on that reading of the sentence, with respect to all lower clauses.

The first of these restrictions can be illustrated as follows. In sentences (1) and (3), the lowest clause is a friend of mine is a busdriver. There is no way of interpreting this, standing alone as an independent sentence, as non-specific. If it is true then it is true because there is some particular friend of mine who is a busdriver, and it is ture of that particular friend. Though it is certainly possible for someone to utter this sentence without having any particular friend actually in mind, it makes absolutely no sense at all to suppose that it could be the case that some non-specific friend of mine is a busdriver, that is, that it could be true that a friend of mine is a busdriver without its being true of any particular friend of mine that he is a busdriver. And equally it makes no sense to suppose that Mary might believe this to be the case. (Even if Mary did go around saying some such thing, we would hesitate to say of her that she believed it, for it would be unclear what belief we would be attributing to her if we did. We would be better advised, in such circumstances, to say that it just wasn't clear what Mary believed.) Thus it appears that the noun phrase a friend of mine, which is necessarily specific with respect to the clause a friend of mine is a busdriver, must also be taken as specific with respect to that clause even in the context Mary believes.... In general, a clause which, standing alone, allows of no non-specific interpretation for a noun phrase that it contains, equally allows of no interpretation of that noun phrase as non-specific with respect to that clause even when that clause is subordinated to some higher verb.

The second restriction which operates to reduce the number of predicted readings for a sentence is that if a noun phrase is interpreted as specific with respect to a given clause in the sentence, then it must also be interpreted as specific, on that reading, with respect to all lower clauses. For sentence (3), this restriction excludes the possibility that the noun phrase a friend of mine is taken simultaneously as specific with respect to the highest, I hope...., clause, and as non-specific with respect to the middle, Mary believes...., clause. Such a reading would amount to saying that there is a certain friend of mine of whom I hope that Mary believes that some friend or other of mine is a busdriver, and this is obviously nonsense. Exactly analogous observations with respect to sentences containing four or more clauses establishes the general validity of this restriction.

To the extent to which any claim based on speakers' intuitions about shades of meaning can be firmly established, it seems that these two restrictions on possible arrays of feature specifications for a sentence do correspond with the facts. Between them, the restrictions reduce the predicted number of readings from $2^{\underline{n}}$ to $\underline{n}$ for a sentence with $\underline{n}$ clauses. (This is, of course, to consider only one indefinite noun phrase. If there are more, we must take the product of the number predicted for each.) To see this, we need only imagine the feature specifications for a sentence arrayed as a linear sequence of pluses and minuses, with left-to-right order corresponding to the 'height' of the clause in the sentence. Then the restrictions operate to ensure that all possible sequences consist of a sequence (possibly null) of minuses, followed by a sequence (non-null) of pluses. Simple arithmetic shows that there are n such sequences of n specifications.

The importance of this observation is that it suggests a very much simpler and more appropriate representational device than an array of feature specifications subject to restrictions which are, from a formal point of view, completely arbitrary. This simpler device would be just a line drawn across the structural representation of the reading of a sentence, to be interpreted by a convention to mean that the noun phrase in question is non-specific with respect to all clauses above (to the left of) the line, and is specific with respect to all clauses below (to the right of) the line. There would, of course, have to be one such line for each indefinite noun phrase in a complement clause, and these lines would therefore presumably have to be subscripted or marked in some other way to indicate which noun phrases they were associated with. Such a system of subscripted lines would capture simply and non-redundantly both the number and the nature of the possible readings of sentences with indefinite noun phrases.

It is worth observing at this point that logical representations in which the scope of the existential quantifier is used to indicate specificity (cf. examples (9) and (12) of the previous chapter) constitute a system of just this kind. Formally, a quantifier is no different from a line subscripted for a particular noun phrase in a sentence, and just like our subscripted line, it can appear in any one of the 'clauses' of a logical formula. Although I shall argue later in this chapter that using the existential quantifier in the role of specificity indicator leads to some incorrect predictions about the meanings of opaque constructions, it is clear that such an analysis is of the appropriate kind at least as far as its general formal characteristics are concerned.

I would point out in conclusion that an argument against a semantic analysis of specificity based on differences in the semantic feature representations of particular constituents, and in favour of an analysis in terms of the scope relationships between constituents, would be much more secure against the background of a general theory of scope phenomena, that is, a general account of just what it is about a semantic contrast which makes variation in the scope of a symbol, rather than different choices of symbols, an appropriate representational device. Unfortunately, logicians give definitions of the scope of particular symbols or types of symbol without ever, as far as I know, having given an explication of scope in general. I cannot pretend to have given a general account of it either, but I do think that the kinds of observation made here about specificity would be central to such an account. What I have attempted to establish is that the ambiguity of sentences with an indefinite noun phrase in an opaque context does not consist in the ambiguity of the noun phrase itself, nor in the ambiguity of the context in which it appears, but is a matter of the semantic relationship between the noun phrase and the rest of the sentence. This conclusion will be important when we come to consider the nature of the system of rules which relate semantic representations to syntactic ones, for what it says is that the syntactic relationships between the constituents of a sentence do not mirror the semantic relationships between them. (At least for one of the readings of an ambiguous sentence this must be so.) The semantic representations therefore cannot be a mere fleshing out of the syntactic ones with semantic markers, but must differ from them configurationally as well.[FN]

Section 2. Specificity and the existential quantifier.

The purpose of the preceding section was to establish what are the minimal formal requirements on a system of representation which is to capture ambiguities of specificity. A number of substantive proposals can be generated by identifying the 'subscripted line' of that discussion with some already recognised constituent of linguistic or logical representations.

FN. The whole of this section is simply an elaboration of a point made by Bach (Nouns and Noun Phrases, p. 107). In a comment on an example of the specific/non-specific ambiguity, Bach says: 'I do not believe it is possible to explain such ambiguities except by means of the notion of scope, because we find a systematic relationship between the number of interpretations and the number of embedded sentences (of the proper type)'. I had read Bach's paper when I wrote the passage above, but had overlooked this remark. Had I not done so, an earlier paper of mine on the topic of non-specificity (Non-specific Noun Phrases in English, 1968) might also have been improved.

The point of this would be not just to avoid adding to one's theoretical apparatus a wholly new primitive symbol just for the purpose of representing specificity. More importantly, it would enable us to capture directly in the representational system some of the entailments of sentences containing indefinite noun phrases. So far we have considered only how to ensure that there will be formally distinct representations for distinct readings of a sentence. Although an adequate semantic system will have to do at least this, we can also require of the system that it should make some positive claims about the meanings of the sentences concerned -- that it should define the semantic relationships between the various readings of a given sentence, and between each of these and the readings of other sentences in the language. By identifying the specificity indicator with some independently significant descriptive element, we would thereby ascribe to the sentences so represented the whole body of entailments normally associated with that element. The particular embodiment that we choose for the specificity operator will therefore commit us to certain positive claims about the meanings of opaque constructions.

There are a number of immediately obvious candidates that we might consider. We might identify the specificity operator with a duplicate of the noun phrase in question, allowing this duplicate to appear in any clause of the structure and taking its position to define scope. This proposal is suggested by the existence of sentences like:

(4) Mary believes of a friend of mine that he is a busdriver.

which paraphrases the specific reading of the sentence:

(5) Mary believes that a friend of mine is a busdriver.

The presence of the noun phrase a friend of mine, co-referential with the subject of the complement but itself within the matrix clause, is apparently sufficient to determine specificity. There are actually variants of this proposal, depending on whether we regard the pronoun he of (4) as derived from an underlying phrase a friend of mine, so that the relationship between (4) and (5) is a matter of deleting the noun phrase in the matrix clause, or whether we treat the he just as a variable or place-holder, and the relationship between (4) and (5) as involving the movement of lexical material from the matrix to the complement clause.

An alternative suggestion would be to use not the whole noun phrase but just its determiner as the scope indicator. Yet another would be to use the phrase there is...., or whatever underlies it, in different positions to mark different readings. This suggestion is based on the existence of the paraphrases:

(6) There is a friend of mine that Mary thinks is a busdriver.

(7) Mary thinks that there is a friend of mine who is a

busdriver.

for the specific and non-specific readings respectively of sentence (5). Since the existential quantifier of formal logic is often read as 'there is a...', 'there is at least one...', 'there is something which...', etc., this latter suggestion is a natural linguistic counterpart to the use of the existential quantifier to mark specificity in logical representations. Unless the phrase <u>there is</u>... is actually to be derived from an underlying symbol formally indistinguishable from the existential quantifier of logic, an analysis based on <u>there is</u>... and one based on a quantifier would differ with respect to the grammatical rules relating semantic to surface syntactic representations, but as far as their semantic implications are concerned they would obviously have a great deal in common. Questions concerning syntax will be discussed in Chapter V, and the rest of the present chapter will be devoted to the semantic implications of such an analysis.

In view of the problems with this analysis which we shall consider shortly, it is worth considering what the motivation in favour of using the existential quantifier to indicate specificity in logical formulae might be. If the specificity operator is to be identified with any device already at hand in the logical system, then a quantifier is a natural choice since, as we have already observed, the general formal characteristics of quantifiers are just those that any device for representing specificity must have. The existential quantifier will be preferred to the universal quantifier since specificity is associated with indefinite noun phrases and, except when such noun phrases are interpreted as generic, they are normally represented in logical formulae by means of an existential quantifier. The strongest form of this argument is the claim that there is no significant difference between the specific interpretation of a noun phrase in an opaque context, and the normal interpretation of noun phrases in non-opaque contexts, and that the former should therefore be represented in exactly the same way as the latter, viz. by means of an existential quantifier at the far left of the formula.

This argument, together with the fact that we want to be able to use just one symbol, in different positions, to indicate non-specific as well as specific readings, obviously suggests that we should use the existential'quantifier in representing non-specific readings too, though it must, of course, appear somewhere other than at the left of the formula in this case. There is actually some independent motivation for the same conclusion. There are valid inferences on the pattern of:

(8) Mary believes that a friend of mine is a busdriver.
     Mary's belief is correct.
     Therefore a friend of mine is a busdriver.

(9) John wanted to catch a fish.
     John got what he wanted. (John's want was satisfied.)
     Therefore John caught a fish.

The conclusions of these arguments have only a specific interpretation, but the arguments are valid even if the first premise is interpreted as non-specific. If the non-specific reading of the first premise is represented with an existential quantifier within the complement clause, for example:

(10)   Mary believes ($\exists x$) (x is a friend of mine and x is a busdriver).

then this permits a very simple and intuitive account of the form of such arguments, for the conclusion of the argument (8) is precisely what follows Mary believes in the representation of the first premise. Given the additional premise that Mary's belief is correct, we can simply strip off the Mary believes to obtain the conclusion. There is little prospect of being able to formalise such arguments completely, since what is required as the second premise depends upon the particular verb in the first premise, and the relationship between the two is something that we are far from having a formal account of at present. Nevertheless, this way of representing the non-specific readings of sentences does contribute to revealing the character of such arguments.

It is important to bear in mind that there are arguments in favour of using the existential quantifier to mark specificity, for there are certainly some arguments against doing so. Quine, for example, has argued at length (J. of Phil., 1956) that formulae such as:

45

(11) (∃x) (x is a friend of mine and Mary believes that x

is a busdriver).

should not be permitted since they lead to incorrect and even
bizarre inferences. Quine's arguments crucially involve
definite descriptions, and the substitutivity of identicals,
which are the topics of the next two chapters, and I shall
therefore postpone a detailed discussion of his arguments until
later. They are by no means the only reason for being dubious
about identifying the specificity indicator with the existential quantifier.

It was pointed out in Chapter I that the problem
that opaque contexts pose for the logician is that certain
patterns of argument which are generally valid elsewhere are
not valid within opaque contexts. Any logical operator within
the context of a verb like <u>believes</u>, <u>wants</u>, <u>expects</u>, etc., is
inferentially almost inert. To see this one has only to
select from an introductory text book of logic any reasonably
complex example of a valid formalised argument, and preface
each premise and the conclusion with the phrase <u>John believes</u>
<u>that....</u> The resulting argument is clearly invalid. (Of
course, the premises and the conclusion might be, as a matter
of fact, true of some person called John, but this is far
from establishing that the conclusion can properly be inferred
from the premises.) This point is often made by saying that
people are by and large not fully rational; they are quite
capable of believing things that are logically incompatible.

From the point of view of the mechanics of the formal system, what is important about this is that if we do assign the same representations to sentences within opaque contexts as we would assign to them when they stand alone, then the usual inference rules must not be allowed to apply to the symbols within the opaque context. If they were allowed to do so, they would generate invalid arguments. But then one might reasonably ask why, if some symbol in a logical representation is non-functional from the point of view of generating valid arguments, there is any reason for supposing that the symbol should be present in the representation at all. One might ask, in particular, why the existential quantifier is preferable to any other logical symbol, or to none at all, in a representation such as (10), if no consequences follow from its presence.

The existence of arguments like (8) and (9) above, which involve inferences from an opaquely interpreted premise to a transparent conclusion, is part of the answer to this objection. It is also maintained by many philosophers that certain inference rules, albeit the most trivial ones, do apply within opaque contexts, and that the argument from irrationality is not as powerful as it looks at first sight. This is the doctrine of 'immediate inference', and it can be illustrated as follows. Suppose we know that Jane believes there is a mouse in her kitchen. Then surely it is legitimate to infer that Jane believes that it is false that there is no mouse in her kitchen. The reason this inference is legitimate is not, as might be thought, that the move from 'There is a mouse in my kitchen' to 'It is false that there is no mouse in my kitchen' is so obvious that we can rely on Jane's making the inference, however muddle-headed a person she may be. The validity of the argument depends upon the fact that if Jane were to maintain, apparently sincerely, that she did not believe the second of these propositions, then this would be sufficient grounds for denying that she believed the first, however vehemently she might claim to. To believe there is a mouse in one's kitchen just is, in some sense, to believe that it is false that there is no mouse in one's kitchen. To claim to believe the one but not the other is thus scarcely different from claiming to believe there is a mouse in one's kitchen and then denying that one believed it. And since the latter situation would not count as evidence that one really did believe that there was a mouse in one's kitchen and no mouse in one's kitchen, then nor should the former.

A similar account can be given for some other familiar inference rules, for example the interchange of existential and universal quantifiers under negation, as in the argument: Jane believes that not all men are self-centred, therefore Jane believes that there is at least one man who is not self-centred. Just as above, Jane could not be said to believe the one but not the other, since to credit her with the one belief <u>just is</u> to credit her with the other. If the doctrine of immediate inference is correct (and it is less convincing

for some verbs, e.g. realise, than it is for believe), then it

does provide some justification for assigning logical structure

to material within opaque contexts. It is clear, however,

that not all of the usual inference rules apply within opaque

contexts, and that the logical symbols appearing within such

contexts are, if not quite inert, at least emasculated.

Therefore if we accept formulae in which the existential

quantifier, or other logical symbols, appear within opaque

contexts, in order to capture those inferences which are

valid, then we must impose some constraints on at least some

inference rules in order to avoid predicting inferences which

are not. A large part of the task of characterising the

logical and semantic properties of opaque constructions thus

consists of investigating which in particular of the usual

inferences are valid and which of them are not. In the next

section I shall examine in detail one way in which using the

scope of the existential quantifier to indicate specificity

apparently leads to wrong predictions about the logical and

semantic properties of the non-specific reading of noun

phrases.

Section 3. Non-specific noun phrases and existence.

The hypothesis to be examined is that the non-specific

reading of a sentence such as:

(12) John hopes that he will catch a fish.

should be represented formally as something like:

(13)   John hopes ($\exists$x) (x is a fish and John will catch x).

The most natural rendering of this in English is:

(14)   John hopes that there is a fish and he will catch it.

There are obviously problems here about tense, for it is compatible with (12) that John's hope should be satisfied by his catching a fish that does not exist now, but only at some future time. Thus we should need, either instead of (14) or in addition to it, the paraphrase:

(15)   John hopes that there will be a fish and he will catch it.

Logical representations which do not indicate time relationships are obviously not rich enough to do justice to a sentence such as (12). In what follows, however, I shall ignore any complications due to tense; nothing in my argument will turn upon it, and it will simplify the discussion to consider only paraphrases like (14) rather than (15).

Quite apart from questions of tense and time, (14) is misleading as a paraphrase of (12), for it suggests that there are two things that John hopes -- he hopes that a fish (at least one) exists, and he hopes to catch it. This might perhaps be the case, but it is also possible that John knows perfectly well that fish exist. He might even be completely indifferent to the fact that they exist. This would be quite compatible with the truth of (12) as long as, on the belief that fish exist, John hopes to catch one. By putting the existential quantifier within the scope of the main verb in a representation such as (13), we seem to commit ourselves to the false claim that a proposition about the existence of fish is part of the content of John's hope.

It is probably true that John's views about the existence of fish are not entirely irrelevant to the truth of (12). We would certainly be reluctant to say that (12) was true if we knew that John positively hoped that fish did not exist (at least until such time as he had caught one), and even perhaps if we knew that he was convinced that fish did not exist. Some reference to the relationship between John and the proposition that fish exist might not be out of place, therefore, in the semantic representation of (12). It should be observed, however, that John's views about the existence of fish have as much bearing on the truth of the specific reading of (12) as they do on the non-specific reading. In the kind of system we are considering, the specific reading of (12) would be represented as:

(16) $(\exists x)$ (x is a fish and John hopes John will catch x). and this does not carry any implication about John's views about the existence of fish. If his views should be indicated in the representation of the non-specific reading then they should surely also be indicated in the representation of the specific reading. Thus even if it could be argued that (13) is not a misleading representation, it would follow that (16) is.

Complicating the problem further is that different

verbs differ with respect to the appropriateness of the existence clause in the representation of the non-specific reading. For verbs of knowing, believing, thinking, assuming, and so on, the implication that the subject 'verbs' the existence of fish (of whatever it is that the noun phrase in question designates), is not unwelcome at all. For example, the sentence:

(17) Mary believes that John caught a fish.

interpreted non-specifically, does seem to entail that Mary believes that at least one fish exists, just as the representation:

(18) Mary believes $(\exists x)$ (x is a fish and John caught x).

suggests. On the other hand there are cases where the claim that the subject 'verbs' the existence clause amounts to sheer nonsense. If, for example, we represent the sentence:

(19) John ordered Mary to shoot a squirrel.

as:

(20) John ordered Mary $(\exists x)$ (x is a squirrel and Mary shoot x).

this would seem to imply that John ordered Mary that there be a squirrel. Even if some sense can be given to this, it is clearly no part of the meaning of (19). For quite different reasons we run into nonsense in connection with a sentence such as:

(21) I want to eat one of those apples.

This sentence has a perfectly acceptable non-specific reading (e.g. I don't mind which of those apples I eat as long as I get one of them), but it surely cannot entail that I want one of those apples to exist.

It appears that in these cases where the subject cannot be said to 'verb' the existence of objects of the kind in question, he must at least be of the opinion that they exist. Furthermore, we have already seen that even where it does make sense to say that he 'verbs' their existence, as for sentence (12), it is also compatible with the truth of the sentence that he does not, in fact, 'verb' that they exist but is merely of the opinion that they do. The solution to our problem might therefore be to say that what is entailed is that the subject either 'verbs' or believes (in some weak sense of believe) that things of the kind in question exist. We would then need only to define some special principles at work in examples like (19) or (21) which have the effect of excluding one of these alternatives. Cases like (17) would easily be explained on the basis of the virtual identity of the two alternatives.

The problem with this suggestion is a formal one. What is proposed is that we represent the non-specific reading of (12), for example, not as (13) but as:

(22)   (John hopes $(\exists x)$ (x is a fish and John will catch x)) or
                (John believes $(\exists x)$ x is a fish and John hopes
                                        John will catch x).

There are some brackets missing from the second disjunct of this representation, and it is here that the problem lies.

53

If we bracket the second disjunct as:

(23)　John believes (∃x) (x is a fish and John hopes John

will catch x).

then this represents John as believing that he hopes something, which is not what (12) means at all.　If, on the other hand, we take the second conjunct of (22) to be:

(24)　(John believes (∃x) x is a fish) and (John hopes John

will catch x).

then, though we no longer have John believing that he hopes something, we do have an unbound variable in the second conjunct.　We have taken the <u>John hopes</u>... clause out of the scope of the <u>John believes</u>..., but we have thereby taken it out of the scope of the existential quantifier.　The variable in the <u>John hopes</u>... clause therefore cannot be regarded as bound by that quantifier.　And this means that the representation does not indicate, as we want it to, that what John hopes that he will catch is a fish.

Inserting another quantifier into the representation, in order to bind the second variable, does not help.　Either we would get:

(25)　(John believes (∃x) x is a fish) and ((∃y) (John hopes

John will catch y)).

which is unacceptable, since the quantifier is to the left of the verb <u>hopes</u>, and thus represents a specific rather than a non-specific hope.　Or else we would have:

54

(26)   (John believes ($\exists$x) x is a fish) and (John hopes ($\exists$y)

John will catch y).

which still fails to indicate that what John hopes to catch is

a fish. If we remedy this, by inserting a y is a fish clause,

(27)   (John believes ($\exists$x) x is a fish) and (John hopes ($\exists$y) (y

is a fish and John will catch y)).

then this has John once again hoping that fish exist. It

therefore does not provide the kind of alternative we need

as the second disjunct of (22), since the whole point of the

second disjunct was to avoid the implication that John hopes

that fish exist.

To reject the hypothesis that lies behind the proposed

representation (22), simply on the grounds that (22) is not, by

the conventions of standard logic, well-formed, might be too

glib a move, for there are apparently acceptable sentences of

English which seem to demand such a representation. For

example, it is hard to see how else to represent the sentence:

(28)   John believes there is a fish in the pond and he wants

to catch it.

other than as:

(29)   John believes ($\exists$x) x is a fish and x is in the pond and

John wants John catch x.

and yet (29) suffers from the same kinds of technical defects

as (22). (See also the examples due to Baker and Karttunen,

quoted by Lakoff in 'Counterparts, or the Problem of Reference

in Transformational Grammar', 1968.) I shall examine examples such as these in more detail later in this chapter and consider there the possibility that it is the formal system that needs to be revised, not our intuitions about what such sentences mean. In particular, the general constraint in standard logical systems that scope relationships should be transitive, may have to be dropped, since it is this which excludes any way of bracketing a formula such as (22) or (29) which is simultaneously both formally and semantically appropriate.

However, even if we suppose that such a move should be made, the problem with the proposed analysis of sentences like (12) is actually a more general one than has been suggested so far. The non-specific reading of the sentence:

(30) John hopes that he will catch a purple fish.

would be represented as:

(31) John hopes ($\exists$x) (x is a fish and x is purple and John will catch x).

and this apparently implies not only that John hopes there are fish but also that he hopes there are purple things. It also implies (and this, though not mentioned above, is also true of (13)), that John hopes that he will catch something. Now it is very likely, and is certainly compatible with the truth of (30), that John knows quite well that fish exist and that purple things exist. It is even compatible with the truth of (30) that he should be quite indifferent to the existence

of fish or of purple things except insofar as, on the
assumption that they exist, he has conceived a desire to catch
a purple fish. It is also possible that John is quite convinced that he will catch something, even if only an old boot
or a tin can, and he might even be indifferent to the idea of
catching something even though, on the assumption that he will,
he would like it to be a purple fish rather than anything
else. What all of this means is that it is not only the first
clause within the scope of the quantifier in (31) that John
might believe rather than hope to be true; the same holds for
any of the clauses within the opaque context, and indeed for
any pair of them simultaneously. In fact if we assume, as
seems natural, that John's believing something is not incompatible with his hoping it too, then it is compatible with (30)
that John should believe the truth of the proposition within
the opaque context, that he should believe that he will catch
a purple fish. Of course it is not compatible with (30) that
he should merely believe this -- at least part of the proposition that he will catch a purple fish must be something that
he hopes will be true. It should also be remembered that John
might not believe any or all of what is involved in the
proposition that he will catch a fish; he can certainly hope
for something that he does not believe will come true.

The situation we have arrived at is the following. We
cannot represent a sentence such as (12) by means of (13),

for (13) suggests that John is not indifferent to the existence
of fish and that he is not indifferent to the possibility that
he will catch something, and either of these claims might be
false. If, to avoid these implications, we devise some way of
including in the formal representations the possibility that
he might merely believe, rather than hope, either that fish
exist or that he will catch something, then (12) must be
assigned a number of different formal representations, each
one corresponding to one of the possible combinations of hope
and belief with respect to each of the clauses of the proposition within the opaque context. And the implication of this,
viz. that sentence (12) is many ways ambiguous, seems
intuitively to be just false. In fact, intuitively, sentence (12) does not say anything at all about what John
belceives. The truth of certain propositions about what he
believes may be necessary conditions on the truth of (12), and
the truth of (12) will in that case entail the truth of those
propositions. But this is not to say that these propositions
are part of what (12) means.

It is a reasonable requirement on formal semantic
representations that they should symbolize what a sentence
means rather than all of the things that it entails. Quite
apart from any other considerations, a sentence may have an
infinite number of entailments whereas a formal semantic
representation must be finite. The (possibly infinite) set of

entailments can then be generated from the representation of meaning by means of inference rules. If we attempt to apply this in principle to sentences such as (12) or (30), then it seems intuitively correct to exclude from the semantic representations any representation of John's beliefs. In fact it was only because representations like (13) threaten to commit us to incorrect entailments, such as that John must hope that fish exist, that we were led to the idea of including his beliefs in the formal representations at all.

I shall presently suggest a solution to this problem which does not involve mentioning John's beliefs at all, but first I should consider the possibility that it might be maintained that sentences like (12) really are ambiguous, at least under emphatic stress. With stress on the word purple, the sentence:

(32) John hopes he will catch a purple fish.

is certainly more likely to suggest that John believes that he will catch a fish and hopes it will be purple, than is the same sentence with stress on the word fish. The latter is more likely to suggest that John believes he will catch something purple and hopes that it will be a fish. How strong this suggestion is, whether it should be regarded as a matter of conversational implicatur, presupposition, entailment, or even, in some stronger sense, part of the meaning of the sentence when so stressed, is another question and a much more difficult one. Furthermore, it is not even clear that the emphatic stress is to be taken as indicating a contrast between what John hopes and what he merely believes. Sentence (32) with stress on _purple_ seems to me quite compatible with John's not really believing that he will catch a fish at all; the stress might be read as suggesting that while John would like to catch a purple fish he would simply hate to catch a fish of any other colour. More important than these points, however, is that even if it were true that such a sentence is ambiguous, and has distinct readings which do contain, as part of their meaning, distinct claims about John's beliefs, it seems undeniable that there is also a reading which is completely neutral and does not say anything at all about what John believes.

This situation is reminiscent of that for negation. It has been maintained that a sentence such as for example:
(33) John did not catch a purple fish.
is ambiguous, at least under emphatic stress. It has been suggested that this sentence can be taken to mean or entail or presuppose, or perhaps something even weaker still, that John did catch a fish, and to assert that the fish was not purple. Alternatively, it is claimed, the sentence can be taken to mean, entail, etc., that John caught something purple and to assert that this thing was not a fish, and so on. However, even if all this is true, there also seems to be a quite neutral reading of this sentence, on which it means

simply that it is false that John caught a purple fish. This reading would standardly be represented as:

(34) NOT ($\exists x$) (x is a fish and x is purple and John caught x). What is important about this reading is that the sentence so interpreted might be true because John did not catch anything, because what he caught was not purple, because it was not a fish or for any combination of these reasons. Thus we cannot infer from (33) on this reading that John did not catch anything, we cannot infer that there are no fish, and we cannot infer that there are no purple things. From the negation of a complex proposition, that is to say, we cannot in general infer the falsity of any one of the component propositions. This corresponds exactly to our observations about opaque contexts. From the fact that John hopes that a complex proposition will turn out to be true, we cannot infer that he hopes that any one of its component propositions will turn out to be true.

This parallel with negation puts our worries about opaque contexts into a new light, for there simply is no corresponding problem about negation. It is not valid to infer, from a negated conjunction, the negation of any individual conjunct. And because it is not valid, systems of logic do not contain any inference rule or rules which would generate such an inference. It is true that standard systems do contain a rule which permits the simplification of conjunctions, that is, the inference from a conjunctive proposition of each of its conjuncts. But this rule is formulated in such a way that it is not applicable to a conjunction within the scope of a negation operator. Why, then, should we ever have supposed in the first place that this rule would be applicable within the scope of an opaque operator? It was this assumption, and only this, which gave rise to the worries about representing a non-specific noun phrase by means of an existential quantifier within the scope of an opaque verb. If we ensure that the rule for simplifying conjunctions does not apply within the scope of an opaque verb, any more than it does within the scope of a negation operator, then these worries simply disappear. We can no longer infer that John hopes that fish exist from the formal representation of the statement that John hopes to catch a fish.

There are other precedents besides negation for restricting the domain of the rule which simplifies conjunctions. The argument:

(35)   If (p and q) then r.

   Therefore: If p then r.

is obviously invalid, showing that conjunctions cannot be simplified within the antecedent of a conditional either. Nevertheless, despite such precedents, the assumption that conjunctions can be simplified within opaque contexts can certainly be found in the literature on opacity. Linsky, for example, ('Referring', p. 67ff.) discusses the analysis of the sentence:

62

(36) George IV wished to know whether Scott was the author of

Waverley.

as:

(37) George IV wished to know whether one, and only one,

individual both wrote Waverley and was identical

with Scott.

Linsky remarks (pp. 71-2): 'Asked whether he wants to know
whether one, and only one, individual both wrote Waverley and
is identical with Scott, George IV might answer that this is
not what he wishes to know, since he already knows that one,
and only one, individual wrote Waverley; what he does not know
is whether the author of Waverley is Scott.' Linsky concludes
on the basis of this that (37) is not an appropriate analysis
of (36), since (37) might be false even though (36) is true.
The argument, however, clearly turns upon simplifying the
conjunction within the opaque context wished to know whether
in (37). Having accepted this as a valid move, it is clear
that we should have to reject the proposed analysis since,
as Linsky rightly points out, it is probably false that George IV
wished to know whether the first of the two conjuncts was true.
If, on the other hand, we block the simplification of conjunction within opaque contexts, then this observation is not
a reason for rejecting (37) as the analysis of (36).

I suspect that the reason why Linsky and others have
assumed the validity of simplification within opaque contexts

without questioning it, is that for the two kinds of opaque operator that have been studied most fully by logicians, simplification creates no problems; it is valid even within the scope of these operators. In the usual systems of modal logic, (38) and (39) are theorems:

(38) Necessarily (p and q) ≡ (necessarily p) and (necessarily q).

(39) Possibly (p and q) ≡ (possibly p) and (possibly q).

The conjunction on the right hand side of each of these equivalences can be simplified, so that from 'necessarily (p and q)' we can infer, for example 'necessarily p'. An example involving the existential quantifier is the argument:

(40) Necessarily there is an odd number greater than five which is prime.

Therefore: Necessarily there is an odd number.

Represented formally this argument is:

(41) Necessarily $(\exists x)$ (x is a number and x is odd and x is greater than five and x is prime.

Therefore: Necessarily $(\exists x)$ (x is a number and x is odd).

In epistemic logic, the logic of verbs like <u>know</u> and <u>believe</u>, simplification presents no problems either, though for a rather different reason. The problem with a verb like <u>hope</u> was that the subject of the verb might not hope but might rather believe or even know, that one of the conjuncts of the proposition within the opaque context was true. Now if the opaque verb concerned is itself <u>believe</u> or <u>know</u>, then these two possibilities are one and the same. Thus for a sentence such as:

(42) John believes he will catch a fish.

represented as:

(43) John believes ($\exists$x) (x is a fish and John will catch x).

there is no point in going through the intermediate stage of inferring that John either believes that fish exist or believes that fish exist. As long as one's logical system is restricted to such verbs, and is not extended to verbs such as want, hope, etc., then one can afford to ignore the complications that we have been considering, and permit a direct inference from (43) to:

(44) John believes ($\exists$x) (x is a fish).

by allowing the rule which simplifies conjunctions to apply within opaque contexts.

Considering the precedents of negative and conditional statements, it seemed quite extraordinary that simplification should ever have been imagined to be a general rule, applicable in all contexts and thus in opaque contexts in particular. Now we see that there are also precedents for accepting it as a valid rule, and precedents which are closer to home since they themselves concern opaque contexts, even if only of a very restricted class. However, it seems clear that in a logical system designed to deal with opaque contexts in general, simplification must be blocked with opaque contexts. Even the slightest deviation from the narrow range of the verbs know and believe can lead to problems. For example, although (45) is a valid argument, (46) is not.

(45)   John knows that Mary caught a fish.

Therefore John knows that there are fish.

(46)   John doubts that Mary caught a fish.

Therefore John doubts that there are fish.

Of course, in this case, it is plausible to ascribe the failure of the inference to the negative aspect of the meaning of doubts, since we already know that simplification is invalid in negative contexts. It is less obvious that we should analyse surprise as containing a negative element in order to account for the invalidity of the argument:

(47)   It is surprising that Mary caught a fish.

Therefore it is surprising that there are fish.

There is also Linsky's argument, which fails, presumably, because there the verb know is within the scope of another opaque verb, the verb wish, which does not permit simplification.

Section 4.   The conjunctive analysis of noun phrases.

It was pointed out in Section 2 of this chapter that if all the usual inference rules must be prevented from applying to a logical symbol within an opaque context, this throws some doubt on the assumption that that symbol does actually appear in those contexts. It is important, therefore, to observe that it is not the presence of the existential quantifier within opaque contexts which is thrown into doubt by the conclusion that simplification is not valid. In a representation such as:

(48) John hopes (∃x) (x is a fish and John will catch x).

it is the conjunctive structure of the proposition within the opaque context, not the existential quantifier itself, which is the source of the trouble. And it is an inference rule that applies to conjunctions, not a rule specially concerned with the existential quantifier, that must be prevented from applying to (48).

In fact, no disastrous consequences appear to follow from assuming that the existential quantifier occurs within the opaque context in (48). If we take (48) to be equivalent to the English sentence:

(49) John hopes there is a fish that he will catch.

or, with allowance for tense:

(50) John hopes that there will be a fish that he catches.

and if we take care to avoid the temptation to simplify, then it appears that the analysis is at least logically equivalent to the original sentence:

(51) John hopes that he will catch a fish.

if not synonymous with it. As an analysis, therefore, it is unobjectionable. Perhaps it can be critised on the grounds of the inapplicability of some other inference rule. For example, it is not obvious that (51) entails:

(52) John hopes that not everything is not a fish that he

will catch.

but then it is not obvious that (51) does <u>not</u> entail this either. Intuitions about such inferences just seem to be too insecure to support a strong argument in either direction.

If it is the case that it is not the existential implication of the analysis (48) that causes the trouble, but rather the conjunctive structure of the proposition within the opaque context, this is an important fact, for it suggests an alternative to accepting the analysis (48) and then blocking the simplification of conjunction. The conclusion of Section 1 was that in order to represent specificity, we need to employ some formal device with the effect of a line drawn across a structural representation at some level of embedding, that is, some symbol, subscripted for a particular noun phrase, and capable of appearing in any one of the clauses of a complement construction. If, for typographic convenience, we use the arbitrary symbol (Sx) instead of an actual line, then the general form of the representations of the specific and non-specific readings of sentence (51) must be:

(53) (Sx) John hopes John will catch (a fish)$_x$.

(54) John hopes (Sx) John will catch (a fish)$_x$.

Now even if we decide, on semantic grounds, that the existential quantifier should be used in place of this arbitrary (Sx) symbol, we cannot simply substitute $(\exists x)$ for (Sx) in these representations. In standard quantificational logic there are other constraints on the formal representation of noun phrases. In particular, the lexical material within a noun phrase is not permitted to co-exist alongside the bound variable as it does in (53) and (54). It must instead be spelled out as a separate 'clause', as in the structures:

(55) ($\exists$x) x is a fish and John hopes John will catch x.

(56) John hopes ($\exists$x) x is a fish and John will catch x.

It is this move which is responsible for there being a conjoined proposition within the opaque context in representations of the non-specific readings of sentences, and it is therefore this move which requires that a special restriction be placed on the inference rule that simplifies conjunctions. But this move was no part of what was argued for in Section 1 on the basis of the general properties of the phenomenon of non-specificity. We should therefore consider the possibility of not making it. We are not bound to take over the structures of any system of logic, in all their details, as the semantic representations of our grammar, and if it would simplify the system to depart from the conventions of standard quantificational logic, and assume that the existential quantifier may appear in structures like (53) and (54),[FN] then we should

---

FN. There are systems of logic ('many-sorted logics') in which different types of quantifier are recognised, each ranging over different classes of variables. For example, there might be a quantifier restricted to range over just fish, and in this case there would obviously be no need of a clause x is a fish in the representation of our example (51). I believe it has been suggested informally by McCawley that quantifiers in semantic representations should be subscripted to indicate their range. Thus we might write fish under the existential quantifier in (55) and (56) and omit the x is a fish clause. This proposal differs from the proposal to employ structures like (53) and (54) rather than (55) and (56) only, as far as I can see, in that it would

obviously do so. Linguistic arguments have been put forward in favour of a conjunctive analysis, as in (55) and (56), of the lexical content of noun phrases, and I shall consider these arguments shortly. First, however, let us consider what advantages would follow from rejecting such an analysis.

If we assume that the semantic representations for the specific and non-specific readings of sentence (51) are to be just like (53) and (54) except for containing the existential quantifier, thus:

(57) $(\exists x)$ John hopes John will catch (a fish)$_x$.

(58) John hopes $(\exists x)$ John will catch (a fish$_x$.

rather than (55) and (56), then the advantages that would appear to follow from this assumption are of two kinds. First, we would no longer need a special restriction to block simplification of conjunctions in opaque contexts, because no conjunction is present in a structure like (58). Secondly, since (57) and (58) are obviously more similar structurally to the surface structure (51) to which they correspond than are (55) and (56), the system of grammatical rules which correlates semantic representations with surface structures should be simplified. As it turns out, however, both of these apparent advantages are illusory.

When a sentence such as:

---

run into appalling problems in connection with selection restrictions between verbs and noun phrases, and would also require more complex rules for mapping semantic representations onto surface structures.

(59)　John will catch a fish.

is _not_ embedded within an opaque context, simplification does lead to valid arguments. Thus, ignoring questions about tense, sentence (59) does entail both that there is a fish, and that John will catch something. On a conjunctive analysis, as in logic, (59) will be represented as:

(60)　$(\exists x)$　x is a fish and John will catch x.

and the entailments of (59) can be generated from this representation by simplifying the conjunction. If, on the other hand, (59) is represented simply as:

(61)　$(\exists x)$　John will catch (a fish)$_x$

then, since there is no conjunction here to simplify, we must devise some other appropriate inference rule to generate these entailments. On the assumption that (61) could be mapped onto the surface structure (59) by a simpler set of grammatical rules than would be needed for (60), it looks as though we are weighing this new inference rule on one side against the inference rule for simplifying conjunctions plus some grammatical rules on the other side.

This is not in fact the case, however, for even in a system containing (61) rather than (60), we should still need a rule for simplifying conjunctions. This is quite obvious from examples which contain an explicit conjunction in surface structure. For example, the sentence:

(62)　John will catch a fish and Mary will catch a frog.

quite clearly entails both (63) and (64):

(63)   John will catch a fish.

(64)   Mary will catch a frog.

and the system must therefore contain an inference rule which
generates these entailments. Thus the balance is actually
between two inference rules on one side and an inference
rule plus some grammatical rules on the other. A decision
between these two alternatives obviously cannot be made at
this level of generality.

What, then of the advantage of dropping the special
restriction on the rule that simplifies conjunctions? This too
is an illusion. It is true that the problems connected with
the simplification of conjunctions within opaque contexts
would no longer arise in connection with the representation of
non-specific readings of sentences, for noun phrases would no
longer appear as conjoined clauses in formal representations.
Once again, however, there are other sentences in the language
which have overt conjunctive structure and which pose exactly
the same problems about simplification. Consider, for example,
the sentence:

(65)   Mary hopes that the soufflé will rise and the sauce

won't curdle.

If the sauce is intended for the soufflé, and neither would be
good to eat alone, then it is possible that though Mary hopes
that they will both turn out well, she really wouldn't care
one way or the other about the sauce if the soufflé failed to

rise, or about the souffle if the sauce curdled. And this situation appears to be perfectly compatible with the truth of (65). This example is simply another illustration of the fact that a person may have a certain attitude towards a composite situation without having that attitude to each aspect of the situation. This is the factual counterpart of the formal restriction on simplifying conjunctions, and we must therefore recognise that simplification is not valid as applied to sentence (65).

It may be felt that this conclusion is too strong, and that there is a reading of (65) from which we <u>can</u> infer both (66) and (67):

(66) Mary hopes that the souffle will rise.

(67) Mary hopes that the sauce won't curdle.

It is therefore worth pointing out in passing that almost any familiar version of the grammar of English will predict that a sentence such as (65) is ambiguous, unless it is constrained in some way for which there is no apparent independent motivation. Such a sentence could be generated either from a deep structure in which the complement to the matrix verb is a conjoined sentence, or from a deep structure consisting of the conjunction of two clauses, each one containing a complement clause. The two sources for (65) would be something like (68) and (69) respectively:

(68) Mary hopes ((the souffle will rise) and (the sauce won't

curdle)).

(69) (Mary hopes (the soufflé will rise)) and (Mary hopes

(the sauce won't curdle)).

The first of these will give the surface structure (65) almost
directly, the second as the result of conjunction reduction.

Now (69) represents simply the conjunction of two
propositions, and since conjunctions can in general be
simplified, we should regard (69) as representing the second
reading of (65), the reading on which it does entail both (66)
and (67). On the other hand, since (68) represents a conjoined proposition within an opaque context, we can take this
to represent the first of our two readings of (65), the
reading on which it is invalid to infer (66) and (67). Thus
the situation is not, as might have been feared, that certain
genuine entailments are lost if simplification is outlawed in
opaque contexts, but rather that the grammar is sufficiently
rich that it provides an alternative source from which these
entailments can be derived. (It should also be noted that
examples such as these show that opacity involves much more
than just the failure of existential generalization and the
substitutivity of identicals.)

So far it has been shown that if we consider the inference rules as well as the grammatical rules of the system,
there would be no obvious gain from giving up the conjunctive
analysis of noun phrases. As far as the facts about non-
specificity and existence are concerned, it seems to make

little difference whether we employ structures like (57) and (58) or structures like (55) and (56). In both cases we shall need an inference rule that simplifies conjunctions, and in both cases this rule must be prevented from applying within opaque contexts. The entailments of noun phrases in non-opaque contexts can either be captured by assigning them conjunctive representations such as (60) and then simplifying the conjunctions, or else by applying a special inference rule to a representation such as (61). The similarities between the lexical content of noun phrases and conjoined clauses are brought out in the first case in the body of rules that maps surface structures onto semantic representations, and in the second case in the body of inference rules that generates entailments from semantic representations.

If there is <u>syntactic</u> motivation for deriving noun phrases from conjoined clauses in underlying structures, then the first of these alternatives will obviously be preferable. I shall therefore turn now to the arguments that have been presented in favour of this analysis. The proposal actually consists of two parts. One is to analyse all noun phrases as derived from predicate nominals, that is to derive a sentence such as:

(70) I saw a cow.

from a structure like that which underlies the sentence:

(71) I saw something which was a cow.

The other part of the proposal is to treat the relative clause containing this predicate nominal as a conjoined clause rather than as a clause subordinated to an NP node, that is, to derive (71) in turn from a structure like that which underlies the sentence:

(72) I saw something and it was a cow.

Bach (Nouns and Noun Phrases, 1968) presents a number of arguments for the first part of the analysis; Postal (Restrictive Relatives, 1967) has a number of arguments for the second. Postal also argues that pronouns like the something and the it in (72) should be represented simply as referential indices, and Bach that they should be represented as variables bound by quantifier-like operators in underlying structures. Taken together, these ideas amount to deriving a sentence like (70) from a structure virtually identical with the standard logical formula:

(73) $(\exists x)$ (I saw x and x is a cow).

I shall not discuss all of Bach's arguments for the predicative analysis of noun phrases. The strongest of them all consist of the observation that some phenomenon normally associated with clausal structures may also be associated with noun phrases. There is the familiar case of negation. Bach argues that analysing out the noun phrases in the sentence:

(74) The professors signed a petition.

in the fashion:

(75) The ones who were professors signed something which was
                                            a petition.

would permit the correct prediction not only of the number, but also of the nature, of all the possible negations of sentence (74), viz.

(76) The professors DIDN'T sign a petition.

Neg the ones who were professors signed something which was a petition.

(77) The PROFESSORS didn't sign a petition.

The ones Neg who were professors signed something which was a petition.

(78) The professors didn't sign a PETITION.

The ones who were professors signed something Neg which was a petition.

There has been considerable discussion of constituent negation in the linguistic literature but I shall make only two comments here. First, a general account of negation, applicable to all types of constituent, is presumably to be preferred to one that deals only with noun phrases, but it is not at all obvious that this type of clausal account of noun phrase negation could be extended to other types of constituent that can be negated, such as adverbs.

Secondly, Bach's argument conflicts with some of his own assumptions. The sentence:

(79) He didn't sign a petition.

is ambiguous in exactly the same way as it is the negation of (74) One of its readings parallels (77) above, viz:

(80) HE didn't sign a petition.

and to explain this, Bach would have to analyse (80) as:

(81) The one Neg who was him signed something which was a

petition.

But, if I have understood him correctly, Bach intends that his clausal analysis should not apply to pronouns, such as the he in (79). Just as in the logical system on which this syntactic analysis is modelled, this pronoun would be represented as a bound variable. To extend the analysis of constituent negation to pronouns would be possible, but it would lead to other unwelcome consequences. Bach suggests that there will be a definiteness operator in underlying structures; if we represent this as (Dx), and ignore temporarily the analysis of the phrase a petition, then the analysis of (79) that we can construct on the basis of Bach's discussion should be something like:

(82) (Dx) (x sign a petition)

with a Neg element to be inserted in some appropriate position. Now it is, of course, quite possible to provide a formula along these lines into which Neg can be inserted in accordance with Bach's theory of constituent negation, thus:

(83) (Dx) (Dy) (Neg (x is y) and x sign a petition)

This formula, with its negated identity clause, is very similar to the paraphrase (81), and thus provides an analysis of (80) parallel to the one Bach gives for (77). However, if we do extend Bach's analysis to pronouns in this way, consistency will require that an identity clause is present also in the representation of the affirmative sentence:

(84) He signed a petition.

This sentence would thus have to be analysed as something like:

(85) (Dx) (Dy) (x is y and x sign a petition).

As long as infinite regress can be avoided, there is probably nothing that would positively rule this out as a possible deep structure, but the necessity for such identity clauses underlying all pronouns detracts seriously from the idea of using variables and quantifier elements in deep structure, since the major advantage of this idea is the simplification it permits in the representation of pronominal cross-reference. To a large extent this is lost if, on the basis of Bach's argument about negation, we are forced to derive pronouns, as well as noun phrases with lexical content, from underlying clauses.

Another of Bach's observations is that noun phrases are interpreted in relation to tense. For example, the noun phrase the President in the sentence:

(86) Several years ago I met the President in Baltimore. can be taken to refer either to the person who was President at the time of meeting, or to the person who is President now. Bach suggests treating this ambiguity of reference as an ambiguity of meaning, and deriving the phrase the President from either the one who was President, or the one who is President, i.e. from underlying clauses in which tense is explicitly marked. Although a great many noun phrases are ambiguous in this way, Bach maintains that the range of possible

interpretations is always predictable -- the clause underlying the noun phrase always has either present tense or 'narrative' tense (roughly, the same tense as the main verb of the sentence). Some general conditions on the tense element in underlying clauses that are reduced to noun phrases in surface structure will therefore give the right results.

One can cite examples which are apparently exceptions to Bach's generalization. Thus the sentence:

(87)   Tomorrow I shall make a kite.

obviously lacks a reading with present tense reference for a kite, and the sentence:

(88)   Yesterday I ate a pork pie.

lacks a reading with present tense reference for a pork pie. It should be noticed also that even though (87) can perhaps be paraphrased as:

(89)   Tomorrow I shall make something which will be a kite.

the temporal references of the two clauses are not strictly identical, since something will be a kite only after I have made it so. However, 'creative' verbs like make, and 'destructive' verbs like eat are exceptional precisely in their special implications about the past, present or future existence of their objects. The fact that a general theory of tense and reference does not, without special modification, account for these exceptional cases is therefore hardly an objection to the theory.

More interesting is the possibility of an alternative

explanation of Bach's observations. Bach's analysis does provide an explanation, and not merely a representation, of these facts, for he points out that if there were no conditions on the tense element in a relative clause that is reduced, the reduction transformation would violate the principle that deletions should be recoverable. On Bach's proposal, relative clause reduction goes through only if the tense element is identical to that of the main clause, or if it is the present tense. Thus recoverability (up to ambiguity) is secured, and the semantic facts are simultaneously predicted. On the other hand, the semantic facts might be taken as evidence for a scope analysis of tense relationships. Tenses and time adverbs interact very closely, and the notion of the scope of an adverb is a familiar one. For example, a sentence like:

(90) We decided to leave on Tuesday.

is ambiguous; it has different readings depending on how the scope of the time adverb on Tuesday is taken. What is being suggested is that a general account of this kind might be developed to deal with the tenses of verbs as well as with time adverbs. A noun phrase might be interpreted as either inside or outside the scope of the time indicator of the sentence in which it occurred. If inside, the referent of the noun phrase would be whatever the descriptive content of the noun phrase is, was, or will be, true of at the time indicated in the sentence; if outside, the noun phrase would refer simply to whatever it was true of at the time of utterance.

Composite tenses would be handled quite naturally within such a system; the time relevant to the referent of a phrase would be determined by the interaction of any tense elements contained within it, with any tense elements in whose scope it occurred. In order to account for Bach's observations, relative clause reduction would be permitted only when tense within the relative clause was unmarked.

I cannot pretend to have the details of such a system worked out, but there are some indications that this is the correct approach to tense. Sentences with the verb <u>will</u> conform to Bach's generalization about the interpretation of noun phrases only for a non-specific reading of the noun phrase. For example, the noun phrase <u>a beautiful girl</u> in the sentence:

(91) John will marry a beautiful girl.

may be taken to refer to a girl who is now beautiful, or to refer to a girl who will be beautiful at the time John marries her, though she may be plain, or even not have been born, at the time of utterance. This noun phrase may also be interpreted either as specific or as non-specific; the sentence may be used to make a prediction about a particular beautiful girl, or to make the much weaker prediction that whoever John marries will be beautiful. The specific reading, however, requires a present tense interpretation of the noun phrase -- the noun phrase must be taken to refer to a girl who is <u>now</u> beautiful. People certainly can be referred to in terms of their future properties as well as their present ones, and someone might well believe that John will marry a certain girl who, though plain now, will be beautiful by the time she is married. But if this is the sense intended, then (91) will not do; the proper form in such a case is (92):

(92) John will marry a (certain) girl who will be beautiful.

For the specific reading, that is, if a future reference is intended it must be explicitly marked.

The interest of this is that the specific/non-specific contrast is a matter of scope. If the noun phrase is within the scope of the opaque verb, it is non-specific; if it is outside the scope of that verb then it is specific. Given a scope analysis of tense, we would therefore actually predict that on the specific reading, a noun phrase cannot pick up a temporal reference from the verb of a sentence in which it appears. For on this reading, the noun phrase will be outside the scope of that verb. The interaction of specificity and time reference would be explained on the assumption that both are a matter of the relative scope of a noun phrase and a verb.

Another observation of the same kind is that demonstrative noun phrases also lack one of the interpretations that Bach's generalization predicts. The sentence:

(93) I used to sit by the statue of Napoleon.

is ambiguous between reference to a presently existing statue and one which used to exist. Because of the latter possibility, the sentence:

(94) I used to sit by the statue of Napoleon before it was

melted down.

makes sense. By contrast, the sentence:

(95) I used to sit by that statue.

with a demonstrative noun phrase, can be taken to refer only to a presently existing statue, and the sentence:

(96) I used to sit by that statue before it was melted down.

is correspondingly anomalous. These facts can also be accounted for if we assume that the time reference of a noun phrase is a matter of its scope with respect to the main verb of the sentence. It is a general fact about demonstrative noun phrases (though I shall not attempt to establish it here) that they are never interpreted as within the scope of other elements in the sentences in which they occur. The hypothesis that tense in a noun phrase is a matter of scope, together with the fact that the scope of a demonstrative phrase is always maximal, automatically predicts that a demonstrative phrase will not pick up its time reference from the tense of the sentence in which it occurs. Thus the phrase that statue in (95) and (96) must be taken to refer to a presently existing statue, not to one that used to exist.

A scope analysis of tense, if the details can be worked out satisfactorily, would therefore appear to account not only for the facts observed by Bach, but also for cases which would be exceptions to his generalization. The reason for considering this alternative to Bach's analysis is that it does not require that noun phrases be derived from underlying clauses. Derivation from underlying clauses is needed only if it is supposed that tense must be explicitly marked in noun phrases, for then a verb must be supplied to carry this tense marking. On the scope analysis of tense, however, only the scope of the noun phrase with respect to the rest of the sentence need be indicated. The time reference of the phrase would follow automatically from this (together with the tense of the sentence), and there would be no need for an explicit indication of tense in the noun phrase.

Another of Bach's arguments to the effect that clausal structure underlies simple noun phrases is the familiar observation that phrases like heavy smoker, early riser, former president, etc., cannot be paraphrased as smoker who is heavy, riser who is early, president who is former. The only natural way of indicating the role of the adjective in these phrases is by means of a paraphrase containing an adverb, thus someone who smokes heavily, someone who rises early, the person who formerly was president. There are also ambiguous examples such as graceful dancer, good cook, which have one reading which is naturally captured by the simple paraphrase dancer who is graceful, cook who is good, but also another reading for which this is not sufficient. Unless we assume, counter-intuitively, that the words graceful and good are themselves ambiguous, the difference between the two readings of these phrases must be treated as a difference in the grammatical role of the adjective. An analysis based on the paraphrases dancer who is graceful, someone who dances gracefully, does exactly this and it is difficult to think of a more natural way of doing it. And this analysis does require that, at least for one of the readings of the phrase, the word dancer is derived from the clausal structure someone who dances.

This analysis is not without its problems. In a footnote (p. 103) Bach mentions a comment of Langendoen's to the effect that this analysis "explains neatly the ambiguity of phrases like a good czar as (1) 'a czar who is good' and (2) 'one who "czars" well' ('good as a czar')". How seriously we are supposed to take the suggested paraphrase 'one who "czars" well' is not clear. Chomsky has emphasized (personal communication) that while the idea of deriving a good dancer from one who dances well might perhaps be extended to the derivation of a good doctor from one who doctors well, the suggestion is extremely implausible for other nominals, e.g. a good Under Secretary of State. If deriving the adjective from an underlying adverb means deriving the noun from an underlying verb, we shall have to posit an enormous number of abstract verb forms whose function is solely to be obligatorily converted into such nouns. This criticism, however, does not constitute an argument against the hypothesis that clausal structure underlies simple noun phrases. Some alternative analysis, such as one who is good as a czar, one who is good as an

Under Secretary of State, is still needed, and there appears
to be no plausible proposal for such an analysis that does not
involve the derivation of noun phrases from underlying relative
clauses.

Even if there are alternatives in the case of Bach's
other arguments for the derivation of noun phrases from
underlying relative clauses, this latter argument does appear
to hold. I shall therefore turn now to the second part of the
proposal under examination, which is that these relative
clauses should in turn be derived from conjoined clauses.
Bach gives much less attention to this part of the proposal,
but he does assume it in his proposed representations for the
sentence:

(97) She wants to marry a man with a big bank account.

The specific and non-specific readings of this sentence are
to be represented respectively as:

(98) Some x [$\hat{\ }_S$x has a big bank account and she wants to

marry x].

(99) She wants [$\hat{\ }_S$some x [$\hat{\ }_S$x has a big bank account and she

marry x]].

Both of these representations contain conjunctions, though
there is none in the surface structure (97), and the representations are structurally very similar to those which
would be assigned by a system of quantificational logic.
As pointed out earlier, however, this conjunctive analysis
is not a necessary correlate of the employment of a

specificity operator resembling the existential quantifier, but should be argued for independently.

Postal's arguments for the conjunctive analysis of relative clauses fall into three groups. The first are based on Bach and Peters' observations about pronominalization. He points out quite rightly that those observations make nonsense of a rather strong identity condition on noun phrases which he himself had previously proposed, viz:

(100)   If two disjoint noun phrases have the same heads, i.e. heads identical in meaning and reference index, then all their other structure, in particular, modifiers, must be identical, or the deep structure in which they lie enters the garbage component rather than the surface structure assignment (transformational) component.

This condition was designed to prevent the pronominalization transformation from operating on such structures as:

(101) knight_{52} axed (knight_{52} (knight_{52} was in a plight)).

(102)   (knight_{52} (knight_{52} in a plight)) axed (knight_{52}

(knight_{52} not in a plight)).

Since it is the modifiers, the relative clauses, which create the problems in these cases, and since condition (100) cannot after all be used to avoid these problems, Postal concludes that relative clauses should not be present in noun phrases at the stage at which pronominalization takes place. He argues later that they should be present in underlying structures as clauses conjoined to the main sentence, presumably to be moved into their eventual positions in surface structure by some transformation applying after the pronominalization transformation.

Postal's observations, however, do not support anything like so strong a conclusion, for there are other, less radical, cures for the puzzles about pronominalization. We might, for example, simply weaken the identity condition on pronominalization to an inclusion relationship between the 'antecedent' noun phrase and the one to be pronominalised. This would avoid the Bach-Peters paradox and also prevent pronominalization in (101) and (102) above. But this move does not require the analysis of relative clauses as conjunctions.

The second set of arguments in Postal's paper concern opaque contexts, in particular the substitutivity of identicals in opaque contexts. Since this is the topic of Chapter IV, I shall postpone discussion of these arguments until then. They do not, as far as I can see, support the conjunctive analysis of relative clauses.

The third kind of argument that Postal employs consists of observations such that the sentence:

(103)   The boy who smiled smiled.

is redundant in much the same way as the sentences:

(104)   The boy, who smiled, smiled.

(105)   The boy smiled and the boy smiled.

Postal also refers to Lakoff's observation that the phrase:

(106)   the boy who is big who is big

is not only redundant, but is also in danger of being transformed into the non-synonymous phrase:

(107) the big big boy

These observations seem to indicate at most that the content of relative clauses constitute entailments of the sentences in which they occur. The redundancy of the examples simply illustrates this fact in a rather effective way. Certain significant details of this claim must be spelled out more precisely, to account, for example, for the differences in interpretation of the definite article in (103) and (105). But even if such discrepancies could be overcome, it certainly does not follow that a sentence transformed into a relative clause must be coordinated rather than subordinated to the main clause in the underlying structure. This conclusion follows only on the incorrect assumption that the underlying representation of a sentence must consist of a conjunction of all propositions that the sentence entails.

The only other point that I can find in Postal's paper that is relevant to this analysis of relative clauses, and it is a point that Bach makes too, is that non-restrictive relative clauses are very similar in certain ways to conjoined clauses, and that restrictive relative clauses are similar in certain ways to non-restrictive relative clauses. For example, both restrictive and non-restrictive relative clauses can be reduced to give preposed adjectival constructions; this accounts for the ambiguity of a phrase such as:

(108)   the friendly Americans

However, as Postal notes, using this similarity as an argument for analysing restrictive relative clauses as conjoined
clauses leaves one with the problem of giving an account of
what it is that distinguishes restrictive and non-restrictive
relatives, for one can no longer treat this distinction as
a contrast between subordinate and coordinate clauses in
underlying structure.

All that really comes out of these arguments, then,
is the claim that a sentence entails the propositions
embodied in the sentences which underlie its relative clauses.
Properly stated (with due allowance for determiner differences,
and, probably, reference to presupposition rather than
straightforward entailment) there is certainly some truth in
this claim, but it does not force us to accept the analysis.
As was pointed out at the beginning of this section, an
inference rule operating on structures with subordinated
relative clauses would be just as effective in generating
such entailments.   The proposal that noun phrases should be
represented as predicate nominals in underlying restrictive
relative clauses does have some support, but there appears
to be little or no motivation for the claim that these
relative clauses are coordinate rather than subordinate.

Section 5.   Specific noun phrases and existence.

In Section 3 we considered a problem that arises in

connection with non-specific noun phrases if the specificity operator is identified with the existential quantifier. In Section 4 it was observed that this problem was not essentially connected with the existential quantifier but was a consequence of adopting the conjunctive analysis of noun phrases which is standardly associated with the existential quantifier in formal logical representations. I shall now consider the implications of using the existential quantifier in representations of the specific reading of noun phrases. A problem arises here which is not simply a matter of the formal apparatus associated with the existential quantifier but is due to the interpretation of the existential quantifier itself.

In giving some reasons, in Section 2, for identifying the specificity operator with the existential quantifier, it was suggested that a noun phrase interpreted as specific though within an opaque context does not differ significantly in interpretation from a noun phrase in a non-opaque context. In particular, since a sentence containing an indefinite noun phrase normally entails that something of the kind described by that noun phrase exists, it might be assumed that the same is true of a sentence containing a specifically interpreted noun phrase in an opaque context. Only this could justify representing such a sentence by means of an existentially quantified formula. It appears, however, that this assumption is false.

A sentence such as:

(109) John has caught a unicorn.

must be false because unicorns do not exist. But it appears
that many speakers of English are prepared to accept that
a sentence such as:

(110) John wants to catch a unicorn.

could be true, even on a specific interpretation of a unicorn,
despite the non-existence of unicorns. Certainly, if John
believes that unicorns exist, and believes that a certain
unicorn answering some description exists, then what goes
on in John's mind could be just the same whether unicorns
really existed or not. The question is whether, given that
unicorns do not exist, it is possible to describe what goes
on in John's mind in the words of (110). If it is, then
this would argue against representing (110) as:

(111) $(\exists x)$ (x is a unicorn and John wants John catch x).

for the rules of the logical system permit us to infer from
this:

(112) $(\exists x)$ (x is a unicorn).

that is, unicorns exist. Even if, in view of the remarks
of the previous section of this chapter, we give up the
conjunctive aspect of the logical representation, and
represent (110) instead as:

(113) $(\exists x)$ John wants John catch $(\text{a unicorn})_x$.

the conclusion that unicorns exist should surely follow.

These observations suggest that the existential
quantifier should not be used to represent specificity. The
same is not true, however, of the English phrase there is...
which is often taken to be the counterpart of the existential
quantifier, for those speakers who do not find the non-
existence of unicorns incompatible with the truth of (110)
also apparently do not find it incompatible with the truth
of:

(114) There is a unicorn that John wants to catch.

Apparently there is... can be used non-existentially. Before
accepting this conclusion, however, we might consider the
possibility of reconciling representations such as (111),
which are existentially quantified, with the absence of an
existential entailment. Worries about the use of the
existential quantifier in connection with sentences about
unicorns and other mythical or fictional beings such as
Pegasus, Santa Claus, etc., have been examined at some
length by philosophers. The problem can be illustrated
by means of the sentence:

(115) A tiger visited Winnie the Pooh.

If this sentence is represented as:

(116) $(\exists x)$ (x is a tiger and x visited Winnie the Pooh).

then it would appear that we can infer:

(117) $(\exists x)$ (x is a tiger).

that is, that at least one tiger exists. But (115) cannot

entail the existence of tigers since the tiger who visited Winnie the Pooh was Tigger, and Tigger does not exist. Therefore (115), which is true, would still be true even if tigers did not exist. If, on the other hand, (115) is <u>not</u> to be represented as (116), then how is it to be represented? This is, after all, the way in which analogous sentences, such as:

(118) A social worker visited Mrs. Smith.

are standardly represented, and if (118) and (115) have to be treated as having quite different logical forms, this would mean that we could never decide on the logical form of a sentence until we knew whether it was intended to describe a real or merely a fictional state of affairs.

It has been proposed as a solution to this puzzle that (116) <u>can</u> be retained as the representation of (115), without our being forced to accept that it entails that tigers exist, if we regard (115) and (116) as being within the scope of some reality-conceding phrase such as 'According to the familiar story...'. This removes the worry about the existential entailment of (115), because within the familiar story, this entailment does hold -- it is quite true that according to the familiar story there exists at least one tiger, viz. Tigger.

Could not a similar account be given of sentence (110) above, to explain why (110) can be held to be true in the face of the non-existence of unicorns? We would not, of course, want to preface (110) with the phrase 'According to the familiar story...', but some other phrase might be found which would be suitable. A natural candidate would be 'According to John's beliefs...', thus:

(119)   According to John's beliefs, John wants to catch a (certain) unicorn.

or, more naturally,

(120)   John thinks he wants to catch a (certain) unicorn.

This sentence can be represented in such a way that there is no temptation to say that it entails the existence of unicorns, even though its representation does contain the existential quantifier. Thus:

(121)   John thinks $(\exists x)$ (x is a unicorn and John wants John catch x).

The want here is represented as specific, since the quantifier is to the left of the phrase John wants..., but because the quantifier is to the right of John thinks..., we are committed only to John's thinking that unicorns exist and not to their actual existence. The representation corresponds roughly to the sentence:

(122)   John thinks there is a unicorn he wants to catch.

The trouble with this is that it does not properly capture the meaning of (110), for according to (110) John does want something, and yet (120) and (122) say only that

he thinks he does. The scope relationships between the
quantifier and the opaque verbs in (121) are correct, but
the scope relationship between the two opaque verbs themselves is incorrect, for the verb <u>wants</u> is within the scope
of the verb <u>thinks</u>. By analogy with similar constructions,
such as:

(123)   Bill thinks John wants to catch a unicorn.

the sentence (120) should be interpreted as saying, roughly,
that one of John's thoughts is a thought about one of his
wants. Of course John might have such a thought, but the
sense of (110) that we are trying to capture has nothing to
do with that possibility. If we are going to bring John's
thoughts into the analysis at all, the most we should want
to say is that John thinks there is a unicorn and he wants
to catch it, not (120) or (122). In fact, unless we are
prepared to make what John thinks part of the analysis of
a sentence such as:

(124)   John wants to catch a (certain) fish.

then we should probably not make it part of the analysis
of (110), for the mental state of John's that we are concerned with in (110) is precisely similar to the one involved
in (124) except for the difference between unicorns and
fish.

It should be noted, however, that there is a precedent
for paraphrases such as (120) or (122). The sentence:

(125) John thinks he knows who lives next door.

might, by analogy with:

(126) Bill thinks John knows who lives next door.

be interpreted as saying that John has a certain opinion, to the effect that he knows who lives next door. But a much more common interpretation of (125) is simply that John has an opinion about who lives next door. This is really very similar to the situation for sentence (110). As far as John's mental state is concerned, no significant difference is implied by saying that John knows something rather than that he thinks it. The difference between the two has to do with how things actually are in the real world, with whether what John thinks is the case really is or not. When we want to avoid the implication that John is right, we use think rather than know -- except, that is, with a WH-complement. For whatever reason, sentences like:

(127) *John thinks who lives next door.

are ungrammatical in English. And it is this gap which the sentence (125) fills; it is taken to mean exactly what (127) would mean if it were grammatical. In other words, to describe the situation in which John 'knows' something except that he is wrong about it, we embed the John knows... sentence within John thinks....

The paraphrase (120) of sentence (110) is exactly parallel to this. In order to describe the situation in which John wants to catch something except that it does not

exist, we have embedded the John wants... sentence within

John thinks.... Despite this very close parallel, however,

I think (120) does not, after all, serve as a useful analysis

of the sentence (110). For one thing, even in spite of

the analogy, my intuitions say that (120), unlike (125), can

only be taken literally, i.e. as saying that John has a thought

about a want, and that it therefore does not have the meaning

necessary to serve as a paraphrase for (110). Even if it

did, the structure of (120), just like the structure of (125),

does not illuminate that interpretation. Rather, (120)

and (125) themselves stand in need of explication, and so

very little would be gained by taking them as the model for

the analysis of (110). The treatment which works for

sentences like (115), which are to be taken wholly within

the context of a fiction of some kind, is not, it seems,

adequate for sentences like (110) which combine references

to the real world with reference to imaginary entities.

Rather than placing the whole of sentence (110)

within the context of a reality-conceding phrase, it looks

as if it is just the noun phrase a unicorn which, lacking

the usual existential entailment, should be treated in this

way. We might therefore consider, instead of (120), the

paraphrase:

(128) John wants to catch something that he thinks is a

unicorn.

corresponding to the representation:

(129)   ($\exists$x) (John thinks x is a unicorn and John wants John catch x).

This, however, will not do, for it makes John's belief that a unicorn exists a matter of his believing, wrongly, of something that does exist, that it is a unicorn. This is certainly a possible source for John's belief, but it is not the only one. Furthermore, if this _is_ the case, then it is arguable that sentence (110) is false for then (110) says that something which, ex hypothesi, is not a unicorn, is a unicorn. This will be discussed in more detail in Chapter IV, since it concerns the description under which something is referred to. I shall simply assume, for the moment, that what is needed in connection with sentence (110) is not John's believing of something that exists that it is a unicorn, but his believing of a unicorn that it exists.

Notice, however, that if we try to express this latter situation, either by:

(130)   John believes a unicorn exists and he wants to catch it.

or by:

(131)   John wants to catch a unicorn that he believes exists.

then we simply have to give up the existential interpretation of indefinite noun phrases, at least in these contexts. Up to this point, we responded to the threat that a sentence like (110) poses for the representation of specificity

with the existential quantifier, by continuing to assume
that specificity entails existence and thus that the existential analysis is correct, and by trying to explain away
sentence (110) as elliptical for some other sentence that
does not entail the existence of unicorns. In working out
the details of this move, however, we seem to have rejected
all alternatives except the one we set out to avoid, i.e.
that specific noun phrases simply do not entail existence.
And, as it happens, there is some rather strong evidence in
support of this conclusion. Sentences such as:

(132)   I have to write a paper.

(133)   I would like you to make a telephone call.

can be interpreted specifically or non-specifically. I
might, for example, want you to call my Aunt Alice and tell
her I shall be late for supper, or I might simply want you
to make sure the telephone is in order, in which case I
wouldn't care what call you made. The specific interpretations of these sentences can be paraphrased as:

(134)   There is a (certain) paper I have to write.

(135)   There is a (certain) telephone call I want you to
                                            make.

These are perfectly acceptable English sentences, not
deviant or odd in any way. Yet they definitely do not
entail existence.

    With verbs such as <u>write</u> or <u>make</u>, which we might
call 'creative' verbs, we have to be careful about existence

entailments in any case, not just in opaque contexts. The sentence:

(136)   John is writing a paper.

does not mean, or even entail:

(137)   There is a paper and John is writing it.

in the way that the sentence:

(138)   John is copying a paper.

means, or at least entails:

(139)   There is a paper and John is copying it.

for the paper that John is writing does not really exist until he has written a great deal, perhaps all, of it. But notice that the claim that (132) and (134) do not entail the existence of a paper does not rest simply on this. It is not just that the paper I have to write does not <u>now</u> exist. It is quite compatible with the truth of (132) and (134) that it should never exist at all, since, as is so often the case, I might never write the paper I have to write. Thus these sentences do not entail either (140) or (141):

(140)   There is a paper.

(141)   There will be a paper.

and they thus constitute strong evidence for the claim that the specific/non-specific contrast is not to be analysed in terms of existence entailments.

Paraphrasing specific and non-specific noun phrases with <u>there is</u>... tends to suggest an analysis in terms of

102

existence entailments, but there are other ways of paraphrasing them which bring out other semantic aspects of
the contrast and might therefore be a better guide to the
correct analysis. We have said, for example, that the
specific reading of the sentence:

(142) John wants to catch a fish.

means that John has a certain fish in mind, while the non-
specific reading is compatible with his having no particular
fish in mind. The sentence:

(143) John has a certain fish in mind.

might itself be taken to entail the existence of fish, for
it might be taken to be equivalent to :

(144) There is a fish and John is thinking of it.

but there is also another sense, in which one can have a
certain fish in mind without its actually having to exist.
All that this sense involves is imagining to oneself a fish
with some individuating characteristics. I do not want to
go into the detailed phenomenology of this, and questions
such as whether one can imagine to oneself a fish-in-general,
without any particular characteristics, are questions that
I shall deliberately avoid. All I wish to suggest is that
an essential difference between the specific and non-specific
readings of a sentence like (142) is whether or not John is
able or prepared to ascribe some particular characteristics
to the fish he wants to catch, characteristics which distinguish

it from other fish. The contrast, that is to say, is not
a matter of whether a fish exists, but of whether a fish can
be individuated.

Another way of expressing this is to say that the
specific reading of sentence (142) says that some fish
(whether or not it exists in the real world) has the property
being-wanted-to-be-caught-by-John. This is what Quine calls
the 'relational' interpretation; the sentence says that John
and some fish stand in the relation wants-to-catch. The
non-specific reading, on the other hand, though it does
ascribe a property to John, does not ascribe a property to
any fish. Now if it makes sense to say that a certain fish
has a certain property, it must be possible, at least in
principle if not in practice, to say which fish has that
property, i.e. to individuate the fish in question. That
individuation is at the heart of the specific/non-specific
contrast is supported by the contrast between sentences (132)
and (133) and the sentence:

(145) I would like you to make me a cup of tea.

The specific reading of this sentence, and its paraphrase:

(146) There is a cup of tea that I would like you to make.

are extremely unnatural. The only explanation for this
that I can think of is that cups of tea, unlike papers and
telephone calls, are not the kind of thing we normally
individuate, or could imagine how to individuate, independently

of their spatio-temporal and physical properties, i.e. independently of their real physical existence. Where such individuation is problematic, the specific readings of sentences are bizarre.

Talk of individuation, though it is obviously more appropriate than talk of existence entailments, is only the beginning of an answer of course, for it is not itself a completely clear notion. There are serious problems concerning the principles of individuation for things that do not exist. If, for example, I am hallucinating a pink elephant, and John is hallucinating a pink elephant, does it even make sense to ask whether they are the same pink elephant or different ones? (See Geach, J. of Phil., 1967, for further discussion of such puzzles.) Nevertheless, the way we use our language strongly suggests that we do operate with some such principles, however difficult they are to state and however unreliable. Even for things that do exist, just how much characterization is necessary to count as having picked out some individual is a very difficult question to answer. We might in principle demand some description of the individual which is true of no other individual, but this is a much stronger requirement than we actually impose in practice. To back up my claim that there is a certain fish that I want to catch I certainly do not have to be able to describe the fish in question in such a way that there is no possibility that you, or even I, might mistake some other fish for it. On the other hand, if the very most that I can say about it is that it is a blue fish, you would have some reason to doubt that I do have a particular fish in mind.

Since almost exactly the same problems arise when one attempts to say what counts as a sufficiently individuating description to warrant the use of the definite article, one might suspect that a necessary condition on the truth of the specific reading of a sentence like:

(147) John wants to catch a fish.

is that there should be some true sentence of the form:

(148) John wants to catch the such-and-such fish.

where 'such-and-such' is replaced by some descriptive phrase. The non-specific reading of (147), by contrast, would not entail any such sentence. However, this is too strong a condition. It says that if it is true that:

(149) I have to write a (certain) paper.

then there must be some true sentence of the form:

(150) I have to write the such-and-such paper.

There do exist sentences of this form, for example:

(151) I have to write the paper that I forgot to write
                                last term.

but they are not very common, and in fact a sentence like (149) seems to be justified on the basis of something much weaker than a definite description, for example by:

106

(152) I have to write a paper on the relation between

marihuana use and arthritis.

It is interesting that the which-question criterion for

specificity also fails in these same cases. Normally one

can distinguish the specific from the non-specific reading

of a sentence such as (147) for example, by asking whether

the question:

(153) Which fish does John want to catch?

is an appropriate question to ask. For the non-specific

reading of (147), there is no possible answer to such a

question, but for the specific reading there must in

principle be an answer to it, even if no-one actually knows

the answer. For the specific reading of (149), however, it

seems that there does not necessarily have to be an answer

to the question:

(154) Which paper do you have to write?

The most that can be demanded is that there should be an

answer to the question:

(155) What paper do you have to write?

What-questions are odd things; they are in many cases only

marginally acceptable, for example:

(156) What pencil did you buy?

A detailed study of them might perhaps shed some light on

the notion of individuation.

The conclusion to be drawn from this discussion is

that the specific reading of a sentence containing an

indefinite noun phrase in an opaque context should not be represented by an existentially quantified formula. The specificity operator is to be defined in terms of some notion of individuation, not in terms of existence. Curiously, however, this seems to be too weak an analysis for the non-specific reading. Many of the problems about the non-specific reading discussed in Section 3 are dissolved away if we analyse the non-specific reading of, for example:

(157)   John wants to catch a fish.

as something like:

(158)   John wants that some fish should have the property
                        that he catches it.

rather than as:

(159)   John wants that there should be a fish that he catches.
The analysis in terms of individuation and properties, applied to the non-specific reading, does therefore seem to have advantages over the analysis in terms of existence. But on the other hand it is surely not true that John would be satisfied if some merely fictional or imaginary fish should have the property in question. In fact, since one cannot catch fish that do not exist, it does not even make sense to suppose that this is what John wants to do. (Of course, John could want it to be true, within some story, that he caught a fish.) We are in danger, therefore, of having to give up one of our basic principles, viz. that specific and

103

non-specific readings should be distinguished by differences in scope of <u>one and the same symbol</u>. The non-specific reading seems to require an operator with existential import, and the specific reading to require an operator without it.

One way out of this conclusion would be to say that indefinite noun phrases are <u>never</u> to be analysed in terms of of existence. Sentences containing indefinite noun phrases do very often have existential entailments. For example, the sentence:

(160) I read some books today.

entails:

(161) Some books that I read today exist.

(ignoring, once again, the tense of the existential proposition). But it certainly seems odd to say that (160) <u>means</u> (161). Since (160) and (161) are logically equivalent, it is possible to represent the former along the lines of the latter without running the risk of generating any incorrect entailments. Instead of devising distinct representations for (160) and (161), and setting up the inference rules to capture the fact that they entail each other, we can simply use a representation appropriate for one to do service for both, and thus incidentally get by without needing inference rules to relate them. But we have just been examining examples in which an indefinite noun phrase carries no existential entailment and for which a representation in terms of existence is therefore incorrect. These examples, together

with the non-synonymy of pairs like (160) and (161), suggest
that sentences which contain indefinite noun phrases but
which are not explicitly existential sentences, should always
be assigned a representation which is neutral with respect
to existential entailments. Inference rules could then be
set up to generate existential entailments in just those
cases for which they exist. It appears, in fact, that it
is the property that the sentence predicates of the referent
of the noun phrase which determines whether or not that
referent must exist in the real world. If the property is
wanted-to-be-caught-by-John, real existence is not required.
If the property is having-been-caught-by-John, on the other
hand, or being-read-by-me-today, then real existence <u>is</u>
required. This will explain the difference between the
specific and non-specific reading of sentence (157) that
was noted above. The property that is ascribed to a fish
on the specific reading is wanted-to-be-caught-by-John, which
does not entail the real existence of the fish. The property
that, on the non-specific reading, John wants some fish to
have is being-caught-by-John, which does entail the real
existence of any fish having this property.

Of course, distinguishing those properties which can
hold only of really existing individuals from those which
can hold of non-existent ones, might appear to be just our
original task of distinguishing transparent contexts from

opaque ones. But those noun phrases whose referents need
not really exist and those which exhibit the specific/non-
specific ambiguity are not exactly the same, though the
classes do overlap to a considerable extent. Verbs that
tolerate non-existent referents for their object noun phrases
but not non-specific ones are write to, talk to, address,
pray to, etc.. For example, the sentence:

(162) John wrote to someone.

is not ambiguous with respect to specificity. It has no
non-specific reading; one cannot write to no-one in particular
in the way that one can, for example, look for a pencil but
no particular pencil. (John might, of course, have written:
'To whom it may concern...', but this does not establish
that there is a non-specific reading of (162) for we can
still say that John wrote to the person(s) who were concerned.)
On the other hand, sentence (162) would still be true if the
person John wrote to was Santa Claus or even some less public
fictional individual whom John mistakenly believes to
exist.

A verb of the opposite type, which takes a noun phrase
which may be read as non-specific but which does entail
existence, is manage. The sentence:

(163) John managed to catch a fish.

is ambiguous. It may be taken to describe the situation
in which John's intention was simply not to return from his

day by the river fishless, i.e. to catch some fish or other, and he succeeded in this. On the other hand it may be taken to say that John intended to catch a particular fish and succeeded in this. The phrase:

(164) The fish that John managed to catch...

is, strictly, appropriate only given the truth of the specific reading of (163), though admittedly this distinction is a fine one and much less striking than for a phrase like:

(165) The fish John wanted to catch...

However, sentence (163) could not be true, on either reading, if fish did not really exist. The sentence:

(166) John managed to catch a unicorn.

for example, is bound to be false given the non-existence of unicorns (unless, of course, it is taken as a whole as within the context of a story).

In view of these observations, it is clear that at least two different things may be meant by the claim that existential generalization fails for a given sentence. Existential generalization may fail because the sentence is being read non-specifically and thus is not being taken to ascribe any property to any individual (really existent or otherwise). On the other hand, and quite independently of this, existential generalization may fail in the sense that it is not valid to infer the real existence of an object of the kind described. Also, as pointed out in Chapter I, existential generalization may be said to fail because of considerations connected with the description under which something is referred to. These three cases do not coincide exactly. Which one we take as a defining criterion for the class of opaque contexts is a terminological question which is of little importance compared with the importance of recognising that there are these distinctions to be made. In fact, in many discussions of opacity it looks as though talk of the failure of existential generalization involves the confusion of these different cases.

What I have been arguing for is that existential generalization in the sense in which it is relevant to the specific/non-specific contrast is <u>not</u> concerned with real existence. The notion of existential generalization in the sense which has to do with individuation rather than real existence is obviously central to the explication of the specific/non-specific contrast, and it is also this sense which correlates with the use of <u>there is...</u> in English. Though there is more to be said on the subject than I have been able to say here, there therefore appear to be obvious advantages to using an existence-neutral operator (such as our (Sx)) in the formal representation of <u>all</u> sentences with indefinite noun phrases. The function of this operator will be simply to indicate the scope relationships between the noun phrase and other parts of the sentence, that is,

to indicate which properties are being ascribed to which
individuals. Inference rules operating on such representations
must then be used to generate entailments concerning real
existence when and where these inferences are valid.[FN] It
appears, from the observations presented above, that these
inference rules will have to be sensitive to particular
lexical items, or, at least, to certain semantically defined
classes of lexical items. Perhaps in the characterization
of these classes, though I have none to offer here, the
answer will be found to the important outstanding question,
which is why the correlation between contexts which are
ambiguous with respect to existential generalization in the
sense of individuation, and contexts for which existential
generalization in the sense of real existence fails, though
not a perfect correlation, is as strong as it is.

Section 6. Logical relationships between the readings.

The non-specific reading of a sentence such as:

FN. I have suggested that the validity of such inferences
will depend on what property the sentence predicates of the
individual in question. However this treatment also allows
for some flexibility about inferring real existence depending
on the type of entity the noun phrase refers to. It has
often been observed that there is something odd about inferring
from a sentence like: There is an aspect of the problem that
I don't understand that there exist aspects, or aspects of
problems. The same kind of bizarreness attends, to a greater
or lesser degree, statements about the existence of, for
example, consequences, considerations, numbers, facts, climates,
hairstyles, etc. etc..

(167)   John wants to catch a fish.

has been characterised so far mostly in a negative fashion.
By contrast with the specific reading of the same sentence,
the non-specific reading does not imply that John has a
particular fish in mind.   The specific reading thus seems to
be the 'stronger' of the two, to 'say more' than the non-
specific reading.   We may therefore consider the hypothesis
that its meaning includes that of the non-specific reading,
i.e. that it entails the non-specific reading of the
sentence, though not vice versa.

The truth of this claim might be questioned on a
number of grounds, but these do not all stand up to scrutiny.
It is conceivable, for example, that John, asked if he wants
to catch a fish, says 'no', but then asked if he wants to
catch the fish that is eating his tadpoles says 'yes'.   But
this obviously does not establish that the specific reading
might be true and the non-specific reading simultaneously
false.   As pointed out earlier, the fact that someone will,
apparently quite sincerely, make two statements that contradict each other does not always count as evidence even that
he believes both, yet alone that both are true.   John might
be confused.   Or he might have forgotten about his desire to
catch a fish until reminded of the existence of the one that
eats his tadpoles.   Notice in the latter case, however,
that once he has remembered his desire to catch that fish,

he will presumably now answer 'yes' to the question whether
he wants to catch a fish. There is a dispositional sense
of want, in which one can be said to want something even if
one is not consciously aware at the time, for whatever reason,
that one does. It is this that is involved in the situation
we have just described, but since it is equally applicable
to the specific and the non-specific readings of the
sentence, it cannot be used to pull them apart and show that
the former does not entail the latter.

Another possibility that one might consider is that
John does want to catch a particular fish, will point to it
and announce his desire to catch it, but will deny that he
wants to catch a fish because he does not realise that the
fish he wants to catch is a fish. This, however, is clearly
a matter of the description under which something is referred
to. A particularly interesting case of this is where there
are, for example, fifty-seven fish that John wants to catch
but, because he has not counted them, or has miscounted
them, he denies that he wants to catch fifty-seven fish.
The description under which something is referred to obviously
does affect the validity of inferences from opaque constructions but, as will be argued in Chapter IV, it affects
inferences on both the specific and non-specific readings.
Moving from a transparent interpretation of the description
on the specific reading, to an opaque interpretation of it

on the non-specific reading, or vice versa, and then
exhibiting the inferences as invalid, clearly should not
be taken as evidence that the specific reading does not
entail the non-specific.

A more substantial argument to the effect that the
specific reading does not entail the non-specific is based
on the claim that the non-specific reading can be paraphrased with the word any, for example that the non-specific
reading of (167) above can be paraphrased as:

(168)   John wants to catch any fish.

The claim, then, is that not only is the non-specific reading
compatible with John's not having decided on a particular
fish, but this reading actually entails or means that he has
not done so.   In fact it goes further, for it says that the
non-specific reading entails that he has not even decided
which kind of fish he wants to catch.   Perhaps no-one would
actually claim that the sentence (168) with any is logically
equivalent to the non-specific reading of (167), for presumably allowance has to be made for defective or atypical
specimens of fish.   We should therefore take the claim to
be, roughly, that the non-specific reading of (167) entails
that John would be happy to catch any characteristic or normal
fish, whatever that means precisely.   Now if this is so, the
non-specific reading will have a positive aspect to its
meaning that the specific reading lacks; it will entail that

John is indifferent between different fish that he might catch, which is clearly not the case for the specific reading. Hence the specific reading would not entail the non-specific one.

This account of the non-specific reading seems to me to be too strong, however. It would mean that we could never report a non-specific want, belief, intention, expectation, etc., correctly unless we knew everything relevant to it. It would not be proper to use a sentence like (167) unless one were sure that the colour, size, breed, etc., of fish were completely irrelevant to John's want. It would not be proper to use a sentence such as:

(169) John believes an elephant is in the garden.

if one suspected that John also had an opinion about the size and colour of the elephant. For the description contained in the non-specific noun phrase must, it is being claimed, provide a _complete_ specification of the kind of thing that would satisfy John's want, or the kind of thing he believes is in the garden. Notice that this would also mean that if a sentence such as:

(170) John wants to catch a green fish.

is true on its non-specific reading, then sentence (167) would be false (unless, of course, John had two separate desires, one to catch any fish, and another to catch any green fish, i.e. he wants to catch two fish). Now, if the remarks of Section 3 about simplification in opaque contexts are

correct, it is certainly the case that (170) does not entail (167). But to say that it is incompatible with (167)
seems to go much too far. Thus this attempt to establish
that the specific reading does not entail the non-specific
reading also breaks down.

Nevertheless it is true that the specific reading
does not entail the non-specific, and the reason for this
does have to do with simplification. Sentence (170) does
not, we have said, entail (167) because John might be completely indifferent to catching a fish except insofar as he
wants to catch a green one. Sentence (167) is, for example,
compatible with John's believing he will catch a fish, not
caring much about this either way, but, on the assumption
that he will catch one, wanting the one he catches to be
green. Now in exactly the same way, the specific reading
of (167) does not entail the non-specific reading, for there
might be a particular fish that John wants to catch and yet
he might be completely indifferent to the idea of catching a
fish in general. He might, that is, want to catch a fish
only if it is that particular one, just as he might want
to catch a fish only if it is a green one; he might, assuming
he is going to catch a fish, want it to be that one, just as,
assuming he is going to catch a fish, he might it to be a
green one. Thus, just as (170), though not incompatible
with (167), does not entail it, so the specific

reading of (167), though not, of course, incompatible with the non-specific reading, does not entail it.

On the other hand, this conclusion does not show that the specific reading does not, in some sense, 'include' the non-specific reading. We can, in fact, provide a representation of the specific reading that differs from the representation of the non-specific reading just in that it contains an extra clause. The reason that this does not force us to say that the specific reading entails the non-specific, is that this clause is within the opaque context, and simplification within opaque contexts is not valid. Thus we might regard the specific reading of (167) as saying that there is a particular fish such that John wants that he should catch a fish and that it be that particular fish, and we could therefore say that the specific reading of (167) can be represented as:

(171) John wants (Sx) (x = a & John catch x).

for some individual constant a which designates a particular fish, just as the non-specific reading of (170) can be represented as:

(172) John wants (Sx) (x is a fish and x is green and John

catch x).

Of course, since (167) does not tell us which individual fish it is that John wants to catch, but only that there is one, we should not really use an individual constant in the representation; all that is justified is something like:

(173)   (Sy) (y is a fish & John wants (Sx)(x = y & John

catch x)).

This doubly quantified formula is unwieldy, and I am not seriously suggesting it as the standard representation of the specific reading of (167). If, however, we wish the logical relationship between the specific and non-specific readings to be captured by our system, then we shall need to have inference rules that allow us to derive something like (173) from the standard representation of the specific reading of sentence (167).

The claim that the specific reading does not entail the non-specific for reasons connected with the simplification of conjunctions within opaque contexts suggests two hypotheses, both of which appear to be true. One is that for the limited class of opaque contexts in which simplification is valid, it should also be valid to infer the non-specific reading from the specific. It was pointed out in Section 3 that for epistemic verbs, such as know and believe, simplification is valid even within the opaque context. For example, the argument:

(174)   Mary believes there is a green fish in the pond.

Therefore Mary believes there is a fish in the pond. is valid (at least, given a theory of immediate inference, and ignoring possible complications due to the opacity of

the descriptive content of noun phrases). And, as predicted,
the argument:

(175) There is a fish that Mary believes is in the pond.

Therefore Mary believes there is a fish in the pond.
is also valid. The same point can be made for the adjective
possible; both of the following arguments are valid.

(176) It is possible that there is a green fish in the pond.

Therefore it is possible that there is a fish in the pond.

(177) There is a fish such that it is possible that it is

in the pond.

Therefore it is possible that there is a fish in the pond.
Curiously, though simplification is valid also for necessary,
thus:

(178) It is necessary that there is a green fish in the pond.

Therefore it is necessary that there is a fish in the pond.
the argument from specific to non-specific seems dubious:

(179) There is a fish such that necessarily it is in the pond.

Necessarily there is a fish in the pond.
However this argument is valid within standard systems of modal
logic (see Hughes and Cresswell, 1968, p. 144). I cannot go
into a detailed discussion of modal logic here, but I would
point out that for necessary, the specific reading must be
defined with care, since the sentences:

(180) There is a fish such that necessarily it is in the pond.

(181) Necessarily there is a certain fish in the pond.
are apparently not equivalent, and the argument with (181)

122

as premise rather than (180), viz:

(182)   Necessarily there is a certain fish in the pond.

Therefore necessarily there is a fish in the pond.
does appear to be valid.

The second hypothesis about the inference from specific
to non-specific is that in negative contexts, where simplification is clearly not valid but the inverse of it is, we
should find that the relationship between specific and non-
specific readings is reversed, i.e. that there is some
temptation to infer the specific reading from the non-specific,
though no temptation to infer the non-specific from the specific.
Before going into details I should make clear what I do not
mean by this. Since in general if p entails q, then (not q)
entails (not p), where the specific reading does entail the
non-specific, the negation of the non-specific reading should
entail the negation of the specific. Thus since the argument (175
is valid, then the argument:

(183)   It is false that Mary believes there is a fish in the

pond.

Therefore it is false that there is a fish that Mary

believes is in the pond.
is also valid. Since the argument:

(184)   There is a fish that John wants to catch.

Therefore John wants there to be a fish that he catches.
is not valid, we should not expect the argument:

(185) It is false that John wants there to be a fish that

he catches.

Therefore it is false that there is a fish that John

wants to catch.

to be valid either. This is a straightforward fact about the
truth conditions on conditional statements, and is not
especially connected with opaque contexts.

The hypothesis that I wish to consider is based on the
fact that while simplification within negative contexts is
invalid, i.e. the argument:

(186) Not (p & q).

Therefore not p.

is invalid, the converse argument:

(187) Not p.

Therefore not (p & q).

is valid. We should therefore expect the argument:

(188) John believes that not (p & q).

Therefore John believes that not p.

to be invalid, but the argument:

(189) John believes that not p.

Therefore John believes that not (p & q).

might conceivably be valid. Similarly for the 'negative'
verb <u>doubts</u>, it is clear that the argument:

(190) John doubts that (p & q).

Therefore John doubts that p.

is invalid, but there is some plausibility to the converse

argument:

(191)   John doubts that p.

Therefore John doubts that (p & q).

Analogous examples for the specific/non-specific
contrast rather than overt conjunctions are:

(192)   John doubts that he killed a spider.

which has the readings:

(193)   There is a spider that John doubts that he killed.

(194)   John doubts that there is a spider that he killed.

and here too, the argument from (193) to (194) is quite
obviously invalid while the argument from (194) to (193) has
some plausibility. With negative verbs, that is to say, if
either reading entails the other, it is the non-specific that
entails the specific. I think it can be argued, however,
that just as the specific reading does not really entail the
non-specific in positive contexts, though it might appear
to, so the non-specific reading does not really entail the
specific in negative contexts, though it might appear to.
For example, the argument from (194) to (193) is not really
valid, since to doubt p means to believe (or suspect, etc.)
that not p, and not simply not to believe that p. And John
might have no opinions about any particular spider at all,
thus (193) might be false, even though (194) is true.

Though the predicted inversion of the relationship
between specific and non-specific readings thus does appear
to hold for negative opaque verbs, there are enormous

complexities in the interpretation of sentences containing a negative element as well as an indefinite noun phrase in an opaque context that I can only begin to touch on here. There are scope ambiguities in sentences with negation and indefinite noun phrases, even in transparent contexts. Thus the sentence:

(195) John did not kill a spider. (It is false that John

killed a spider.)

can be taken to mean either that there is a spider that John did not kill, or that it is false that there is a spider that John killed. (This contrast is very like, if not identical to, the specific/non-specific contrast in opaque contexts, but I shall not attempt here to give a general account of indefinite noun phrases in negative contexts or to define this connection.) There are also scope ambiguities in sentences with both negation and certain opaque verbs, even without indefinite noun phrases. Thus the sentence:

(196) John does not believe that p.

may be taken to mean either that John believes that it is false that p, or else that it is false that John believes that p. (See Klima, Negation in English, for further discussion.) Putting these ambiguities together with the familiar specific/ non-specific ambiguity of indefinite noun phrases in opaque contexts, we would predict that the sentence:

(197) John does not believe that he killed a spider.

has the six readings:

(198)   a.   There is a spider such that it is false that John
believes he killed it.

       b.   It is false that there is a spider that John believes
he killed.

       c.   It is false that John believes there is a spider
that he killed.

       d.   There is a spider that John believes he did not kill.

       e.   John believes it is false that there is a spider
that he killed.

       f.   John believes that there is a spider that he did
not kill.

The reader may satisfy himself that the sentence has all of
these readings except the last. The absence of this reading
shows that 'Neg-hopping' cannot operate across a specificity
operator; the string:

(199)   John believes (Sx) **Neg Fx.**

cannot be converted into:

(200)   John doesn't believe (Sx) **Fx.**

although for a string in which the specificity operator does
not intervene between the verb and the **Neg,** for example:

(201)   (Sx) John believes **Neg Fx.**

'Neg-hopping' does apply, to give:

(202)   (Sx) John doesn't believe **Fx.**

I also point out in passing that there are interactions
between the specificity operator and 'negative' verbs such as

doubt. It has already been remarked that doubt p means
something like believe not p (or perhaps suspect not p, etc.)
rather than not believe that p. The negation, that is to say,
is interpreted as internal to the opaque context. The
sentence:

(203) John doubts that he killed a spider.

therefore should only have three of the readings of (198),
in particular the readings d, e and f. However, there is a
further constraint that excludes the last of these. The
specificity operator cannot be interpreted as intervening
between the believe and the negation element that are combined
in the word doubt. There is no reading, that is, which
corresponds to:

(204) John believes (Sx) Neg Fx.

It has just been observed that for negative opaque
verbs, the usual relationship between specific and non-
specific readings is reversed. There is another type of
example for which the non-specific reading appears, at
least at first sight, to entail the specific. This is the
case of factive opaque verbs, but here we also find the
usual temptation to infer the non-specific reading from
the specific. In this case, therefore, it is not that the
usual logical relationship is reversed, but that the two
readings virtually fall together, since there is a temptation
to infer each from the other. The sentence:

(205) John regrets having killed a spider.

for example, is ambiguous with respect to specificity. There may

be a particular spider that John regrets having killed -- your

pet tarantula, perhaps. Or it may be that John regrets the fact

that there is a spider that he killed. But the ambiguity

of this sentence is apparently harder for speakers to detect

than the ambiguity of a sentence like:

(206) John wants to kill a spider.

and even when one has observed that it is ambiguous, the two

readings seem much less distinct.

The argument from non-specific to specific in a case

like (205) rests on the fact that both readings presuppose:

(207) John killed a spider.

This sentence does not contain an opaque context, and is not

ambiguous with respect to specificity. If John killed a spider

then there is a spider that John killed. But if John regrets

having killed a spider, and his having killed a spider

is his having killed a certain spider, then it seems to

follow that John regrets having killed a certain spider. This

argument, however, is not valid and for much the same reasons as

simplification in opaque contexts is not valid. For John might

regret having killed a spider and yet, having done so, be quite

indifferent to which particular spider he killed; he regrets

having killed that spider only inasmuch as it involves having

killed a spider, and he might in fact be quite relieved that,

having killed a spider, it was that one that he killed. Notice

that there are differences among factive verbs as to the extent
to which the readings tend to fall together. The difference
between the two readings of:

(208) John knows that he killed a spider.

or of:

(209) John admitted having killed a spider.

is much more apparent than for (205), and the temptation to
infer the specific reading from the non-specific is much
less. This difference will be discussed in more detail
at the end of Chapter III, in connection with the relationship
between definite noun phrases and indefinite ones, particularly
the relationship between a sentence such as (205) and the
sentence:

(210) John regrets having killed the spider that he killed.

CHAPTER III.   OPACITY AND DEFINITE NOUN PHRASES.

Section 1.   The referential/attributive ambiguity.

Since indefinite noun phrases are ambiguous in opaque contexts, and since there obviously exist syntactic and semantic connections between indefinite and definite noun phrases, it is natural to ask whether definite noun phrases exhibit a similar kind of scope ambiguity in opaque contexts. And it is possible, in fact, to distinguish (at least) two readings of a sentence such as:

(1)   John wants to talk to the boy who failed the exam.

This sentence can be taken to mean that John wants to meet a certain boy, a boy who happens, as a matter of fact, to be the one boy who failed the exam.   The sentence can also be taken to describe the situation in which there is no-one independently specifiable that John wants to talk to -- he simply wants to talk to whichever boy it was who failed the exam.

This ambiguity is much less striking than the specific/ non-specific ambiguity of indefinite noun phrases; the difference between the two readings is not so great.   It was pointed out in the previous chapter that a question such as:

(2)   Which boy does John want to talk to?

can be answered only if the specific reading of the corresponding assertion:

(3)   John wants to talk to a boy.

is true.   If sentence (3) is true only when read as

non-specific, then the question (2) is unanswerable. But this question is both appropriate and answerable given the truth of either of the readings of sentence (1) that we are interested in, and so the which-question criterion fails to distinguish them. It is also true that the phrase:

(4) The boy John wants to talk to...

can be used properly only if sentence (3) is true on its specific interpretation; if (3) is true only when interpreted as non-specific then there is no-one to whom the phrase (4) refers. Once again, however, this criterion fails to distinguish the different readings of definite noun phrases. The phrase (4) will have a referent if sentence (1) is true on either of the readings in question.

The ambiguity of definite noun phrases in opaque contexts is therefore not identical to the specific/non-specific ambiguity. In fact, both readings of (1) apparently entail the specific reading of the sentence:

(5) John wants to talk to a boy.

that is:

(6) There is a boy that John wants to talk to.

(Note: It is possible to have some reservations about this claim, and I shall discuss it again in more detail in Section 8.) The notion of John's having a particular boy in mind, however, which we used in the previous chapter to distinguish between specific and non-specific readings,

132

does serve to clarify the ambiguity of definite noun phrases. According to one of the readings of sentence (1), which I shall call the 'attributive' reading, John does not have any particular boy in mind, but simply wants to talk to whoever failed the exam. On the other reading, the 'referential' reading, John does have a particular boy in mind as the boy he wants to talk to, and the boy he has in mind is the boy who failed the exam. However, if we are more precise, we shall see that this notion of having someone in mind is being used in a slightly different way in connection with definite noun phrases than in connection with indefinite ones. The specific reading of the sentence:

(7) John wants to talk to a boy who failed the exam.

implies that John has a certain boy in mind as the boy he wants to talk to--he has decided which boy he wants to talk to. The non-specific reading of (7), by contrast, does not imply this. But both the referential and the attributive reading of sentence (1) imply that John has a particular boy in mind as the boy he wants to talk to. After all, as pointed out above, for both readings there is an answer to the question:

(8) Which boy does John want to talk to?

The difference between the referential and attributive readings of sentence (1) is a matter of whether or not John has any particular boy in mind as the boy who failed the exam. The non-specific reading of (7) implies that there is no boy in particular that John wants to talk to, that John has not decided which boy who failed the exam he wants to talk to. The attributive reading of (1), on the other hand, implies that there is only one boy who failed the exam, and there can therefore be no question of John's deciding which boy who failed the exam he wants to talk to, but only of John's knowing or not knowing which boy failed the exam. We must therefore not conclude that the referential/attributive ambiguity and the specific/non-specific ambiguity are the same, simply on the grounds that the notion of having someone particular in mind can be used in characterising both kinds of ambiguity.

There _is_ a relationship between the two ambiguities, however, though it is an indirect one, and before I can discuss it, I must try to distinguish the referential/attributive ambiguity from the other ambiguity mentioned in Chapter I, the ambiguity of the descriptive content of noun phrases. Even if John does have a particular boy in mind as a boy he wants to talk to, and this boy is, in fact, the boy who failed the exam, it can still be maintained that the sentence:

(9) John wants to talk to the boy who failed the exam.

is false, if John does not _realise_ that the boy he has in mind is the boy who failed the exam, that is, if he does not recognise the description 'the boy who failed the exam' as a description of the boy he has in mind. This question, the question of whether the description used in the sentence is one which John does or does not recognise as a description of the person (or thing) in question, is the topic of the next chapter and, although it will not be easy, I want to avoid any further discussion of it in the present chapter. I shall therefore assume, throughout this chapter, that the descriptive content of the ambiguous noun phrase _is_ true of someone or something, that John (in general, the subject of the opaque verb) _knows_ that it is true of someone or something, and that if either he or the speaker is supposed to have an opinion as to who it is true of, then his opinion is correct. That is, as far as the present chapter is concerned, I shall disregard the dependence of the truth value of a sentence on the particular description under which something is referred to. It should be clear that the referential/attributive ambiguity is still present in a sentence such as (9), even when the ambiguity of descriptive content is thus factored out.

Bearing this in mind, we can now say that the referential and attributive readings of sentence (9) differ with respect to whether John is supposed to have an opinion as to which boy failed the exam. The attributive reading implies only that John knows that a boy did fail the exam; the referential reading implies that he knows of some boy

that _he_ failed the exam. Thus the attributive reading
requires the truth of the non-specific reading of:

(10)   John knows that a boy failed the exam.

that is, the truth of:

(11)   John knows that there is a boy who failed the exam.

But the referential reading requires the truth of the specific
reading of (10), that is, the truth of:

(12)   There is a boy whom John knows failed the exam.

Hintikka (Knowledge and Belief, Chapter 6) relates the
distinction between pairs like (11) and (12) to the notion
of 'knowing who'. The truth of (12) warrants the claim
that John knows who (which boy) failed the exam, but the
truth of (11) does not. The concept of 'knowing who' will be
discussed in more detail in Section 6 of this chapter. It
may be noted here, however, that there is another kind of
paraphrase which also apparently picks up the same distinction.
The specific reading of an indefinite noun phrase is sometimes distinguished from the non-specific reading by paraphrasing it with an _of_ phrase, thus:

(13)   John knows of a boy that he failed the exam.

picks out the specific reading of sentence (10). The same
kind of paraphrase can also be used to distinguish the
referential from the attributive reading of a definite noun
phrase. Thus:

(14)   John wants of the boy who failed the exam to talk to him.

though it is not very elegant English, apparently picks out
the referential reading of sentence (9) at the expense of
the attributive reading. (With verbs such as believes, hopes,
expects, rather than wants, the of NP paraphrase is often a
perfectly grammatical sentence.)

Section 2. The referential/attributive distinction as a scope phenomenon.

Although the referential/attributive distinction is,
semantically, a different distinction from the specific/
non-specific one, the general formal properties of the two
phenomena are apparently the same. If there are two or more
definite noun phrases in a complement clause, their interpretations with respect to the referential/attributive
distinction are independent. Thus the sentence:

(15) John thinks that the boy who failed the exam kicked
the examiner.

can be read in any one of four ways, depending on whether
John is supposed to have a particular boy in mind as the
boy who failed the exam and whether he is supposed to have
a particular person in mind as the examiner. The number
of possible readings of a sentence also depends on the
number of embedded complement clauses. For example, the
sentence:

137

(16)   Mary thinks John wants to talk to the boy who failed
                               the exam.

can be taken to mean (a) Mary has in mind the boy who failed
the exam and she thinks that John wants to talk to him, (b)
Mary thinks that whichever boy failed the exam is such that
John wants to talk to him, or (c) Mary thinks that John
simply wants to talk to whichever boy failed the exam.   Just
as for the specific/non-specific distinction, there appears
to be no fourth reading of the kind that a feature analysis
of the phenomenon would predict, viz. that Mary has a particular boy in mind as the boy who failed the exam, and she
thinks that John does not have any particular boy in mind
but simply wants to talk to whichever boy failed the exam.
Hence the oddity of:

(17)   Mary thinks of the boy who failed the exam that John wants
                to talk to whichever boy failed the exam.

       Arguments analogous to those of Section 1 of Chapter II
for indefinite noun phrases can therefore be given to establish that the referential/attributive distinction is a matter
of scope relationships, and that the readings should be
distinguished formally in terms of the position of some
operator which defines the scope of the noun phrase.   Using
the arbitrary symbol (Tx) temporarily in the role of the
referentiality operator, sentence (16) will thus have the
three possible representations:

(18) (Tx) Mary thinks John wants John talk to (the boy who failed the exam)$_x$.

(19) Mary thinks (Tx) John wants John talk to (the boy who failed the exam)$_x$.

(20) Mary thinks John wants (Tx) John talk to (the boy who failed the exam)$_x$.

The terms 'referential' and 'attributive' are therefore misleading in just the same way as the terms 'specific' and 'non-specific', for they suggest, incorrectly, that there is just a two-way distinction to be made. In fact, since the degree of ambiguity depends on the degree of embedding, we shall want to talk of a noun phrase being referential or attributive with respect to certain of the clauses of a sentence and not with respect to others.

I have taken over the terms 'referential' and 'attributive' from Donnellan (Reference and Definite Descriptions, Phil.Review, 1966), and to avoid possible confusions, I should make it clear that the distinction I have drawn between referential and attributive readings of definite noun phrases in opaque contexts is <u>not</u> in fact the same distinction as Donnellan draws in his paper, though it is very closely related to it. Donnellan discusses the sentence:

(21) Smith's murderer is insane.

(Note: The phrase <u>Smith's murderer</u> does not contain the definite article, but it is reasonable to call it a definite description since it is synonymous with the phrase <u>the person who murdered Smith</u>, and is, in any case, definite according to all the usual syntactic criteria.) Donnellan describes two ways in which this phrase, and thus the sentence (21), can be used. He says (pp.285-6):

> Suppose first that we come upon poor Smith foully murdered. From the brutal manner of the killing and the fact that Smith was the most lovable person in the world, we might exclaim, "Smith's murderer is insane." I will assume, to make it a simpler case, that in a quite ordinary sense we do not know who murdered Smith (though this is not in the end essential to the case). This, I shall say, is an attributive use of the definite description.
> The contrast with such a use of the sentence is one of those situations in which we expect and intend our audience to realize whom we have in mind when we speak of Smith's murderer and, most importantly, to know that it is this person about whom we are going to say something.
> For example, suppose that Jones has been charged with Smith's murder and has been placed on trial. Imagine that there is a discussion of Jones's odd behavior at his trial. We might sum up our impression of his behavior by saying, "Smith's murderer is insane." If someone asks to whom we are referring, by using this description, the answer here is "Jones." This, I shall say, is a referential use of the definite description.

To distinguish the referential use from the attributive use, Donnellan also talks of the speaker having some particular person in mind, or of meaning someone in particular. Thus Donnellan's distinction is very similar to the distinction we made above in connection with the sentence:

(22)   John wants to talk to the boy who failed the exam.

when we said that this sentence either might or might not
be taken to mean that John has a particular boy in mind.

Notice, however, that Donnellan's example, sentence (21),
does not contain an opaque context. The existence of two
distinct ways of using a definite noun phrase is not supposed
to be tied to opaque contexts but to be a feature of definite
noun phrases in general. Furthermore, Donnellan explicitly
says that he does not regard sentence (21) as an ambiguous
sentence, but as an unambiguous sentence that can be <u>used</u>
in two different ways (to make two different statements,
which may differ in truth value). By contrast, the examples
that we discussed above all involved opaque contexts, and
the referential/attributive distinction drawn there was
intended to be a distinction between possible readings of
these sentences, that is, the sentences were claimed to be
ambiguous.

The relationship between Donnellan's distinction,
and the distinction between referential and attributive
readings of a definite noun phrase in an opaque context,
can be brought out as follows. Suppose that John utters
the sentence (21), viz:

(23) Smith's murderer is insane.

Now since John could, according to Donnellan, have been using
this sentence in two different ways, to make either of two
different statements, then there are presumably two different

things that John might have been thinking, and the sentence:

(24)   John thinks that Smith's murderer is insane.

will be ambiguous, since it can be taken to report either of these distinct thoughts. Thus what appears as a distinction between uses of a phrase in a transparent context, such as (23), and is a matter of whether or not the speaker has any particular person in mind, appears as a distinction between possible readings of a phrase in an opaque context, such as (24), and is a matter of whether or not the subject of the opaque verb is supposed to have a particular person in mind.

Of course, since the sentence (24) itself contains the phrase Smith's murderer, we should expect the distinction between referential and attributive uses to show up here too, as well as the referential/attributive ambiguity. And this is in fact the case, at least for the referential reading of (24). On this reading, I, the speaker, mean to convey that John has a particular person in mind as the person who murdered Smith, but it can still be asked whether I have any particular person in mind, that is, whether I am using the phrase referentially or attributively in Donnellan's sense. Those linguists who maintain that a 'performative clause' sits atop the underlying representation of any sentence have a natural way of distinguishing all of these possibilities. The sentence (24) is supposed to

142

be equivalent to:

(25) I say to you that John thinks that Smith's murderer
                                        is insane.

and in representations based on (25) there will be three
possible positions for the referentiality operator (Tx).
Thus:

(26) (Tx) I say to you that John thinks that (Smith's
                              murderer)$_x$ is insane.

(27) I say to you (Tx) John thinks that (Smith's murderer)$_x$
                                        is insane.

(28) I say to you that John thinks (Tx) (Smith's murderer)$_x$
                                        is insane.

The difference between (26) and (27) is Donnellan's
distinction between the two ways in which the speaker might
use the phrase Smith's murderer; the difference between (27)
and (28) is the difference between the referential and
attributive readings of the phrase Smith's murderer in an
opaque context. The 'performative clause' analysis is
useful here in illustrating the continuity between these
two distinctions, but it seems to me to be a weakness of
this analysis that it does not permit a distinction to be
drawn between differences of use and differences of meaning,
but assimilates the former to the latter.

        Donnellan goes into the distinction between referential
and attributive uses of definite noun phrases in considerable

detail in his paper, and I hope that his exposition will clarify, at second hand, the nature of the distinction between referential and attributive readings of definite noun phrases in opaque contexts. It is the latter, however, which we shall be primarily concerned with in this chapter. The task, just as in the previous chapter, is to provide formal representations of the different readings. We have already established that the general form of these representations must be like (18)-(20), with a scope operator to indicate referentiality. I shall now consider the possibility of identifying this abstract scope operator with some more familiar constituent of semantic representations.

Section 3. Definite noun phrases and the universal quantifier.

In the previous chapter, we considered identifying the arbitrary specificity operator (Sx) with the existential quantifier of formal logic, or with its linguistic counterpart. This was a natural hypothesis to explore because the existential quantifier is used in formalising sentences with indefinite noun phrases in non-opaque contexts. We may consider identifying the abstract referentiality operator, then, with whatever device is used for formalising sentences containing definite noun phrases in non-opaque contexts.

This is not such a straightforward matter as for indefinite noun phrases, however, for even in formal logic,

yet alone in linguistics, there is some disagreement as to
how definite noun phrases should be formally represented.
Russell (On Denoting, Mind 1905) maintained that a sentence
like:

(29) The present king of France is bald.

should be regarded as of a form which I shall render roughly
as:

(30) ($\exists$x) (x is presently king of France & (y) (either y is
        presently king of France or y = x) & x is bald).

This is even more roughly rendered in English as:

(31) There is someone who is presently king of France and
       no-one else is presently king of France (i.e. everyone
       either is that person or else is not the king of France),
       and the person in question is bald.

Thus the analysis contains an explicit existential clause
to the effect that there is a present king of France, and
an explicit uniqueness clause to the effect that there is
only one king of France. If either of these conditions is
not met, then the sentence (29) must be regarded, on this
analysis, as false. Thus if there is no king of France or
if there is more than one king of France, then it is false
that the king of France is bald.

Strawson (On Referring, Mind 1950) maintains that
this is incorrect, and that although indeed sentence (29)
is not true if there is no king of France or more than one,
it is not false either. Strawson introduced the notion of

a presupposition of a statement, a presupposition being a
proposition that must be true in order that the statement
should be either true or false. Thus we can regard the
existence and uniqueness conditions of Russell's analysis
as the presuppositions of (29), that is, as necessary conditions for either the truth or falsity of (29). The 'baldness'
clause in the analysis of (29) will represent what (29)
actually asserts, and is thus a necessary condition for the
truth, though not the falsity, of (29). On this analysis, (29)
is true if and only if there is one and only one king of
France and he is bald, and it is false if and only if there is
one and only one king of France and he is not bald. If there
is no king of France or more than one, (29) is assigned no
truth value at all.

It is not at all clear from the philosophical literature on presuppositions what their status is supposed to be
with respect to representations of logical form. Should they
be explicitly represented in formulae? If so, then they
must presumably be marked in some way as presuppositions
rather than as straightforward entailments, since their
contribution to the truth value of the proposition is different
from the contribution of straightforward entailments. Even
if they are so marked, notice that the formula expressing
the conditions for the truth of a statement will not be
simply the negation of the formula expressing the conditions

for its falsity, or the conditions for the truth of its contradiction. Only those parts of the formula which correspond to straighforward entailments rather than to presuppositions, must be negated in order to derive the conditions for the falsity of the statement. The necessary conditions for the truth of a statement and the necessary conditions for the truth of its contradiction overlap, since the presuppositions of the statement are necessary conditions for both. Therefore if the presuppositions are included in the representations of logical form, we lose the usual simple relationship between negation and contradiction. If, on the other hand, it is assumed that the presuppositions of a statement are not to be included in the formula representing its logical form, then, since the presuppositions are relevant to its truth value, and to what can be inferred from it, either it must be possible to apply certain rules to the representation of logical form to generate the presuppositions, or else the presuppositions must be explicitly stated elsewhere in some fashion or other.

To deal with this topic satisfactorily would require a thesis to itself and I shall not spend any more time on it here. Some decision has to be made if we are to proceed any further, however, and since, as I shall show shortly, it seems possible in the case of definite noun phrases to predict their presuppositions on the basis of formal representations which do not express them explicitly, I shall assume that they are not to be included directly in our semantic representations. Thus (30) is not the kind of representation we need for (29); the existence and uniqueness clauses of (30) have to be dropped. There is no way of simply dropping them out of (30) and retaining what is left, but we can get the same effect if we observe that (30) is logically equivalent to:

(32) $(\exists x)$ (x is presently king of france & (y) (either y is presently king of France or y = x)) & (z)(z is presently king of France $\supset$ z is bald)

which can be read into English as roughly: There is someone who is presently king of France and no-one else is presently king of France, and anyone who is presently king of France is bald. Thus the 'baldness' clause has been taken out of the scope of the existential quantifier and expressed as a conditional statement universally quantified. We can now omit the whole of the existentially quantified expression from (32). It expresses the presupposition of sentence (29), and what is left is:

(33) (z) (z is presently king of France $\supset$ z is bald)

which is a plausible representation of what (29) is supposed actually to assert rather than presuppose.

Taking (33) as our representation of (29), we can actually predict the existence presupposition of (29),

148

because the universal quantifier is also claimed to presuppose existence. Strawson (Introduction to Logical Theory, p.173ff.) considers a situation in which someone says:

(34) All John's children are asleep.

and he comments: "Obviously he will not normally, or properly, say this, unless he believes that John has children (who are asleep). But suppose he is mistaken. Suppose John has no children. Then is it true or false that all John's children are asleep? Either answer would seem to be misleading. But we are not compelled to give either answer. We can, and normally should, say that, since John has no children, the question does not arise." That there should exist children of John's is thus to be regarded as a presupposition of (34), and of any statement involving the phrase all John's children. If (34) is represented as:

(35) (x) (x is a child of John's $\supset$ x is asleep).

then we can express the presupposition as that the antecedent of the conditional should not be vacuous. And by analogy with this, we can state that a presupposition of the statement represented by (33) is that someone should be presently king of France.

Although I have quoted this example of Strawson's, I think some comment is needed. The phrase John's children seems to be equivalent to the children of John, and thus itself to be definite. If this is true, that is, if (34) can also be expressed as:

(36)   All of the children of John are asleep.

then the presupposition of existence might be due to the presence of the definite article in (36), rather than to the presence of the word all. In other words, representing definite descriptions by means of the universal quantifier might not allow us to predict the existence presupposition after all, because Strawson's illustration of the existence presupposition of the universal quantifier might not in fact demonstrate that the universal quantifier carries a pre-supposition of existence, but only that a universal quantifier together with a definite description carries a presupposition of existence. What we need is an example with a universal quantifier but no definite description (and nothing equivalent to one) and then we can ask whether the universal quantifier does indeed, all on its own, carry a presupposition of existence. Thus we might consider the example:

(37)   All children like ice-cream.

represented as:

(38)   (x) (x is a child $\supset$ x likes ice-cream).

As normally used, sentence (37) does suggest that there are children, and it would be an odd thing for someone to say if he thought that no children existed. We must be careful, for the formula (38) is usually assumed also to be readable as: Anything which is a child likes ice-cream, if anything is a child then it likes ice-cream, and so on, and it is not quite so clear that these sentences presuppose the existence of children. There can be some doubt, therefore, as to the validity of the claim that statements of the form All x is y invariably presuppose the existence of some x's. If this claim is correct, however, then whatever decision we make as to how to represent this presupposition of the universal quantifier, using the universal quantifier to represent definite noun phrases will predict the existence presupposition of definite noun phrases.

The other presupposition of (29), the presupposition of uniqueness, will also, I think, turn out to be predictable from our semantic representations, though it is not predictable within standard systems of logic. In logic no singular/ plural distinction is made. Even the existential quantifier is to be read as 'there is at least one...', rather than as 'there is exactly one...'. If it is required to represent a statement to the effect that there is exactly one thing that is F, then an explicit uniqueness clause is required, as in (30), which says that nothing other than that thing is F. If we want to epxress the fact that there are exactly two things that are F, then we must use two existential quantifiers together with a clause saying that nothing else is F. The singular/plural distinction (or a singular/dual/plural distinction) is, on the other hand, one of the most common

151

and fundamental of distinctions found in natural languages, and an adequate system of semantic representation for natural languages will surely employ such a distinction. If so, then the uniqueness presupposition of a singular definite description such as the present king of France will follow automatically from the fact that the noun phrase is singular and yet is to be read as universally quantified. The present king of France will be rendered as something like all one king of France, and though there is no such surface form in English, it is exactly parallel to the grammatical phrases: all three kings of France, all four kings of France, all ninety-seven kings of France, etc.. (Note that if there are two kings of France we would use the word both rather than all, which suggests that even in English there is a trace of a dual category.) This will bring the presupposition of uniqueness of the singular definite noun phrase into line with the numerical presuppositions of the three kings of France, the four kings of France, etc., and also with the many kings of France, etc.. (The simple plural definite noun phrase the kings of France, with no quantity expression, carries a presupposition of existence but none of uniqueness or of any other number; if we spell out its presuppositions, analogously to the singular phrase, as: there are people who are kings of France and no-one else is, it is clear that the 'and no-one else is' here is doing no work.)

152

The hypothesis that we are considering, that the should be represented by means of the universal quantifier, like all and every, is a plausible one even disregarding the philosophical literature on definite descriptions, for the actual surface forms of English suggest it. We found it helpful earlier to paraphrase definite noun phrases by means of whoever... or whichever.... Thus the attributive reading of our original example is brought out by the paraphrase:

(39) John wants to talk to whoever (whichever boy) failed

the exam.

Though I shall not argue for it in detail here, the most plausible derivational source for these words is everyone who..., everything which..., every N which.... Thus the conclusion reached on the basis of the logical behaviour of definite phrases looks as if it will also provide a satisfactory syntactic analysis.

In the previous chapter we considered the identification of the specificity operator for indefinite noun phrases with the existential quantifier. We are now considering the identification of the referentiality operator for definite noun phrases with the universal quantifier, and we have just seen some reasons for regarding this identification as an attractive one. However, the universal quantifier is usually assumed to correspond to words like all, every, each, any, in English, and not to the definite article. We must therefore examine the behaviour of these words in opaque contexts, to make sure that the idea of representing definite noun phrases with the universal quantifier does not conflict with anything we need to say about all, etc..

Section 4. All, every, each, and opaque contexts.

The sentence:

(40)   John wants to talk to every boy in the room.

is ambiguous in very much the way that sentence (1) above is ambiguous. It can be taken as saying that there are certain boys whom John wants to talk to and that these boys are (or at least include) every boy in the room. Or it can be taken as saying that, assuming there are boys in the room, John wants it to be true that he has talked to every one of them. This ambiguity, however, co-exists in (40) with another ambiguity which is characteristic of the word every even in transparent contexts. This is the collective/distributive ambiguity. Unambiguous examples can be constructed, such as:

(41)   Every boy in the room saw John.

which is distributive and can be paraphrased as:

(42)   Each boy in the room saw John.

and:

(43)   John was surrounded by every boy in the room.

which is collective and does not entail:

154

(44) John was surrounded by each boy in the room.

There are also ambiguous examples, with verbs which represent actions which can be undertaken either individually or collectively, such as:

(45) Every boy in the room sang the national anthem.

but in such a case, both the collective and the distributive readings entail:

(46) Each boy in the room sang the national anthem.

and the difference is simply a matter of whether or not they sang it together.[FN] Sentence (40) can similarly be taken as meaning that John wants to talk to each boy in the room individually, or as meaning that he wants to talk to all the boys together. I think it is clear that both of these readings are still ambiguous with respect to whether John has any particular boys in mind or whether he simply wants to talk to whichever boys are in the room.

Since we wish to represent this latter ambiguity (which I shall call a referential/attributive ambiguity,

---

FN. It appears that some speakers deny that the collective reading of (45) entails (46). This is similar to the situation for examples like John and Mary went to the store which can be taken to mean either that they went together or that each went separately. There are speakers who maintain that the 'together' reading does not entail John went to the store, although the 'separately' reading obviously does. To my mind both readings quite clearly do have this entailment, and the example thus differs from John and Mary met, since John met is ungrammatical. This difference between what one might call 'necessarily collective' and 'contingently collective' examples is not, however, central to my discussion.

just as for noun phrases with the definite article) by means
of the scope of the universal quantifier, it would be as
well to make sure that the collective/distributive ambiguity
is not going to require the same kind of formal representation, for since the ambiguities are distinct we obviously
cannot represent both in the same way. The sentence:

(47) John showed all of the boys a picture.

can be represented in the two following ways, with differing
scope relations, ($\underline{b}$ = boys, $\underline{p}$ = picture)

(48) (b) (Ep) (John showed p to b).

(49) (Ep) (b) (John showed p to b).

The collective reading of (47) clearly cannot be represented
by means of (48), for (48) is consistent with John's having
shown each boy a different picture. If either formula is
to be used for the collective reading, then, it must be (47),
and (48) must be reserved for the reading: each boy is such
that there is a picture that John showed him. However,
there is another possible reading of (47), the reading:
there is a picture such that John showed it to each boy
individually. This is a distributive reading but involves
only one picture. The formula (48) obviously does not capture
this reading, and so we are left with (49) for both the
collective and distributive readings when only one picture
is involved. The conclusion must be that quantifier position
does not capture the collective/distributive contrast. It

is in fact fairly clear that it is the collective reading
which this type of representation fails to capture. Although
the collective reading of (47) seems to entail that there
is a picture that John showed to each of the boys, the
collective reading of (50):

(50)   John gave all of the boys a picture.

does not entail that there is a picture that John gave to
each of the boys, because if he had given it to one, he could
not have given it to anyone else.   But the counterpart of (49),
viz:

(51)   (Ep) (b) (John gave p to b).

would conventionally be taken to entail that John gave the
picture to each of the boys.

Some other type of scope analysis of the collective/
distributive contrast may be possible.   One might, for example,
try to capture the collective reading in terms of there being
just one instance or event of giving, rather than a number of
such events.   Thus one might base an analysis on paraphrases
like:

(52)   There was an event which was such that everyone was
            such that John gave him a picture.
(53)   Everyone is such that there was an event such that
            John gave him a picture.

However, (52), at least when expressed in formal logical
symbols, still apparently entails that John gave each person
a picture.   I can at present see no way of patching up this

analysis satisfactorily. Rather than digress any longer on the proper analysis of the collective/distributive distinction, however, I shall take it as shown that, however this distinction _is_ to be captured formally, it will _not_ be in terms of the scope of the universal quantifier. Thus we are free to use the scope of this quantifier to capture the referential/ attributive distinction.

The referential/attributive ambiguity of a sentence like (40) can be regarded, just like the referential/attributive ambiguity of definite noun phrases, as a matter of whether or not John is supposed to know who is in the room. Thus John may want to talk to every boy in the room, in the attributive sense, simply on the assumption that there are boys in the room, and without knowing who they are. Taken referentially, however, if it is true of every boy in the room that John wants to talk to him, then John must presumably have some particular boys in mind as the boys who are in the room. There seems to be an interesting interaction between the collective/distributive distinction, and this 'knowing who' criterion for the referential sense. It seems to me, though the intuition is not absolutely clear, that if (40) is taken both as referential and as distributive, that is, as saying that it is true of the boys in the room that John wants to talk to each of them individually, then John must know who is in the room in the sense of being able to list, or

otherwise pick out, each boy who is in the room. If the
sentence is taken as referential and collective, on the other
hand, that is, as saying that it is true of the boys in the
room that John wants to address them collectively as a group,
it is sufficient for John to be able to designate in some
fashion what group of people is in the room, and not necessary
that he should know which individuals are in the group. Thus
John's knowing that it is the members of the botany club who
are in the room, even if he does not know who is a member of
the botany club, would seem to be sufficient for the collective
referential reading of (40), though not for the distributive
referential reading.

Since our original interest was whether noun phrases
with the definite article can be represented by means of the
universal quantifier, we should now consider definite noun
phrases in the light of these observations, and ask whether
the definite article has the same semantic properties as
every or all. In a wide range of examples, a collective
interpretation of a definite noun phrase is, if not obligatory,
at least much more natural than a distributive interpretation.
Thus the sentences:

(54) John gave the boys a picture.

(55) John talked to the boys.

would most naturally be interpreted, I think, as collective.
The distributive sense can be expressed by using each in

159

conjunction with the definite article, as in:

(56) John gave the boys a picture each.

(57) John talked to each of the boys.

but if we wish to express the sense of (56) with the definite
article alone, without the aid of each, then we have to say:

(58) John gave the boys pictures.

and even this is not unambiguous. On the other hand, it is
possible to use a simple definite noun phrase with predicates
which can only be true of individuals and not of collections,
for example:

(59) The boys saw John.

(60) The boys craned their necks.

which shows that a distributive interpretation of the definite
article is not absolutely excluded. Assuming, then, that it
will be possible to state where and when a definite noun
phrase is collective or distributive, and assuming that some
means can be found for representing the collective/distributive
distinction, there seems to be nothing connected with this
distinction which would invalidate the representation of
definite noun phrases by means of the universal quantifier,
even though we also want to use this to represent all, each,
every, etc..

The proposal does run into trouble, however, of the
following kind. The sentence:

(61) John wants to have all the pictures.

whether it is taken referentially or attributively, is compatible with John's already having some of the pictures, (and is compatible with his knowing that he has). But it would be odd to say:

(62)   John wants to have the pictures.

if one were aware that John already had some of them.   It might be suggested that the explanation of this difference is the tendency to interpret the simple definite article as collective wherever possible, together with the fact that John's having some of the pictures already is incompatible with the collective interpretation of the sentence.   It might be argued that if John already has some of the pictures then even if he were then to get the others, this would not count as having them collectively.   This explanation will not work, however, because the difference between (61) and (62) also shows up in (63) and (64):

(63)   John had hoped to have all of the pictures.

(64)   John had hoped to have the pictures.

The latter is odd if it is known that John did have some of the pictures, but the former is quite acceptable, <u>even</u> if interpreted as collective.

What seems to be going on in these examples is that <u>all</u> can be used to contrast with <u>some</u>, but <u>the</u> cannot.   And this, of course, is true in general, and not only in opaque contexts.   Thus (65) is odd, though (66) is not.

(65)   I didn't see the boys but I did see some of them.

(66) I didn't see all the boys but I did see some of them.

But the difference between the and all is more than just this. Like many discussions of definite descriptions, the discussion in Section 3 concentrated on singular definite noun phrases at the expense of plural ones. And though analysing the king of France as all one king of France looks both acceptable and attractive, analysing the boys we met as all boys we met is by no means so plausible. The sentence:

(67) The boys we met are orphans.

may be true only if all boys such that we met them are orphans, but it is not obvious that it is false if not all boys such that we met them are orphans. If you were to ask:

(68) Are the boys we met orphans?

it would be odd to reply:

(69) No, some of them are.

though this would be quite appropriate as an answer to the question:

(70) Are all the boys we met orphans?

It is the same point, I think, which underlies the fact that the only negation of (67) is:

(71) The boys we met are not orphans.

while the sentence:

(72) All the boys we met are orphans.

has the two negations:

(73) Not all the boys we met are orphans.

(74) All the boys we met are not orphans.

of which the former is obviously much the more natural.

It looks as though a simple definite noun phrase in the plural not only does not contrast with _some_, but does not even admit the possibility that the sentence might be true of some but not all things of the kind described. Although I suggested at the end of Section 3 that plural definite noun phrases have no presupposition analogous to the presupposition of uniqueness of singular definite noun phrases, the observations of the previous paragraph suggest that there is a presupposition that the sentence is true either of all, or of none, of the things that fall under the description contained in a plural definite phrase. Treating this as a presupposition will permit us to say that sentence (67) is not true if not all the boys we met are orphans, but is not false either. We can say that in those circumstances the sentence is neither true nor false, and that there is likewise no straightforward answer to the question (68). This is, in a sense, to say that _the boys we met_ is interpreted collectively, for it is presupposed that the predicate _are orphans_ is true of all of them if it is true of any of them. But this interpretation is 'collective' in a rather different sense from the one with which we were concerned earlier. To see this one has only to observe that a sentence such as:

(75) The boys sang the national anthem.

which has the 'all or none' presupposition, is still

ambiguous between the boys' singing the national anthem individually and their singing it together, that is, between a distributive and a collective reading in the sense of the earlier discussion.

If I am right about there being an 'all or none' presupposition associated with plural definite noun phrases, then it will not be possible after all to represent definite noun phrases with the universal quantifier, since there is no way, as far as I can see, of predicting this presupposition as we were able to predict the uniqueness presupposition of singular definite noun phrases. However, something very like this presupposition seems also to be associated with generic noun phrases. Thus the sentence:

(76) Women enjoy washing dishes.

will certainly be true if all women enjoy washing dishes, but one hesitates to say it is false if not all women do. Similarly the question:

(77) Do women enjoy washing dishes?

is not naturally answered by a straightforward 'no' simply on the grounds that some women do not, though one could give that answer to the question:

(78) Do all women enjoy washing dishes?

on those grounds. There is also only one negation of a generic sentence like (76), viz:

(79) Women do not enjoy washing dishes.

which also, just like the affirmative statement, leaves no

room for disagreements between different women about the matter. This contrasts with the sentence:

(80) All women enjoy washing dishes.

which has the two negations:

(81) Not all women enjoy washing dishes.

(82) All women do not enjoy washing dishes.

There are further similarities between generic noun phrases (at least, plural ones with no determiner) and definite noun phrases. For example, a generic phrase, like a definite one, is most natrually taken collectively. Thus the sentence:

(83) Birds build a nest.

is rather odd, because it suggests that they build only one between them; one would more naturally say:

(84) Birds build nests.

These examples should be compared with (54) and (58) above. Parallel to (59) and (60), we also, however, have the distributive examples:

(85) Boys like John.

(86) Boys crane their necks (when girls go past).

Most importantly, however, generic and definite noun phrases are similar in interpretation in opaque contexts too. Thus the sentence:

(87) John wants to kill Russians.

exhibits the referential/attributive ambiguity but, like (62)

165

and (64) above, does not show a contrast with some. Thus (87), and especially:

(88) John had wanted to kill Russians.

are odd in the context of John's having already killed some Russians.

These observations suggest that definite noun phrases differ semantically from phrases with every, all, etc., in just the way that generic noun phrases do. Therefore, however generic phrases are to be represented formally (and this will presumably not be by means of the universal quantifier), we should represent definite noun phrases in the same fashion. This would give us the advantages of the analysis in terms of the universal quantifier which were outlined in the previous section, but avoid the disadvantages of that analysis which have been discussed in the present section. The referentiality operator (Tx), then, is to be identified with whatever formal device is used in representing generic phrases.

This identification does require, of course, either that generic phrases and definite phrases be in free variation or that they be in complementary distribution with some general principle predicting which occurs where. In actual fact we seem to have a mixture of both states of affairs. There are contexts in which both generic and definite phrases can appear, with little or no difference in sense, for example:

(89) Animals with backbones that we have examined have hearts.

(90) The animals with backbones that we have examined have

hearts.

There are contexts in which a generic phrase may appear but
where a definite phrase is either deviant or must be taken
as elliptical, for example:

(91) Animals with backbones have hearts.

(92) The animals with backbones have hearts.

Sentence (92) requires, unlike (91), that a certain set of
animals be contextually indicated in some fashion. There
are also contexts in which definite phrases may appear, but
not generic ones, for example:

(93) The people in the next room are singing.

(94) People in the next room are singing.

Although (94) contains a plural noun phrase with no determiner,
this phrase cannot be interpreted as generic but is equivalent
to the phrase some people in the next room. Although I
cannot give a complete analysis of generic phrases here, the
principle at work in these examples is apparently that where
the set of things described by the noun phrase is a closed
set, a definite noun phrase is used; where the set is open,
a generic phrase is used. One way in which this difference
shows up is in the difference between sentences such as:

(95) The cows in this field wear bells.

(96) Cows in this field wear bells.

The latter sentence carries an implication of some kind that there is an essential connection between being a cow in this field and wearing a bell, for example that it is because they are in this field that the cows have, for some reason, to wear bells, or perhaps that there is a rule that only cows wearing bells are allowed into this field. And this suggests that any other cow that is not in this field, if it were in this field would also wear a bell. Sentence (95), by contrast, carries no such implication, or at least far less of one; it says only that cows which <u>are</u> in this field (and this is a closed set of cows) wear bells.

I have one further point to make about the formal representation of definite noun phrases. In Chapter II the conjunctive analysis of noun phrases was discussed in some detail, though virtually no evidence was found to support it. In standard quantificational logic, something like the conjunctive analysis is employed in connection with the universal quantifier as well as the existential quantifier. For the universal quantifier, however, the clause which represents the lexical content of the noun phrase is not a conjunct in the formula but a conditional clause. For example, the sentence:

(97) All children like ice-cream.

is represented as:

(98) (x) (if x is a child then x likes ice-cream).

which in English is roughly:

(99)   Everything is such that if it is a child then it likes
                                        ice-cream.

Now though (99) may be logically equivalent to (97), one
hesitates to say that they are synonymous.   In particular, it
seems odd to say that sentence (97) is about everything,
as (98) suggests; it seems rather to be just about all children.
If we give up the conjunctive analysis of noun phrases, and
its counterpart for the universal quantifier, the conditional
analysis of noun phrases, then this counter-intuitive suggestion is avoided.   Furthermore, we have a uniform treatment
of the lexical content of all noun phrases, rather than two
quite different treatments for phrases with _some_ and phrases
with _all_.   Sentence (97) would be represented as:

(100)   (x) (children)$_x$ like ice-cream.

and only the nature of the quantifier differentiates this from
the representation of the corresponding sentence with _some_
rather than _all_.   If the operator for generic phrases is
formally (though not semantically, of course) just like the
universal quantifier, the same point can be made in connection
with this generic operator.   The connection between (97)
and (99), or between their generic counterparts, must then
be captured by an inference rule rather than by a grammatical
rule.

Section 5.   Referential and attributive noun phrases and existence

   In Section 5 of Chapter II, we observed that in at least

some cases, a sentence containing an indefinite noun phrase which is within an opaque context but is interpreted transparently (i.e. as specific), is not regarded as entailing the existence of anything of the kind that the noun phrase describes. Thus the sentence:

(101)   John wants to catch a (certain) unicorn.

and even:

(102)   There is a (certain) unicorn that John wants to catch.

are regarded by many speakers as quite compatible with the non-existence of unicorns.

There were two kinds of case in particular for which it seemed obvious that specificity does not entail existence. One was the case of fictional or mythical entities, such as unicorns. The other was the case of entities whose existence is planned or projected, that is, which someone wants or hopes or intends to create. An example of this second kind is the sentence:

(103)   I want you to dig a (certain) hole.

which, somewhat surprisingly, can be paraphrased as:

(104)   There is a (certain) hole that I want you to dig.

For examples other than these two types, that is, examples for which an existential interpretation is both possible and plausible, it seemed less clear that an indefinite noun phrase could be used without an existential implication. Thus the sentence:

170

(105) John wants to catch a (certain) mouse that lives in

my kitchen.

would normally be taken to imply that there is a mouse that

lives in my kitchen. There _may_ be a weaker way of reading it,

as compatible with John's believing, incorrectly, that there

is a certain mouse living in my kitchen. There certainly

does seem to be such a reading of a sentence like:

(106) John wants to catch a (certain) mouse which he (mistaken-

ly) thinks lives in my kitchen.

that is, a reading compatible not only with John's being

wrong in thinking that the mouse he has in mind lives in my

kitchen, but compatible with his being wrong in thinking that

it exists at all.

So far I have simply summarized my remarks about

existence entailments of indefinite noun phrases in Chapter

II. I shall now consider the analogous question for definite

noun phrases, the question of whether definite noun phrases

have existential presuppositions in opaque contexts, as they

do in transparent ones. There are two parts to this question.

For indefinite noun phrases, the opaque (i.e. non-specific)

reading quite obviously does not entail the existence of

anything. The non-specific interpretation of:

(107) John wants to catch a unicorn.

is quite compatible with the non-existence of unicorns.

But for definite noun phrases it is not so obvious that the

opaque (i.e. attributive) reading does not presuppose existence, and so we must consider both the referential and attributive readings of definite noun phrases in what follows. I shall not consider, however, the case of definite predicate nominals (by which, for present purposes, I mean any definite noun phrase following the verb be or become). The presuppositions of these phrases will be discussed in detail in Section 7.

Definite noun phrases describing familiar fictional or mythical characters seem to be tolerated just as indefinite noun phrases are. A sentence such as:

(108) John wants to meet the man in the moon.

could surely be true (i.e. neither false nor without truth value) even though there isn't really any man in the moon. Another example is the sentence:

(109) John believes that the seven dwarfs are alive and well
and living in Mexico.

It might seem doubtful that there could be a referential reading of these sentences since no-one can actually be acquainted with the man in the moon or the seven dwarfs. Nevertheless it does not seem to follow that John could not know who they are. If we are prepared to say that John knows who the seven dwarfs are (were?), then we should also be prepared, I think, to say:

(110) John believes of the seven dwarfs that they are alive
and well and living in Mexico.

Thus even a referential reading of (109) is compatible with

the referent of the noun phrase being only a fictional individual. An example which shows that the attributive reading is also compatible with merely fictional existence is:

(111) John wants to visit the town where Cinderella lived.

As far as I know, the Cinderella story does not specify which town she lived in, so nobody could know which town it was. Even so, sentence (111) may surely be true.

As pointed out in Chapter II, although it is clear that noun phrases referring to fictional entities are tolerated, it is not clear how to analyse sentences containing them. For a completely transparent sentence, such as:

(112) The seven dwarfs were friends of Snow White.

one can account for its compatibility with the non-existence of the seven dwarfs (and of Snow White) by treating the whole sentence as if it were within the context of some phrase such as 'Within the familiar story...'. But one cannot capture the sense in which a sentence like (110) is true by regarding it as an elliptical version of the sentence:

(113) In the familiar story, John believes of the seven dwarfs
        that they are alive and well and living in Mexico.

or of the sentence:

(114) John believes of the seven dwarfs that in the familiar
        story they are alive and well and living in Mexico.

One might, perhaps, paraphrase it as:

(115) John believes of the seven dwarfs of the familiar story
        that they are alive and well and living in Mexico.

173

with the reality-conceding phrase just within the noun phrase itself, and not having scope over any other part of the sentence. But this simply is, I think, to say that there need be no real-world referent for the noun phrase in order for the sentence to be true. It does not in any way explain why one can believe something of something that does not really exist although one cannot kick something that does not exist. Allowing the 'story' operator to appear just within the noun phrase does not explain why (115) might be true but (116) is false.

(116) John kicked the seven dwarfs of the familiar story.

Opaque contexts with 'creative verbs tolerate non-existence with definite noun phrases just as for indefinite ones. Consider, for example, the sentence:

(117) I want you to build the largest wheelbarrow in the world.

Unless by chance there are two or more wheelbarrows of the same size, and larger than any other wheelbarrows, then there must already be some wheelbarrow which is the largest wheel-barrow in the world. But this is not the wheelbarrow I want you to build. I want you to build a wheelbarrow that does not yet exist. And, of course, since you may never build such a wheelbarrow, the wheelbarrow I want you to build may never exist. Nevertheless the sentence (117) may be true. It appears, however, that it is only the attribu-tive reading of (117) that tolerates merely planned existence

rather than actual existence. Paraphrasing the sentence
with of NP, which we have found brings out the referential
sense, gives:

(118)   I want of the largest wheelbarrow in the world that
you should build it.

and this sentence is compatible only with my wanting,
illogically, that you should build what is already at this
minute the largest wheelbarrow in the world. This indicates
that the referential reading does presuppose existence, and
that it is only the attributive reading which does not. I
have been unable to find any examples with 'creative' verbs
for which this is not the case.

For noun phrases other than those describing familiar
fictional entities, and verbs other than 'creative' verbs,
it is very hard not to read an existential presupposition
into a sentence, whether it is taken attributively or
referentially. The sentence:

(119)   John wants to talk to the man who broke the window.
does seem to presuppose that some man broke the window, whichever of the two readings we consider. I note in passing that
the uniqueness presupposition of definite noun phrases also
seems to be present. Thus the sentence:

(120)   John wants to talk to the man in the next room.
would be an odd sentence for someone to use if he believed
there were several men in the next room, whatever John

believed. The situation for definite noun phrases is like
that for specific indefinites, where we observed that there
is, at the very least, an extremely strong tendency to read
the sentence as entailing existence. Just as for indefinite
noun phrases, however, it may just be possible to read the
sentence as entailing merely that John believes that something
of the kind in question exists, especially if the speaker
explicitly states that it does not really exist. Thus the
sentence (119) may be regarded as acceptable even if it is
widely known (though not to John) that no-one broke the window.
At least for the sentence:

(121)   John wants to talk to the man he believes broke the

window.

there seems to be a weak reading which is compatible with
John's being mistaken that anyone broke the window, and even,
for the referential reading which says that he has a particular
man in mind, compatible with that man's not really existing.

So far, all of these observations about definite noun
phrases and existence presuppositions have paralleled those
for indefinite noun phrases and existence entailments. The
only significant departure is that the opaque (attributive)
reading of the definite may presuppose existence although
the opaque (non-specific) indefinite does not entail existence.
This is actually an important point, because what it means
is that the presuppositions of a definite noun phrase, even

when the noun phrase is interpreted opaquely, are transparent.
Thus though we may represent the attributive reading of a
sentence like (120) as:

(121a)   John wants (Tx) John talk to (the man in the next

$$\text{room})_x.$$

and paraphrase it informally as:

(121b)   John wants to talk to whichever man is in the next

room.

by contrast with:

(121c)   (Tx) John wants John talk to (the man in the next

$$\text{room})_x.$$

and:

(121d)   Whichever man is in the next room is such that John

wants to talk to him.

nevertheless the existential and other presuppositions (i.e.
uniqueness for singular phrases, 'all-or-none' for plural
ones) of the definite noun phrase are not to be regarded as
solely within the scope of the opaque verb. It is not sufficient for the truth of sentence (120), even on its attributive
reading, that John should want there to be one and only one
man in the next room and to talk to that man. And it is not
sufficient for John to believe that there is one and only
one man in the next room and want to talk to him. It must
be the case that there _is_ one and only one man in the next
room and John wants to talk to whichever man is in the

next room. Thus the sentence as a whole has these presuppositions; the speaker is committed to the existence and uniqueness implications himself and cannot use the sentence simply on the grounds that John accepts them as true. Whether it is a _necessary_ condition on the truth of (120) that John should believe there is one and only one man in the next room, is another question, and it is a difficult one to answer without running up against complications due to the ambiguity of descriptive content which I do not want to discuss at this stage. It seems to me, however, that at least if we take the description 'man in the next room' as one which John recognises and would be prepared to use himself, then the sentence does ascribe this belief to John. If this is so, then the presuppositions of an opaquely interpreted definite noun phrase must be taken to hold _both_ transparently _and_ opaquely.

There are two special points which should be made, however, in connection with the attributive reading and existence presuppositions. The first point is that where uniqueness of reference is guaranteed, the presupposition of existence is either very weak or entirely absent. By a guarantee of uniqueness of reference, I mean a guarantee that _if_ there is a so-and-so, then there is only _one_ so-and-so. And when there is such a guarantee, one can apparently use the phrase _the so-and-so_ in an opaque context without thereby committing oneself to the existence of the so-and-so.

178

There are two types of phrase that I know of for which there is such a guarantee. One is phrases with superlative adjectives, as in:

(122) John wants to meet the cleverest girl in the room. There may be no cleverest girl in the room, either because there are no girls in the room at all, or because two girls are equally clever, but if there is a cleverest girl in the room then there is, of course, only one. And sentence (122) seems to be compatible with there being no cleverest girl in the room, or at least to be more compatible with it than sentence (123) is with there being no girl who climbed Mount Everest.

(123) John wants to meet the girl who climbed Mount Everest. The second type of example involves a role or office or position that only one person can fill at a time. The sentence:

(124) John wants to meet the captain of the cricket team. seems to be acceptable even if there is no captain of the cricket team (and the speaker and hearers know there is none). At least, like (122), it seems less unacceptable in those circumstances than the sentence (123) if it is known that no girl climbed Mount Everest. It is worth observing that the phrase the present king of France, which, since Russell, has been treated as the paradigm case of a definite description, is a phrase of this special kind. Notice also that

179

it is only the attributive readings of these sentences which are atypical with respect to the presupposition of existence. If sentence (124), for example, is taken referentially, so that it can be paraphrased as:

(125) John wants of the captain of the cricket team to meet

him.

then it does seem to presuppose the existence of a captain of the cricket team.

Just why the existence presupposition is absent, or at least much weaker, in these types of case, I do not know, though I suspect that it is not merely an accident that it correlates with the guarantee of uniqueness of reference. Notice that for both kinds of example, there is no indefinite noun phrase corresponding to the definite one. There is no phrase *a cleverest girl in the room, and the phrase a (present captain of the cricket team is semantically, even if not syntactically, odd. Perhaps, then, the real precondition on the proper use of a definite noun phrase is uniqueness of reference, and existence is required only insofar as it is needed to establish uniqueness of reference. For a phrase such as the man in the next room, unlike the cleverest girl in the class, the only situation in which one can be confident that there are not two or more equally good candidates for the description man in the next room is if one knows that there is only one man in the next room, and this will involve knowing that there is a man in the next room. Another possible explanation (which may perhaps turn out to be the same explanation cast in syntactic terms) is that phrases like the oldest girl in the class, or the (present) captain of the cricket team, are only superficially definite noun phrases. In surface structure they contain a definite article rather than an indefinite one, and they must do so. Just because the definite article is fully predictable, it need not be assumed to be present in the underlying structure. The phrases which describe roles or offices can actually appear in surface structure in some positions without any article. One can say:

(126)   Tom is captain of the cricket team.

so one might analyse at least some instances of the captain of the cricket team as someone who is captain of the cricket team. This is indefinite, so when it is interpreted opaquely one would expect it, like non-specific indefinites in general, not to imply existence. The trouble with this suggestion is ' that one would then expect this phrase not to presuppose existence, but to entail it, in transparent contexts. This is partly true and partly false, but I must postpone further discussion of this idea until Section 7 since it involves predicate nominals.

It should perhaps be pointed out here, however, that there are phrases which do guarantee uniqueness of reference

but which nevertheless presuppose existence in opaque contexts.
These are phrases containing the only. Thus the sentence:

(127) John wants to meet the only man in the room.

seems to presuppose that there is only one man in the room;
it would be odd to use this sentence if one knew there were
several men in the room, regardless of what John believed.
It seems, then, that we must either give up the guarantee
of uniqueness as a criterion for the absence of a presupposition of existence in opaque contexts, or else we must disregard
the word only in considering whether there is a guarantee of
uniqueness. It is obvious that we must, in any case, disregard
the definite article itself, for otherwise all singular
definite noun phrases would carry such a guarantee. The
phrase the man in the room will, of course, if it applies to
anyone, apply to only one man. The point is that the phrase
man in the room could apply to more than one man, unlike the
phrase (present) captain of the cricket team or oldest man in
the room. There is in fact some evidence that the only of
a phrase such as the only man in the room should also be
disregarded in determining whether there is a guarantee of
uniqueness. Notice that sentence (127) cannot be read as
saying that John wants it to be the case that only one man
is in the room and that he should meet that man. John
could want this, knowing that the room was packed with men;
he could want all but one to leave. But (127) cannot be

182

used to describe this situation. Thus the _only_ must apparently not be treated as part of the descriptive content of the
noun phrase; it must not be treated as part of the condition
that a person must fulfill if John is to want to meet him.
Therefore if the guarantee of uniqueness is determined by
the descriptive content of the phrase, the phrase the only
man in the room will not carry such a guarantee. I shall
have more to say about phrases containing the only in Section
7.

The second point to be made about attributively
interpreted definite noun phrases and the presupposition of
existence is that an explicit recognition of the possibility
of non-existence can be built into the sentence. Thus one
can say:

(128)   John wants to meet the girl in the next room if there
                                                    is one.

This sentence may be taken as expressing a conditional
statement, thus:

(129)   If there is a girl in the next room, then John wants
                                              to meet her.

which does not entail that John has any want at all. But (128)
can also be taken as an unconditional statement about a
conditional want of John's, thus:

(130)   John wants that if there is a girl in the next room
                                          he should meet her.

Thus it can be John, rather than the speaker, who is allowing

183

for the possibility that there is no girl in the next room.
By contrast, if (128) is read referentially, it can be paraphrased as:

(131)   If there is a girl in the next room, then John wants of
                         her that he should meet her.

but to paraphrase it as an unconditional statement about a
conditional want produces:

(132)   John wants of the girl in the next room that if she
                         exists he should meet her.

which is decidedly odd. This difference shows up a general
difference between referential and attributive phrases in
connection with the existence or non-existence of a referent.
To use a phrase referentially and then allow that there
exists no referent for it, is to allow that a certain individual does not exist. Unless its referent is a fictional
individual, this can presumably only mean that someone has
conjured up the individual in question in his imagination,
and, as we saw earlier in this section, it is only with some
hesitation that one is prepared to accept as true a sentence
containing a noun phrase referring to such an individual. On
the other hand, if one uses a noun phrase attributively and
then admits that there exists no referent for it, what one
is admitting is that no-one is such that he has the property
designated by the noun phrase. Thus one is not saying that
a certain individual does not exist, but is saying that the

property does not individuate anyone, and there is nothing odd about this idea at all.

Section 6.   On knowing who.

In Section 1 of this chapter, a close relationship was posited between three notions, the notion of knowing who someone is, the notion of knowing of someone that he..., or wanting of someone that he..., suspecting of someone that he..., etc., and the notion of the referential reading of a definite noun phrase in an opaque context.   It was claimed that a sentence such as:

(133)   John wants to talk to the man in the bowler hat.

has both a referential reading and an attributive reading with respect to the phrase the man in the bowler hat. It was claimed that the referential reading can be paraphrased, somewhat inelegantly, as:

(134)   John wants of the man in the bowler hat to talk to him.

and that this entails:

(135)   John knows who the man in the bowler hat is.

which in turn can be paraphrased as:

(136)   John knows of someone that he is the man in the bowler

hat.

The attributive reading of (133), on the other hand, was claimed to entail only the non-specific counterpart of (136), viz:

185

(137) John knows that there is someone who is the man in
the bowler hat.

The notion of knowing who someone is is not an easy
one to analyse and the literature that exists on it is somewhat confused. Since it is closely tied up with my account
of the referential reading of definite noun phrases, however,
I shall attempt to give some explication of it. I begin by
stating my intention to ignore, as I have throughout this
whole chapter, the ambiguity of the descriptive content of
noun phrases. This ambiguity is analysed in the following
chapter and I shall not attempt to relate it to the notion
of knowing who someone is until the end of that chapter.
As will become clear shortly, we shall have quite enough
ambiguity to cope with in our examples of knowing who someone is, without considering this one too. Thus all of the
examples in this section are to be read as implying that
the subject of the verb knows accepts all of the descriptions
that appear in the opaque context, in the sense that he
thinks that there is someone who can be so described, and,
furthermore, that if he has an opinion as to who or what
in particular can be so described, then this opinion is
correct. Thus, for the examples already cited, we are to
ignore the possibility that they might be true even if John
does not realise that there is anyone who can be described as
'the man in the bowler hat', or if he is wrong about who can

186

be so described. Given this assumption, it follows, I think, that sentence (135) will be true only if John can give a correct answer to the question:

(138) Who is the man in the bowler hat?

The discussion can also be simplified by restricting it to cases in which John's answer to such a question is a definite noun phrase. John might, in reply to (138), say:

(139) A friend of Bill's.

that is:

(140) $\left\{ \begin{array}{l} \text{He} \\ \text{The man in the bowler hat} \end{array} \right\}$ is a friend of Bill's.

He might even perhaps say something like:

(141) $\left\{ \begin{array}{l} \text{He} \\ \text{The man in the bowler hat} \end{array} \right\}$ came here to interview the vicar.

Whether or not these really count as answers to a question like (138), I shall not consider them further here, but will restrict my attention to replies such as:

(142) The leader of the orchestra.

that is:

(143) $\left\{ \begin{array}{l} \text{He} \\ \text{The man in the bowler hat} \end{array} \right\}$ is the leader of the orchestra.

Thus what I shall be concerned with is the relationship between sentences of the form:

(144) John knows that the ..... is the -----.

and sentences of the form:

(145) John knows who the ..... is.

where the dots and dashes are filled in with descriptive phrases. Sentences of the form (144) will thus contain two definite noun phrases within an opaque context. Though we are to ignore the ambiguity of descriptive content, the existence of a referential/attributive distinction would lead us to predict that such sentences are (at least) four ways ambiguous, since either of the two noun phrases could, at least in principle, be interpreted either referentially or attributively. It is confusions between these four possible readings of sentences of the form (144) which are responsible, I think, for many of the puzzles about the notion of knowing who someone is, and I shall therefore attempt to disentangle them from each other. In order to do so I shall first ignore the verb knows, and opaque contexts in general, and consider simple questions and answers of the form:

(146) Who is so-and-so?

(147) So-and-so is such-and-such.

There are two ways at least in which one can take the question:

(148) Who is so-and-so?

These can be distinguished, very roughly, as:

(149) Which person has the property so-and-so?

(150) What property does the person so-and-so have?

If I am pointing to a man and I ask:

188

(151) Who is that man over there?

then I am surely intending to ask the second kind of question, for, as long as my pointing gesture is successful, there is no question as to which <u>person</u> the description 'that man over there' applies to. If I <u>had</u> been asking the first kind of question, then the reply:

(152) The man in line with the end of your index finger.

ought to be an appropriate one. On the other hand, if I am standing in front of a building which has flames pouring out of its windows, and I ask:

(153) Who is the man in charge of this building?

then I am more likely to be intending my question as a question of the first kind, that is, I want you to point out, or otherwise indicate, the <u>person</u> to whom the description 'the man in charge of this building' applies. The reply:

(154) He's the only man who has ever jumped off the Empire
State Building and survived.

will not be the kind of response I had hoped for. It is, however, a quite satisfactory answer to question (151) as it would normally be understood.

It is not easy to keep these two kinds of question apart. In practice one may often not know which of the two is intended. Thus the question:

(155) Who is Mary's boyfriend?

out of context, can quite naturally be taken either way. If

Mary is standing nearby entwined around some boy, and I am looking at him as I ask (155), then you would be more likely to treat it as a question of the second kind; if Mary has just asked me to pass a note to her boyfriend, you are likely to take it as a question of the first kind. Even if it is clear which kind of question is intended, the range of acceptable answers will usually overlap. In order to get across to me which person the description 'so-and-so' applies to, you must, unless he is actually there to point to, use another name or description. And this might be the name or description which would be a good answer to the corresponding question of the second kind. The second kind of question is a request for an _interesting_ description or a _significant_ name, for if I have a certain person in mind and am able to pick him out in order to ask a question about him, then necessarily I know _some_ description of him, even if it is only 'that man over there'. In asking for other descriptions, therefore, I am presumably asking for interesting ones. By contrast, an answer to a question of the first kind should not be too interesting, because it may then be of no use for identificatory purposes. Since in this case one is to supply a description as a means of indicating a certain person, one's answer should consist of a description such that one knows, or such that it is reasonable to expect, that the questioner already knows which person _it_ applies to. Notice also that I can answer the second kind of question indirectly too, by giving a relatively uninteresting description, such as 'the man we were just talking about', as long as that description will in turn lead you to some interesting ones.

It is the second kind of question that is related to comments like 'He is somebody', 'He is nobody', 'He isn't anyone special'. Thus if I ask:

(156) Who is the man you just waved to?

when I can obviously see which *person* you waved to and am therefore unlikely to be asking the first kind of question, then you can reasonably reply:

(157) Oh, he's no-one special.

even if this would not count, in a sense, as having <u>answered</u> my question. But if I ask you:

(158) Who is the Chief of Police in Milwaukee?

you can hardly reply:

(159) Oh, he's no-one special.

The distinction that I have been discussing is also to be found in Donnellan's paper. Donnellan says (Reference and Definite Descriptions, p. 287):

> Suppose one is at a party and, seeing an interesting-looking person holding a martini glass, one asks, "Who is the man drinking a martini?" If it should turn out that there is only water in the glass, one has nevertheless asked a question about a particular person, a question that it is possible for someone to answer. Contrast this with the use of the same question by the chairman of the local Teetotalers Union. He has just been informed that a man is drinking a martini at their annual party. He responds

191

> by asking his informant, "Who is the man drinking a
> martini?" In asking the question the chairman
> does not have some particular person in mind about
> whom he asks the question; if no one is drinking a
> martini, if the information is wrong, no person
> can be singled out as the person about whom the
> question was asked. Unlike the first case, the
> attribute of being the man drinking a martini is
> all-important, because if it is the attribute of
> no one, the chairman's question has no straightforward
> answer.

Donnellan makes the distinction primarily in terms of what
happens when the descriptive phrase used in the question
happens to describe no one. I have made it in terms of
what would be an acceptable answer to the question. But I
think they are one and the same distinction. Thus in the
first situation that Donnellan describes, none of the
following would be an appropriate answer:

(160)   The man standing next to the blonde.

(161)   The man we were talking about just before you came

                                        into the room.

(162)   The man whose name I always forget.

It would not be inappropriate to reply:

(163)   He's no one special.

but (163) would be unlikely to satisfy the chairman of the
Teetotalers Union in the second situation Donnellan describes.

        Donnellan discusses these two imaginary situations
as paradigm examples of the referential and attributive uses
of definite noun phrases. His first example is an example of
a question used in the second of the two ways I outlined

above; the definite noun phrase is used referentially. His second example is an example of a question used in the first of the ways outlined above; the definite noun phrase is used attributively. I wish to claim that a question containing a noun phrase used referentially is to be answered with a noun phrase used attributively, and a question containing a noun phrase used attributively is to be answered with a noun phrase used referentially. (Note: Since the person who asks a question is, typically, different from the person who answers it, and since the way in which one uses or understands a noun phrase depends, typically, if not essentially, on what one knows, a person may answer a question to his own satisfaction but not to the satisfaction of the person who asked it. What counts as having answered a question is therefore more complicated than I have just suggested, because it will depend on whose viewpoint we take.)

It might seem, contrary to my claim, that one can give an attributive answer to an attributive question, and a referential answer to a referential question. My intuition, however, is that in cases where this appears to be so, the answer given is only an indirect answer; it counts as an answer only insofar as it leads the questioner to an answer of the opposite kind. If, for example, I ask:

(164) Who is the world's expert on humming birds?

using the definite description attributively, and you reply:

(165) He is the only man to have jumped off the Empire State

Building and survived.

your answer may or may not be adequate. If for me the phrase

the only man who jumped off the Empire State Building and

survived has a referential use, if I know to whom it refers,

then your answer does tell me who the world's expert on

humming birds is (whether you know who jumped off the Empire

State Building or not). If, as is more likely, I do not

know who jumped off the Empire State Building, then I still

do not know the answer to my question. But if I now ask you:

(166) Who is the only man to have jumped off the Empire

State Building and survived?

and you can supply a referential answer to this question, then

your two answers between them answer my first question. And

if I can find out in some other way the answer to question (166),

then in a way you have answered my question (164) too. How-

ever, if I do not know, and you cannot tell me, and I cannot

otherwise find out, the answer to question (166), then (165)

does not count as having answered the question (164).[FN]

FN. James Thomson has suggested to me that my claim is too
strong, and that one can in some cases quite properly answer
an attributive question with an attributive description. Thus
if it is generally true that the chairman of the disciplinary
committee is the Senior Proctor, regardless of who happens at
any particular time to be the Senior Proctor, then the question:
Who is the chairman of the disciplinary committee? surely can
be answered quite properly and informatively with: The Senior
Proctor. In order to maintain my theory, I should have to
claim that this counts as an adequate answer only inasmuch as
it may mediate a referential answer, that is. to the extent that
the questioner knows or can find out who the Senior Proctor

194

A similar point can be made in connection with a referential answer to a referential question, though natural examples are harder to come by. Suppose I point to a man in a photograph, and ask:

(167) Who is this man?

wanting you to tell me something interesting about him, and you reply:

(168) That man over there.

pointing to someone across the room. This will be an adequate answer to my question only insofar as I can use it as a basis for finding out, from you or someone else, something interesting about the man you are pointing to, or if I already know something interesting about him and simply failed to realise that he was the man in the photograph.

With this account of simple questions and answers in hand, we can no return to sentences of the form:

(169) John knows who so-and-so is.

and:

(170) John knows that so-and-so is such-and-such.

I pointed out that sentences of the form (170) should be (at least) four ways ambiguous on the assumption that either noun phrase can be interpreted either referentially or attributively. In view of the foregoing discussion, however,

---

actually is. The example, however, is persuasive, and I suspect that I should admit to error and recognise the existence of such question and answer pairs.

195

I shall claim that only two of these readings will count as entailing that John knows who so-and-so is. If one of the two noun phrases is interpreted referentially and the other is interpreted attributively, then we can say that John knows who so-and-so is. But observe that the sentence (169) will be interpreted in a different way in each case. Thus, disregarding the surface order of the two noun phrases (though there are, in fact, some restrictions on it), one sentence of the form (170) will warrant two statements of the form (169), though these will differ in sense. For example, the truth of:

(171)   John knows that the world's expert on humming birds is
                    the man standing next to him.

interpreted, as it most naturally would be, as:

(172)   John knows that [attributive noun phrase] is [referential
                    noun phrase].

warrants both:

(173)   John knows who the world's expert on humming birds is.
(174)   John knows who the man standing next to him is.

where (173) is interpreted attributively, and (174) is interpreted referentially. On the other hand, a sentence of the form (170) in which both noun phrases are interpreted referentially or both are interpreted attributively, will not justify a statement of the form (169).

Hintikka seems to have this same point in mind when he says (Knowledge and Belief, p. 148ff.):

196

> When is it true to say "a knows who b is"?
> Clearly a necessary condition is that the person
> referred to by a should be able to give a right
> answer to the question "Who is b?" and that he
> should know that his answer is right. This necessary
> condition is not a sufficient one, however. Any
> correct and informed answer to the question "Who
> is b?" does not show that the answerer really knows
> to whom the term b refers; nor does such an answer
> always suffice to let the questioner know it. If
> you ask me "Who was the teacher of Antisthenes?"
> and I reply "The teacher of Antisthenes was the
> same man as the teacher of Aristippus," my answer
> does not necessarily help you to know who the teacher
> of Antisthenes was, for you may fail to know who
> the teacher of Aristippus was. Similarly, it is
> conceivable that my answer should not even show
> that I know who the former was; for I might likewise
> fail to know who the latter was, although I happen
> to know that the two are identical. (For a similar
> reason, it is still less helpful of me to reply:
> "The teacher of Antisthenes was the teacher of
> Antisthenes," although there is no doubt that I know
> this answer to be true.) The answer "The teacher of
> Antisthenes was the same man as the teacher of Plato"
> is a much better one just because it is ever so much
> unlikelier that you (or I) should be ignorant of who
> the latter was. The moral of these examples is clear:
> a sentence of the form "a knows that b is c" does
> not imply "a knows who b is" except in conjunction
> with the further premise "a knows who c is."

There are several comments to be made about this passage.

The first, although I shall not dwell on it, is that Hintikka's

'necessary condition' is not even a necessary condition unless

some allowance is made for the opacity of the descriptive

content of noun phrases, for there surely is a sense of,

for example:

(175)   John knows who the man over there is.

which is compatible with John's <u>not</u> being able to answer the

question:

197

(176) Who is the man over there?

At the very least, John might not be able to see who is over there.

The second point to be made is that it is not absolutely obvious that "a knows that b is c" in conjunction with the further premise "a knows who c is" does imply "a knows who b is" for it is possible that the person referred to by a has not put his two bits of knowledge together. (This is possible whether or not we take 'b' in these sentences as opaque or transparent with respect to their descriptive content.)

Hintikka uses constants in his formulae attributively. Thus for example he allows that sentences of the form "a knows that b is b" are bound to be true as long as the person referred to by a knows that someone describable as 'b' exists. On the other hand, he treats 'knowing who' as involving a referential noun phrase.   Thus he says (p. 131ff.):

> ..when is it true to say of you, "He knows who is the murderer of Toto de Brunel"? Clearly you know this only if you know a right answer to the question: Who killed Toto? And this you can do only if there is someone of whom you know that he (or she) killed Toto.

It is clear from Hintikka's use of the 'of whom' paraphrase in this passage (especially in view of the way in which he expresses 'of whom' sentences in his formal notation), that Hintikka's condition on knowing who is the murderer of Toto is that one can supply a referential description as the answer to the question: Who killed Toto?. In both of these

quoted passages, therefore, Hintikka is considering only
questions of the form:

(177) Who is so-and-so?

in which so-and-so is used attributively, and the point that he
is making is that an attributive description does not constitute
a proper answer to such a question; only a referential description is adequate. At least I assume this is the point that
his somewhat questionable moral is intended to make.

Hintikka apparently does not, either in these passages,
or anywhere else in his book, recognise questions of the
form (177) with the so-and-so used referentially, and so he
misses the point that his condition also applies in reverse,
i.e. that only an attributive description is appropriate as
an answer to such a question. He also, as one might expect,
allows only one interpretation of sentences of the form: 'a
knows who b is', the interpretation for which 'b' is attributive. I suspect that if he had not overlooked this other
sense of 'knowing who', and the related use of questions of
the form (177), he would have been less likely to complain,
(as he does in the footnote to p. 149), that "The criteria as
to when one may be said to know who this or that man is are
highly variable". It is undoubtedly true that the criteria
are variable, but the variability is at least more under-
standable if one recognises that there are two senses in
which one may be said to know who someone is and that there
are different conditions on each sense.

On the other hand, the circularity of Hintikka's
account is not eliminable, at least it is not eliminated
simply by recognising this ambiguity, for it remains in one
of the two cases. The condition on the truth of a sentence of
the form:

(178) John knows who so-and-so is.

when so-and-so is interpreted referentially, is, roughly, that
John should know of some interesting property that the person
so-and-so has. This is a vague condition, of course, since
what counts as interesting will vary from case to case and
person to person. For the other reading, however, we cannot
even approximate a statement of the truth conditions which is
not circular, for we have said that (178) is true on this
reading if John knows which person has the property so-and-so.
This in turn is true if there is a true sentence of the form:

(179) John knows that such-and-such is so-and-so.

where such-and-such is interpreted referentially, that is:

(180) John knows of such-and-such that he is so-and-so.

And the only account we have been able to give of this is that
it requires that John should know who such-and-such is. What
we have done is to delineate some of the internal connections
between notions like knowing who so-and-so is (on one reading),
knowing (wanting, etc.) of someone that he..., having a
particular person in mind, referring to someone in particular,
using a description referentially. What we have not done is

200

to break out of this circle and give an analysis of one of these notions that does not invoke the others, and I do not know how to do so.

Observe also in this connection that my remarks about the relationship between sentence (171) and sentences (173) and (174), appear to suggest that merely knowing two descriptions that apply to one and the same person (and knowing that they do) is sufficient for knowing who the person they apply to is. But this is not really the case, for one of these two descriptions, I have claimed, must be a referential one, and although I have not been able to say what is involved in being able to use a description referentially, it does rather obviously involve more than just knowing that it is co-referential with some other description that one is in no position to use referentially.

I have as yet said nothing at all about 'knowing who' when it is not a matter of knowing who someone is, that is, about sentences like:

(181) John knows who stole the jewels.

(182) John knows who is standing behind him.

(183) John knows who you had lunch with yesterday.

These sentences ought to be simpler to analyse than the ones we have dealt with so far, since they are presumably to be related to sentences of the form:

(184) John knows that so-and-so stole the jewels.

(185) John knows that so-and-so is standing behind him.

(186) John knows that you had lunch with so-and-so yesterday.

which contain only one potentially ambiguous noun phrase rather than two (ignoring the jewels, and you, of course). The obvious question to ask about these sentences is how the phrase so-and-so in (184) - (186) must be interpreted in order that sentences of this kind should entail sentences like (181) - (183). Here, unfortunately, my intuitions are not so clear, and I suspect that the answer depends on the nature of the predicate. Sentence (181), for example, appears to require a referentially interpreted so-and-so in (184), and closely resembles the sentence:

(187) John knows who the man who stole the jewels is.

If, for example John is asked:

(188) Who stole the jewels?

it would hardly do for him to reply:

(189) Oh, no-one special.

On the other hand it seems possible to take sentences (182) and (183) either way, and the sentence:

(190) John knows who he is pointing to.

unless John has his eyes closed, would only naturally be taken as entailed by the corresponding sentence with attributive so-and-so. Both senses of 'knowing who' therefore appear to be possible when a non-nominal predicate follows the who.

I shall return to the notion of 'knowing who' in the next chapter, following a discussion of the ambiguity of

202

descriptive content, in order to discuss examples like:

(191) John knows that the man who stole the jewels is the
man who stole the jewels.

(192) John knows that the man who stole the jewels stole
the jewels.

and their relation to the sentences:

(193) John knows who the man who stole the jewels is.

(194) John knows who stole the jewels.

Section 7. Predicate nominals and attributive noun phrases.

In the previous section, I distinguished four different
kinds of statement that can be made with a sentence of the
form NP_1 is NP_2 , in terms of whether either or both of the
noun phrases is used referentially or attributively. Given a
distinction between referential and attributive uses of noun
phrases, it would actually have required some explanation if
sentences of this form could not be used in these four different ways. There are, however, two objections that might be
made to talking of the noun phrases in such sentences having
an attributive use.

The sentence:

(195) Smith's murderer is insane.

if the phrase Smith's murderer is used attributively, can be
paraphrased as:

(196) Whoever murdered Smith is insane.

But the sentence:

(197)   That man is Smith's murderer.

in which, I have claimed, Smith's murderer may be used
attributively, cannot be paraphrased naturally as:

(198)   That man is whoever murdered Smith.

In fact this sentence is at best only barely grammatical.

This fact does not, however, show that it is wrong to
say that Smith's murderer in (197) cannot be used attributively.
A noun phrase is, characteristically, used attributively if
the speaker does not know to whom or to what in particular
the description applies. A noun phrase with whoever or whichever is only properly used if the speaker does not know to
whom or to what in particular the description applies.
Therefore in very many cases, when a noun phrase is used
attributively, it can be paraphrased by means of a phrase
with whoever or whichever. Now sentence (197), unlike
sentence (195), actually says who Smith's murderer is, and
so we obviously cannot assume that a person who uttered (197)
has no idea as to whom the phrase Smith's murderer applies.
It is this which is responsible for the oddity of (198).
But the absence of a whoever phrase does not show that the
phrase Smith's murderer cannot have an attributive use in (197),
for Donnellan explicitly states: "It is possible for a definite
description to be used attributively even though the speaker
(and his audience) believes that a certain person or thing

fits that description". The correlation between what a
speaker knows or believes and the way in which he uses a
given noun phrase is not essential to the referential/
attributive distinction, but is merely a matter of what is
usually the case. Thus it is not ruled out that a noun
phrase can be used attributively even in a sentence which
says who or what the description applies to.

Even though this objection cannot be upheld, it might
be objected that to invoke the referential/attributive
distinction to account for the varieties of NP is NP
sentence is unnecessary, since grammars already recognise a
category of (definite) predicate nominal, and the explanation
of the differences could be based on this, rather than on
the notion of an attributively used noun phrase. The
question that must be answered, therefore, is what is the
relationship between the referential/attributive distinction
and the concept of a predicate nominal. Do we need a category
of predicate nominals as distinct from the category of
attributively used noun phrases? Should we say that there
are predicate nominals and other noun phrases, and that the
latter can be used either referentially or attributively?
Or should we say rather that predicate nominals simply are
noun phrases used attributively? And if there is a distinction between the two, which category does the phrase Smith's
murderer in (197) fall into?

Since there is presumably some connection between the

concept of a predicate nominal and the concept of a predicative sentence, one might expect to gain some understanding of the nature of the phrase Smith's murderer in (197) from a distinction between predicative statements of the form NP is NP and identity statements. Unfortunately this distinction is itself a matter of some confusion, but Linsky provides a test which will be a helpful start to answering the questions of the previous paragraph. Linsky says (Reference and Referents, in: Philosophy and Ordinary Language, p. 80):

> Some of the statements which have been counted as identities cannot be interpreted as such. Suppose I explain to my confused son, "Charles de Gaulle is not the king of France". That this statement is not an identity can be shown as follows. From a ≠ b, it follows that b ≠ a, but from "Charles de Gaulle is not the king of France" it does not follow that "The king of France is not Charles de Gaulle". The first of these statements is true while the second is neither true nor false.

Linsky is pointing out that the phrase the king of France when it precedes the verb to be presupposes the existence of someone who is the king of France, while when it follows the verb to be it has no such presupposition. Since his two sentences differ in this way, they are not logically equivalent and therefore cannot both be identity statements. I assume that Linsky would say that it is sentences with definite descriptions following the verb to be that are not identity statements, since they do not presuppose the existence of a referent for the definite description. In this respect they are like

sentences which have quite straightforwardly predicative
expressions following the subject noun phrase. Thus the
sentences:

(199)   Charles de Gaulle is <u>not</u> hungry.

(200)   Charles de Gaulle is <u>not</u> a busdriver.

(201)   Charles de Gaulle is <u>not</u> singing.

(202)   Charles de Gaulle did <u>not</u> step into a puddle.

do not presuppose, or in any way imply, that anyone is hungry,
a busdriver, or singing, or that anyone stepped into a puddle.

Linsky's test, however, picks out only a very small
class of definite noun phrases; there are many sentences
with definite descriptions following the verb <u>to be</u> which
do presuppose the existence of something falling under the
description, and which might, therefore, as far as Linsky's
test is concerned, be regarded as expressing identity statements. It was observed in Section 5 of this chapter that
some definite noun phrases describe roles or offices or
positions that only one person or thing can occupy at any
one time, so that if they are true of anyone then necessarily
they are true of only one person. These noun phrases were
observed to be atypical with respect to existence presuppositions in opaque contexts; if they are interpreted
attributively, they apparently carry no presupposition of
existence, unlike other definite noun phrases. Now it is
just these noun phrases which carry no presupposition of

existence when they follow the verb to be in transparent

contexts. Thus examples like:

(203)   Tom is not the captain of the cricket team.

(204)   The captain of the cricket team is not Tom.

parallel Linsky's examples:

(205)   Charles de Gaulle is not the king of France.

(206)   The king of France is not Charles de Gaulle.

Sentence (204), though not sentence (203), presupposes that

someone is the captain of the cricket team; and sentence (206),

though not sentence (205), presupposes that someone is the

king of France. By contrast, with a phrase such as the man

who murdered Smith, which does not describe a role or an

office, we have:

(207)   Tom is not the man who murdered Smith.

(208)   The man who murdered Smith is not Tom.

both of which presuppose that someone is the man who murdered

Smith. Notice that the sentences:

(209)   Mary was not the first person I spoke to this morning.

(210)   The first person I spoke to this morning was not Mary.

also seem to presuppose that there is someone who is the

first person I spoke to this morning. In view of the fact

that in opaque contexts, phrases containing superlative

adjectives behave like phrases describing roles, in that

neither presuppose existence, it is somwhat surprising that

sentence (209) is not free of a presupposition of existence

as (203) and (205) are. I have no explanation for this fact.

The class of noun phrases that describe roles are picked out by a number of other criteria too. There are corresponding phrases with no article at all, thus:

(211) Charles de Gaulle is king of France.

(212) Tom is captain of the cricket team.

but not:

(213) *Tom is man who murdered Smith.

or:

(214) *Mary is first person I spoke to this morning.

Notice the contrast between (215) and (216):

(215) Bill is the ugliest man on campus.

(216) Bill is ugliest man on campus.

The latter is only appropriate if there was a competition resulting in the selection of Bill as the ugliest man on campus, that is, if the noun phrase describes a position or status.

A further difference appears in cleft sentences. We have:

(217) What de Gaulle is is the king of France.

(218) What de Gaulle is is king of France.

but not:

(219) *What Bill is is the man who murdered Smith.

(220) *What Bill is is man who murdered Smith.

It is worth observing that adjectives can appear in this

context. For example:

(221) What Bill is is crafty.

and some indefinite noun phrases can do so too, thus:

(222) What de Gaulle is is a figurehead.

Following the verb become we find this same class of constituents (adjectives, some indefinite noun phrases, definite
noun phrases that define roles, and the corresponding phrases
with no article at all). Thus:

(223) Mary became bitter.

(224) John became a busdriver.

(225) De Gaulle became the king of France.

(226) De Gaulle became king of France.

By comparison, the sentences:

(227) Mary became the first person I spoke to this morning.

(228) Bill became the man who murdered Smith.

are distinctly odd.

Thus there appears to be a rather well-defined class
of noun phrases which can describe roles or offices. They
do not carry an existence presupposition when they follow the
verb to be. They have counterparts with no article which
can only follow the verb to be, or to become thus:

(229) *King of France came to tea.

(230) *John met king of France.

and when they do follow these verbs, these phrases do not
carry an existence presupposition either. Wherever a phrase

210

without an article can appear, the corresponding phrase with
a definite article can appear, although other definite noun
phrases cannot. A range of predicative phrases can appear
in these same contexts. The obvious hypothesis, then, is
that when one of these definite noun phrases occurs without
a presupposition of existence, it is synonymous with the
corresponding phrase with no article, and it is to be regarded
as a predicative phrase. Thus the reading of the sentence:

(231)   Charles de Gaulle is <u>not</u> the king of France.

which does not have a presupposition of existence (whether
or not there is also another reading), is synonymous with:

(232)   Charles de Gaulle is <u>not</u> king of France.

and they both mean something like:

(233)   Charles de Gaulle does <u>not</u> hold the office, king of
                                               France.

The phrase <u>king of France</u>, without an article, cannot
appear in superficial subject position and it is not obvious
whether this is merely a superficial fact about English syntax,
or whether 'role-descriptions' in general cannot occur as
surface subjects. However, since other predicative expressions
are ungrammatical:

(234)   *Hungry is John.

or at least distinctly odd:

(235)   ? A busdriver is John.

in subject position, it looks as if the sentence:

211

(236)   *King of France is Charles de Gaulle.

is ruled out by something more than a superficial constraint
on the distribution of articles in English.   And if this is
so, then it explains why the sentence:

(237)   The king of France is not Charles de Gaulle.

does presuppose the existence of someone who is the king of
France.   The phrase the king of France in this context cannot
be used as a 'role-description' and thus it has a presupposition of existence just like other definite noun phrases which
cannot be so used.   Thus sentence (237) does not mean:

(238)   The office, king of France, is not held by de Gaulle.

which, like (233) does not presuppose that anyone does hold
the office, i.e. that there is a king of France.   It can only
be taken to mean something like:

(239)   The holder of the office, king of France, is not

de Gaulle.

which does presuppose that someone holds the office, i.e.
that there is a king of France.   It seems to me that there
is probably also a reading of sentence (231) which is like
this, that is, that sentence (231) is ambiguous, and has,
in addition to the reading (233), a reading to the effect:

(240)   Charles de Gaulle is not the holder of the office,

king of France.

which does presuppose that there is a king of France.

   A sentence of the form NP is NP, where the second

212

noun phrase is interpreted as a role-description, does not, by Linsky's test, express an identity statement, and we have seen that in a number of other ways it resembles quite straightforward examples of predicative sentences. Since Donnellan makes it clear that definite noun phrases used attributively do carry presuppositions of existence, it seems reasonable to say that these role-describing definite noun phrases are predicative and are not instances of attributively used noun phrases. Notice that the phrase the man who murdered Smith in the sentence:

(241) That man is the man who murdered Smith.

does not count as a predicative expression in this sense, since it does presuppose existence. Curiously enough, however, the phrase Smith's murderer in the sentence:

(242) That man is Smith's murderer.

does seem to count as a role-description and thus as predicative in this sense, since its negation is compatible with Smith's not having been murdered:

(243) That man is not Smith's murderer.

This just shows, I think, that the phrase Smith's murderer has at least one reading on which it is not synonymous with the phrase the man (the person) who murdered Smith. Other noun phrases of the same superficial form, such as Smith's girlfriend, Smith's brother, Smith's lawyer, can also be used as role-descriptions by our criteria.

It still remains as a question whether, having

separated off this class of predicative noun phrases, any
further distinctions need to be made, or whether the distinction between referential and attributive uses is sufficient
to account for all the facts. The class of definite predicative expressions that we have recognised is undoubtedly
smaller than the class of definite phrases which would
standardly be called predicate nominals, but I know of no
facts which require a wider class of predicate nominals to be
admitted. I do have one rather odd observation about identity
statements to offer, however.

Linsky's condition on identity statements is a necessary
condition. Unless a sentence of the form NP_1 is NP_2 is logically
equivalent to a sentence of the form NP_2 is NP_1 , then at
least one of them cannot be expressing an identity statement.
We might, however, wish to impose a stronger condition than
this as a sufficient condition on identity statements. One
plausible candidate for such a condition is that a sentence
of the form NP is NP expresses an identity statement only if
it can be paraphrased with the phrase 'the same person as'
or 'the same object as'. Now two of the four kinds of NP is NP
sentence distinguished in the previous section do clearly
have paraphrases of this kind. For example, if both the
noun phrases in the sentence:

(244)   Dr. Jekyll is Mr. Hyde.

are used referentially, as would be quite natural, then the
sentence can be paraphrased as:

214

(245)   Dr. Jekyll is the same person as Mr. Hyde.

or as:

(246)   Dr. Jekyll and Mr. Hyde are the same person.

If both of the noun phrases in the sentence:

(247)   The man who stole the jewels is the man who broke the
window.

are used attributively, as would be quite natural, then this sentence can be paraphrased as:

(248)   The man who stole the jewels is the same person as the
man who broke the window.

or as:

(249)   The man who stole the jewels and the man who broke the
window are the same man (person).

On the other hand, for examples which contain one noun phrase used referentially and another noun phrase used attributively, such a paraphrase is somewhat peculiar. Thus the sentences:

(250)   The man you should speak to is that man over there.

(251)   That man over there is the man you should speak to.

though they may be logically equivalent to the sentences:

(252)   The man you should speak to is the same person as that
man over there.

(253)   That man over there is the same person as the man you
should speak to.

(254)   The man you should speak to and that man over there are
the same man (person).

do not seem to be synonymous with these sentences. This correlates with the intuition (of some speakers, at least) that sentences like (250) and (251) do not really express identity statements but predications. They differ in presuppositions from sentences with role-describing definite noun phrases, and other predicative expressions, it is true, but they do not seem to be true identity statements either. This might be taken to suggest that a third category of statements, and of types or uses of noun phrases, must be recognised. In the absence of any other evidence for this, however, we could simply say that an identity statement requires that both noun phrases be used in the same way, referentially or attributively. Whatever the explanation, however, we are left with the rather surprising conclusion that to know that p is true of someone, where p is quite clearly an identity statement and can be paraphrased with 'is the same person as', does <u>not</u> count as knowing who that person is. It is only if one knows something like (250) or (251) that one can properly be said to know who the man you should speak to is, or who that man over there is, and these sentences are not true identity statements.

Section 8.   Logical relationships between definite and indefinite noun phrases.

In Section 5 of Chapter II it was suggested that it

might be a necessary condition on the truth of a sentence with a specifically interpreted indefinite noun phrase in an opaque context, that there should be some true sentence of the same form but with a definite noun phrase in place of the indefinite one. It was not discussed there whether this definite noun phrase should be a referential or an attributive one. In Section 1 of the present chapter it was claimed that both the referential and the attributive readings of the sentence:

(255)   John wants to meet the boy who failed the exam.

entail the specific reading of:

(256)   John wants to meet a boy.

since both provide an answer to the question:

(257)   Which boy does John want to meet?

There _is_ a difference between the entailments of the referential and attributive readings of (255) which is connected with the specific/non-specific contrast, but this concerns not (256) but the sentence:

(258)   John knows that a (one) boy failed the exam.

The referential reading of (255), it was claimed, requires the truth of (258) on its specific reading, while the attributive reading of (255) requires only that the non-specific reading of (258) is true, (disregarding here any questions concerning the opacity of the descriptive content of the noun phrases).

I shall now add a few tentative comments about these

semantic connections between definite and indefinite noun
phrases. They are tentative because the intuitions, both mine
and those of other speakers, on which they are based are far
from confident. In this area of the language there are,
as I have shown, a number of semantic distinctions to be
made, and they are all rather fine ones; it appears that
speakers of the language are not able to operate consistently, or at least confidently, with all of them at once.
It is difficult to describe the logic of this part of the
language, because its logic is, apparently, not precisely
defined.

With this limitation in mind, I would suggest that
for verbs like _thinks_ and _knows_, rather than _wants_, _intends_,
and so on, the observations of the above paragraph do
not all hold. In particular, the inference of a specific
indefinite from an attributive definite is not, or not
obviously, valid. While the sentence:

(259) John knows that that man was arrested.

with referential _that man_, does entail:

(260) There is someone (a man) whom John knows was arrested.

it is doubtful whether the sentence:

(261) John knows that whoever broke the window was arrested.

entails (260). The specific reading of an indefinite noun
phrase, I have said, requires that the subject should have
someone (something) particular in mind. For verbs like
want, _intend_, _hope_, it apparently counts as having someone

particular in mind if one has <u>decided</u> whom one wants to meet
(intends to marry, etc.). And it is apparently sufficient
for this that one should have settled on a criterion that
distinguishes that person from all others; it is not
necessary that one should know whom that criterion picks
out. This is the content of the claim that an attributive
definite entails a specific indefinite.

For epistemic verbs, on the other hand, the specific
reading of the indefinite is, or at least may be, construed
more strongly. It can be taken to require not only that
one has a criterion that picks out just one individual from
the possible range, but also that one knows which individual
that criterion picks out, i.e. to whom (in the referential
sense) the attributive description applies.

Some sense can be made of this difference between
epistemic and non-epistemic verbs in terms of the <u>which</u>-
question criterion for the specific reading of an indefinite.
Consider the discourse:

(262) Q. Which man does John think will win?

      A. John thinks the youngest man will win.

      Q. But which man does John think is the youngest man?
where, given an attributive answer to the first question,
there is still another <u>which</u>-question that can be asked, a
request for a referential description. This may be compared
with the discourse:

(263)   Q.   Which man does John want to win?

       A.   John wants the youngest man to win.

       Q.   But who does John want to be the youngest man?
in which the second question is distinctly odd.   One can,
of course, ask in this context who John <u>thinks</u> is the
youngest man, but because of the difference of the verbs
here, this question is apparently not taken to be part of
the original question.

    Whether or not this is the correct explanation for
the stronger construal of a specific indefinite for
epistemic verbs than for non-epistemic verbs, the difference
does shed some light on the observation of Chapter II,
Section 6, that for factive verbs, the specific and non-
specific readings are semantically closer with non-epistemic
verbs than with epistemic verbs.   For epistemic verbs,
the specific reading is, or may be, construed in the
strong sense outlined above, and thus stands more clearly
distinct from the non-specific reading, which is in
general weaker than the specific.   In fact the argument
(which I maintained was invalid) from the non-specific
reading of a sentence like:

(264)   John regrets having killed a spider.

to its specific reading, seems to be mediated by a related
sentence with an attributive definite noun phrase.   If,
as I have claimed, the specific reading of (264) can be inferred

from a similar sentence with an attributive definite noun phrase, then it should be possible to infer it from the attributive reading of:

(265) John regrets having killed the spider that he killed.

But this in turn seems to follow from the non-specific reading of (264). For even the non-specific reading of (264) entails that John killed a spider, and if he regrets this then he presumably knows that he killed a spider. But then he could hardly fail to know that the description 'the spider that he (I) killed' is true _attributively_ of the spider that he killed, i.e. it is hard to imagine that (265) is false if the non-specific reading of (264) is true.

For epistemic factive verbs, by contrast, the specific reading can be inferred only from a referential definite, and thus the attributive reading of a sentence like:

(266) John knows that he killed the spider that he killed.

cannot be taken to mediate the inference of the specific reading of:

(267) John knows that he killed a spider.

from its non-specific reading. Hence the readings of this sentence do not tend to fall together. Notice that the referential reading of (266), from which the specific reading of (267) _can_ be inferred, can, unlike the attributive reading, quite easily be imagined to be false when the non-specific reading of (267) is true. For the referential reading of (266) requires that John should know _which_ spider he

221

killed, and he might know that he killed one without knowing which.

I maintained in Chapter II that the non-specific reading does not, in fact, entail the specific reading even for a sentence such as (264), though the argument is at least superficially more plausible than in the case of (267). We can now ask where we should drive the wedge that blocks the inference --- between the non-specific indefinite and the attributive definite, or between the attributive definite and the specific indefinite? The latter, I think, is correct; some argument can be made for it, at least, on the basis of the which-question criterion for the specific reading of an indefinite phrase. The question:

(268) Which spider does John regret killing?

can obviously be answered truly but quite uninformatively by:

(269) He regrets killing the spider that he killed.

given that it is true that John regrets killing a spider. This is because John could not, logically, regret killing any spider that he did not kill -- regret has a factive presupposition. This contrasts with the case for non-factives; for example the answer:

(270) John wanted to kill the spider that he killed.

to the question:

(271) Which spider did John want to kill?

is not uninformative, even given that John did want to kill
a spider. Thus (270) is an acceptable answer to the
question (271), while (269) is not an acceptable answer to (268).
Since someone asking (268) presumably is not seeking the
answer (269), his question must either be taken as a request
for a non-obvious attributive description, or for a
referential description, or else must be taken in some other
way, for example with an implication of non-uniqueness as:

(272) Which of the spiders that he killed does John regret

killing?

And these answers cannot be derived automatically from
the fact that John regrets killing a spider. If the
which-question criterion for the specific reading is thus
strengthened to the condition that there must be an _informative_
answer to the relevant which-question, the specific reading
of an indefinite will _not_, after all, be entailed by just
any attributive definite, and the attributive definite
cannot be taken to mediate the inference of the specific
indefinite from the non-specific.

I also note, finally, that a definite noun phrase
which is co-referential with an indefinite noun phrase must
be attributive if the indefinite phrase is non-specific.
Thus in the discourse:

(273) John wants to catch a fish. The fish that he catches...

with a fish read as non-specific, the phrase the fish that he catches is obviously attributive. By contrast, in the discourse:

(274) John wants to catch a fish. The fish that he wants
to catch...

with a fish read as specific, the phrase the fish that he wants to catch may be read either as attributive or as referential.

224

CHAPTER IV.   OPACITY AND DESCRIPTIONS.

Section 1.   The ambiguity of the descriptive content of noun
             phrases.

In Chapter I, two criteria for opacity were given, the
invalidity of existential generalization, and the invalidity
of substituting one description of something for another
description of it. The status of existential inferences from
opaque contexts was examined in some detail in Chapters II and
III, and I shall now consider some problems about semantic
representation which arise in connection with the substitutivity,
or non-substitutivity, of descriptions.

The intersubstitution of alternative descriptions of
one and the same object is a valid inferential procedure in
transparent contexts. The following argument, for example, is
a valid one.

(1)   Tom is a busdriver.

(2)   Tom is Jim's best friend.

(3)   Therefore Jim's best friend is a busdriver.

Within an opaque context, a similar substitution is not valid,
for example:

(4)   Mary realises that Tom is a busdriver.

(5)   Tom is Jim's best friend.

(6)   Therefore Mary realises that Jim's best friend is a
                                          busdriver.

It was pointed out in Chapter I that sentences like (4) and (6) can be read in such a way that, on that reading, the argument is valid. If (4) is read as saying that Mary realises of the person, Tom, that he is a busdriver, then from the fact that the person, Tom, is Jim's best friend, it obviously does follow that Mary realises of Jim's best friend (i.e. Tom) that he is a busdriver. These sentences also have another, stronger, reading, however, and on that reading the argument is not valid. Thus (4) may be construed as saying that Mary realises that 'Tom' is a description (name) of the person Tom, as well as that she realises that the person Tom is a busdriver, and (6) can be construed similarly as saying that Mary realises that 'Jim's best friend' is a description of the person who is Jim's best friend (i.e. Tom), as well as that she realises of that person that he is a busdriver. On these readings, (6) obviously does not follow from (4) and (5), for Mary might well realise that 'Tom' is a description of the person Tom, and not realise that 'Jim's best friend' is a description of him. Thus (6) might be false if (4) and (5) are true. It is this second way of reading such sentences that is called 'opaque' since it is for these readings that the otherwise valid inference rule for substituting descriptions is invalid.

Postal (Restrictive Relatives, 1967) illustrates the contrast between the two readings very clearly by means of examples in which the complement clause is self-contradictory, e.g.

(7) Charley assumed that the book which was burned was not burned.

Interpreted opaquely, this sentence does ascribe a self-contradictory assumption to Charley, the assumption which can be expressed in the words 'The book which was burned was not burned'. Interpreted transparently, the sentence is compatible with Charley's merely having assumed something which is factually false, i.e. with his having assumed of a certain book which in fact was burned that it was not burned. This is because, on the transparent interpretation, the sentence does not ascribe to Charley acceptance of the description 'the book which was burned' as a description of the book which he assumed was not burned. Postal stresses, quite rightly, that the problem that such sentences pose for the linguist is the problem of finding two distinct ways of formally representing their meanings. I shall discuss shortly the particular proposal that Postal makes as to how this is to be done. First, however, it is important to realise that the ambiguity of sentences like (4), (6) and (7) that we have just been discussing is different from the ambiguities with which we were concerned in Chapters II and III.

In Chapter II, we discussed the specific/non-specific ambiguity of indefinite noun phrases in opaque contexts. In the context:

(8) Charley wants to buy a coat like Bill's.

for example, the noun phrase a coat like Bill's can be taken to refer to a particular coat that Charley wants to buy, or

or else we can take the sentence to mean simply that Charley
wants to buy some coat like Bill's though he has no particular
one in mind. Whether or not the sentence is read as ascribing
to Charley acceptance of the description 'a coat like Bill's' as
a description of what he wants to buy, is a question which
cuts right across the specific/non-specific distinction. The
specific interpretation of the noun phrase in (8) is consistent with the opaque interpretation of the descriptive
content of the noun phrase; we can read the sentence as saying
that there is a particular coat that Charley wants to buy and
that he wants to buy it under the description 'a coat like
Bill's'. On the other hand we can read it as saying that
there is a particular coat that Charley wants to buy but
without ascribing acceptance of the description 'a coat like
Bill's' to Charley. Charley might, after all, not know Bill,
or, if he does, he might not know what Bill's coat is like.
His desire can still be reported by sentence (8), but in this
case obviously the speaker must be the source of the description. This reading of (8) is transparent with respect to
the descriptive content of the noun phrase, and also specific,
that is, transparent with respect to existential generalization.

If we now consider the non-specific interpretation of
(8), we see that it too is consistent with either the transparent or the opaque reading of the descriptive content of
the noun phrase. Thus Charley might, having seen Bill's coat
and admired it, say: 'I want to buy a coat like Bill's', and

though he has no particular coat like Bill's in mind to buy, he nevertheless accepts the description 'a coat like Bill's' as a description of the kind of coat he would like. On the other hand sentence (8) is compatible with Charley's having decided what kind of coat he wants to buy but having no idea that the kind of coat he wants is just like Bill's coat.

The two kinds of ambiguity can thus be seen to be independent and to cut right across each other; the one indefinite noun phrase in (8) allows of four different interpretations. This is a very important point and one that seems to have been overlooked, or at least blurred, in previous discussions of opaque contexts. Quine, for example, (Word and Object, p. 146ff.) clearly states that indefinite noun phrases have no interpretation which is opaque for descriptive content, that is, for which the substitutivity of descriptions is invalid. He discusses the specific/non-specific ambiguity of such noun phrases, and then quite clearly suggests that while opacity shows up in connection with definite noun phrases as a matter of the invalidity of substitutivity, it shows up in connection with indefinite noun phrases as a matter of specificity. His view that the two are mutually exclusive may well be due to the fact that in discussing specificity he employs examples containing the indefinite pronoun someone rather than indefinite noun phrases with some lexical content, such as a coat like Bill's. But whatever its source, I think it is clear that this view is incorrect, and this is important

because it means that the two criteria for opacity, failure of
substitutivity and failure of existential generalization, are
not co-extensive.[FN] This is not simply to claim that there
might be sentences which exhibit an ambiguity of the one kind
but not of the other, although there are indeed such sentences.
As pointed out in Chapter I, the sentence:

(9)   Charley recognised a friend of mine.

has no non-specific interpretation but is ambiguous with
respect to the descriptive content of the noun phrase a friend
of mine and may be read as saying that Charley recognised a
friend of mine as a friend of mine, or as saying that Charley
recognised a friend of mine but without any implication that
Charley was aware that the person he recognised was a friend

FN. It was mentioned in Chapter I that there seems to be an
implicit assumption in many discussions of opacity, that the
failure of substitutivity and the failure of existential
generalization are necessarily connected. The idea is apparently that if existential generalization is valid, then this means
that the sentence expresses a proposition about a particular
individual. But if something is true of a particular individual,
it should be true of him whatever description is used to refer
to him, and therefore substitutivity must be valid. What I
am suggesting, on the other hand, is that there are two quite
independent questions. (a) Does the sentence predicate
something of a particular individual? (b) Under what description of that individual does it do so? The claim that these
questions are independent is not, I think, logically incoherent.
But the idea that something might be true of an individual
though only under some descriptions of him, does require
recognizing that a single noun phrase may have two distinct
functions in a sentence -- to pick out, refer to, an individual,
and to provide a particular description of him. Any co-extensive
phrase could equally well fulfill the first of these functions,
but this is obviously not so of the second, which is why
substitutivity is not generally valid. This point will, I
hope, become clearer in Sections 5 and 6 of this chapter. It was
observed in Chapter I that Quine assumes that if existential
generalization is valid then substitutivity must also be valid. It

of mine. What is justified by the other examples we have
considered, however, is the stronger claim that sentences
which exhibit both ambiguities have readings which are simultaneously opaque by one criterion but transparent by the
other. They also, of course, as is generally recognised,
have readings which are transparent by both criteria or
opaque by both criteria.

The same point can be made about definite noun phrases.
For these, the ambiguity of descriptive content cuts across
the referential/attributive ambiguity. The sentence:

(10) Charley thinks that the man who stole his car has been
arrested.

may be interpreted referentially, as saying that Charley has a
certain person in mind and thinks he has been arrested. Or it
may be interpreted attributively, as saying that Charley thinks
it is true that whoever stole his car has been arrested even
though he may not know who the thief is. It is easy to see
that the referential interpretation is still ambiguous, that
it either may or else may not be taken to ascribe to Charley
the belief that the person whom he thinks has been arrested
is the man who stole his car. It is also easy to see that
the noun phrase can be interpreted attributively and as opaque
for the descriptive content, that is, as saying that though
Charley may not know to whom the description 'the man who stole
his (my) car' applies he nevertheless thinks that whoever it
applies to is such that he has been arrested. The fourth

---

is the unwelcome consequences of this assumption that lead him
to deny the legitimacy of 'quantifying into' opaque contexts
(see Chapter II. example (11)).

interpretation that I am claiming that sentence (10) may have
is the interpretation on which the noun phrase is attributive
but transparent for descriptive content, and over this interpretation there might be some scepticism. Suppose Charley
thinks that whoever the man is who broke into his house last
night has been arrested. Suppose, that is, that the sentence:

(11)   Charley thinks that the man who broke into his house

last night has been arrested.

is true when the noun phrase is interpreted as attributive
and as opaque for descriptive content. Then if I know that
the man who broke into Charley's house last night is the man
who also stole Charley's car (whether or not I know who he is),
then I might report Charley's belief in sentence (10) and
sentence (10) would be true if read as attributive and transparent for descriptive content of the noun phrase. (Note:
Even if there is no general agreement over the possibility
of this reading, the fact that referentially interpreted
definite noun phrases, and specific and non-specific indefinite
noun phrases, are ambiguous with respect to descriptive content
is quite sufficient for my point.)

There is a possible criticism that I would like to
forestall, a criticism not of the claim that sentences
like (8) and (10) have the readings that I have outlined, but
a criticism of the theoretical descriptions given of the
readings. One noun phrase may contain another noun phrase,

as the man who stole his car in (10) contains the noun phrase his car, and a coat like Bill's in (8), since it means a coat like Bill's coat, can be said to contain the noun phrase Bill's coat. The ambiguities affect both the containing and the contained noun phrases in such cases, and it might be suggested that those sentences have four possible readings not because the two ambiguities are orthogonal to each other, as I have claimed, but because of the ambiguity of the noun phrases within the larger noun phrases. The relationship between the opacity or transparency of another noun phrase contained within it is an interesting topic and one that I shall return to in a later section. A full account of this relationship is not needed, however, to rebut the suggestion just outlined; all that is needed is to exhibit the four-way ambiguity in opaque contexts of noun phrases which do not have other noun phrases internal to them. I shall not describe at length all their possible interpretations, but I think it should be clear upon consideration that the following two sentences are ambiguous in ways exactly parallel to sentences (8) and (10) respectively.

(12)   Charley wants to buy an inexpensive coat.

(13)   Charley thinks that the burglar has been arrested.

Section 2.   The formal representation of the ambiguity.

Whatever formal device we use to distinguish between the opaque and the transparent readings of the descriptive

content of noun phrases in opaque contexts must obviously
be different from the formal device used to indicate specificity and/or referentiality of noun phrases. If it were not,
we would not be able to indicate the independence of the two
kinds of phenomenon. It may be noted in passing that the same
form of paraphrase may be used informally for the purpose of
disambiguation in both cases. Thus we might say:

(14) Mary realises of Jim's best friend that he is a
busdriver.

in order to pick out the reading of sentence (6) for which
Jim's best friend is transparent with respect to descriptive
content, that is, to avoid the implication that Mary realises
that the person concerned is Jim's best friend. However, this
same paraphrase might also be used, if there seemed to be a
danger of confusion between the referential and attributive
interpretations of the noun phrase, to pick out its referential
interpretation. Despite its usefulness on occasion to avoid
misunderstanding, it is clear that this form of paraphrase
at best only partially reduces the number of possible
readings and is not itself univocal. It embodies implicitly
the assumption discussed above, that a noun phrase is either
opaque according to both criteria or is transparent according
to both, and since this assumption is incorrect, a paraphrase
like (14) is not powerful enough to serve as a model for the
formal representation of noun phrases in opaque contexts.

Since the same kind of paraphrase seems to lend itself
equally well (and equally badly) to the disambiguation of
both kinds of ambiguities, and since this kind of paraphrase,
as noted in previous chapters, seems designed to express the
scope relation between the noun phrase in question and the
opaque verb, it does suggest that the ambiguity of descriptive
content, like the specific/non-specific and referential/
attributive ambiguities, is to be accounted for in terms of
scope. The ambiguity does indeed exhibit the kinds of property that seem to demand an analysis in terms of scope relations. The number of possible readings depends on the degree
of embedding in a sentence. So far all of our examples have
been sentences containing a single complement clause,
and we have observed that they have two readings with respect
to the descriptive content of any noun phrase in the
complement. But more complex examples have more possible
readings. The sentence:

(15) Charley hopes that Mary thinks that Jim's best friend

is a busdriver.

can be taken as fully transparent for the descriptive
content of the phrase <u>Jim's best friend</u>, that is, it can
be taken to mean that Charley hopes of Jim's best friend,
though not necessarily under that description, that Mary
thinks that he is a busdriver. It can be taken to mean that
Charley hopes of Jim's best friend, under that description,
that Mary thinks that he is a busdriver. And it can be

taken to mean that Charley hopes of Jim's best friend, under that description, that Mary thinks of him under that description that he is a busdriver. Notice that if a set of independent feature specifications were an appropriate way of representing the ambiguity, there should be a fourth possible reading, to the effect that Charley hopes of Jim's best friend, though not necessarily under that description, that Mary thinks of him, under the description 'Jim's best friend', that he is a busdriver. This is certainly a possible state of affairs. Charley might, for example, know Tom, who is Jim's best friend, not know that he is Jim's best friend, and yet hope, for some reason, that Mary thinks Tom both is Jim's best friend and is a busdriver. Although one can imagine the situation, however, it is not one which is expressed by a reading of sentence (15). Apparently if the description is taken as transparent with respect to Charley's hope, it must also be taken as transparent with respect to the thought that he hopes Mary has.

As the complexity of sentences increases, the ability to keep their various alternative readings distinguished in one's mind decreases rapidly, even more rapidly, it seems, than for the ambiguity of specificity or of referentiality of noun phrases. I think it is fairly clear, nevertheless, that in all cases there are as many readings, with respect to the descriptive content of a noun phrase, as there are nested complement clauses in which it appears. And it is not only the _number_ of possible readings that is predictable on the basis of an analysis in terms of the relative scope of the noun phrase and the opaque verbs in the sentence. The difference between the possible readings is not a matter of reading the descriptive phrase itself in a number of distinct ways, as one might read _light coat_ or _colourful ball_, but is a matter of construing the role of the phrase in relation to other parts of the sentence in a number of different ways.

We might propose, then, as we did for the ambiguities discussed in the previous chapters, that some symbol subscripted for the noun phrase in question, say (Dx), be allowed to appear in any one of the clauses of the representation of the sentence, in order to indicate whether the noun phrase is to be taken as inside or outside the scope of the various opaque verbs that the sentence contains. This would be the minimal hypothesis, designed merely to capture the number of possible readings and the fact that the differences between them are scope differences. More interesting and substantive claims about the nature of the readings could then be made by proposing to identify this arbitrary symbol (Dx) with some already recognised constituent of semantic representations. I shall argue later that this whole approach to the representation of the ambiguity should be rejected,

but it is worth considering in some detail because the only
proposal that has been made in the linguistic literature,
as far as I know, is a proposal of just this form.

Postal's proposal (Restrictive Relatives, 1967) is
based on the conjunctive analysis of relative clauses together with the derivation of lexical noun phrases from
predicate nominals in relative clauses. (See Chapter II,
Section 4.) In fact the existence of the ambiguity of
descriptive content of noun phrases, together with the success
of Postal's proposed representations, are presented by
Postal as one of the major arguments in favour of these
analyses. The proposal is, in effect, to use the conjoined
clause which is supposed to underly a noun phrase, in the
role of (Dx), that is, to allow this clause to be conjoined
at any one of the clausal levels in the underlying representation, with each of its possible positions defining
its scope on one possible reading of the sentence. These
underlying representations (which Postal regards, I believe,
as syntactic but which I shall consider only in connection
with the semantics of the sentences concerned) will thus
be something along the lines of:

(16)[FN.] x is Jim's best friend and Mary realises that x is

a busdriver.

_____

FN. These representations are adaptations of Postal's. I
think, especially in the light of Lakoff's discussion of
Postal's paper in lectures (Illinois, Summer 1968), that
they do capture the essence of Postal's proposal accurately.
Postal uses numerical referential indices in his representations

(17) Mary realises that (x is Jim's best friend and x is

a busdriver).

where (16) is supposed to express the transparent reading

of sentence (6), and (17) to express its opaque reading.

Some linguists believe that at the highest level of the

underlying representation of any sentence there should be

a 'performative' clause, and if this is written into (16)

and (17), thus:

(18) I say to you that (x is Jim's best friend and Mary

realises that x is a busdriver).

(19) I say to you that Mary realises that (x is Jim's best

friend and x is a busdriver).

the resulting structures portray quite clearly Postal's

notion that on the transparent reading the source of the

description 'Jim's best friend' should be the speaker, and

that on the opaque reading the source of this description

should be Mary, the subject of the opaque verb <u>realises</u>.

---

and also what appear to be some form of variable, though
nothing resembling quantifiers to bind these. To use
referential constants would not, as far as I can see, be
consistent with Postal's intention; he does in any case
note a similarity between his ideas and those of Bach, who
employs something very like the quantifiers and variables
of the predicate calculus. To sort out the exact status of
these constants or variables or whatever they are, would
be a lengthy task and it is one which I shall not undertake
in view of the fact that I shall argue later that Postal's
type of analysis should be rejected. I shall have occasion,
in the next section, to comment on the role of the x's in
my representations (16) and (17) above, but apart from this
I shall simply leave it open as to exactly what formal
properties they are supposed to have.

239

In the next few sections of this chapter I shall make some observations about the nature of the ambiguity of descriptions, and the nature of these representations, which suggest that this treatment is not appropriate.

Section 3. Paradoxes of scope.

It was observed above that the ambiguity of descriptive content of noun phrases cuts across the ambiguities of specificity and referentiality of noun phrases, and that therefore whatever device is used to represent the former cannot be the same as is used to represent the latter. This places some constraints on the representation of specificity and referentiality in Postal's system. He has, in effect, used up the whole of the noun phrase in representing the relative scope of the description, and this leaves little over to function as the scope indicator for specificity and referentiality. We can, of course, simply stick to arbitrary operators like (Sx). It is also possible to maintain that the determiner of the ambiguous noun phrase is to be used for indicating specificity, for, as has often been pointed out in the linguistic literature, the determiner that appears in the underlying representation of a noun phrase which gets 'relativised' is not the determiner which appears in the noun phrase in surface structure. The latter, since it is therefore not part of the conjoined clause which Postal supposes underlies the noun phrase and indicates the scope of the description in underlying representations, is still available for indicating specificity. The obvious similarities between determiners and the quantifiers of logic would make this a natural decision, and intuitively it seems most satisfactory to relate the ambiguities of specificity and referentiality to the determiner of a noun phrase, and the ambiguity of descriptive content to the rest of the material in the noun phrase. This would account for the fact that the ambiguity of descriptive content affects indefinite and definite noun phrases alike, the fact that it is present simultaneously with these other ambiguities, the fact that the ambiguity of specificity, which affects indefinite noun phrases, and the ambiguity of referentiality, which affects definite noun phrases, are very alike in many ways and yet are mutually exclusive. Thus these proposals would seem to add up to a very coherent general picture of opacity. This coherent picture rapidly dissolves into incoherence, however, if the semantic representations of the grammar, and the definitions of scope for the symbols they contain, are supposed to be modelled on those of standard systems of logic.

The problem is the interaction of the ambiguity of descriptive content with specificity or referentiality. I shall illustrate it with respect to specificity. A sentence like:

241

(20) Charley wants to buy a coat like Bill's.

is, as we saw in the previous section, four ways ambiguous.
The noun phrase a coat like Bill's can be taken as specific
or as non-specific, and, in either case, as either transparent
or opaque with respect to its descriptive content. We
therefore need four distinct semantic representations for
this sentence. Using (Sx) to indicate specificity, and
otherwise modelling our representations on Postal's, we
shall have:

(21) (Sx) (x is a coat like Bill's and Charley wants to
               buy x).

(22) (Sx) (Charley wants (x is a coat like Bill's and
               Charley wants to buy x)).

(23) x is a coat like Bill's and Charley wants (Sx)
               (Charley buy x).

(24) Charley wants (Sx) (x is a coat like Bill's and
               Charley buy x).

The first two represent specific readings, the second two
represent non-specific readings. The first and third
represent readings which are transparent for descriptive
content, the second and fourth represent readings which are
opaque for descriptive content. And the problem, of course,
is that (23) is not well-formed, or rather, that it is well-
formed only if the first occurrence of x in it is regarded as
unbound by the (Sx) and, if it is, then the representation

does not indicate any connection at all between what Charley wants to buy and a coat like Bill's. The paradox of scope is that the first conjunct of (23) must be within the scope of the (Sx) if its variable is to be co-referential with the object of Charley buy..., the (Sx) must be within the scope of the verb wants if it is to express the non-specific reading, but the first conjunct must be outside the scope of wants if it is to express the reading which is transparent for descriptive content. Since scope relations, at least in standard systems of logic, are transitive, these three requirements cannot all be satisfied in one formula.

Also worrying, although less so, is the representation (22) which, like (23), represents a reading of the sentence as transparent in one way and opaque in the other. There is no question in (22) of the variables being unbound, but (22) seems to attribute to the sentence (20) a reading which is compatible with Charley's wanting to buy, say, a telescope, or a porcupine, and wanting it to be a coat like Bill's. The representation (22) indicates that there is something in particular that Charley wants to buy and it says what Charley would like it to be, but it does not actually say what it actually is.

In Chapter II, when discussing the formal representation of specificity by means of devices like quantifiers and variables, I made use of forms like (21) and (24) only,

simply in order not to get involved with these problems.
Now that we require our representations to express the transparency or opacity of the descriptive content of noun
phrases as well as specificity, it is clear that those two
forms of representation, even if they are themselves well-
formed, are not sufficient. The problems that arise in
connection with the other two forms do not prove conclusively
that representations along these lines could not be employed
in a linguistic description, but they do show that a linguistic description containing such representations must
also contain some principles governing the binding of
variables, or the notion of non-transitive scope relations,
or an account of the x's in these representations as something other than variables which must or may be bound by
quantifier-like elements. And this must be done in such a
way that it does not destroy the suitability of these
devices for representing pronominalization or any other
syntactic or semantic phenomenon which they are supposed to
underly. And even if it can be done, there are further
problems.

Section 4. Simplification of conjunctions and the opaque reading.

Postal's analysis makes crucial use of the derivation
of relative clauses from underlying conjoined clauses.

244

Relative clauses have to be loosened from the noun phrases in which they appear in surface structure, so that in the underlying structure they can appear in different positions relative to the other clauses of the sentence. At one point Postal writes as if he can imagine no other way of analysing sentences which exhibit the ambiguity. He says: "Clearly no structural account which requires all R [i.e. restrictive relative clauses, JDF] to originate inside the NP they modify can possibly account for this [ambiguity, JDF]". There obviously are other ways of accounting for it, though perhaps less suitable and less elegant. Postal's way is elegant; like all analyses in terms of scope it seems ideally suited to capture both the number of readings and the way in which the readings differ from each other. The very strong appeal of Postal's particular variety of scope analysis stems, I think, from the fact that just reading his representations out into English seems to provide a quite direct and explicit account of what a sentence means on each of its readings. Thus the representation:

(25) Mary realises that (x is Jim's best friend and x is

a busdriver).

seems to express quite directly the fact that Mary realises two things, that someone is a busdriver and that the person is Jim's best friend. The representation of the transparent reading of the same sentence:

(26) x is Jim's best friend and Mary realises that x is

a busdriver.

seems to express quite clearly that what it is being claimed
that Mary realises is simply that a certain person is a
busdriver, and not that that person is Jim's best friend.

However, in Chapter II, we concluded that simplification of conjunctions within the scope of opaque operators
must not be permitted since it produces invalid arguments.
This means that (25) is not equivalent to:

(27) Mary realises that x is Jim's best friend and Mary

realises that x is a busdriver.

and it means that we cannot infer from (25) that Mary
realises that someone is Jim's best friend. But it was
only reading (25) as if it did entail this that made (25)
seem so attractive as a representation of the opaque sense.
Even for verbs like realise, then, the analysis is not
nearly so appealing as it seems at first sight. And for
other verbs, such as wants, hopes, orders, fears, and so on,
it is not appealing at all. Postal does not consider
sentences with these verbs, but if we consider the
sentence:

(28) Charley wants to buy a coat like Bill's.

and the putative representation of its opaque reading:

(29) Charley wants (x is a coat like Bill's and Charley

buy x).

it is hard to find a way of reading this into English which directly expresses the meaning of the sentence. If it is taken as roughly equivalent to the English sentence: 'Charley wants to buy something and wants what he buys to be a coat like Bill's', then perhaps it is not too bad. But if we can read it this way then we can also, by interchanging the conjuncts, read it as: 'Charley wants something to be a coat like Bill's and he wants to buy whatever is'. This, even if it makes sense at all, is hardly a good paraphrase of sentence (28). Examples like this simply emphasize that simplification of conjunctions must not be allowed within opaque contexts because of the odd results that it produces. But if simplification is not allowed, then Postal's way of indicating the scope relationships in sentences is no more attractive than any other way of doing so; all that made it look especially attractive was the illusory impression that to use the conjoined clause underlying the ambiguous noun phrase as the scope operator would be to spell out the meaning and entailments of the sentence explicitly. It has been stressed in previous chapters that the semantic representation of a sentence need not, should not, and probably could not, consist of a list, or conjunction, of all the entailments of the sentence. The fact that Postal's proposed representations do not spell out the entailments of opaque sentences therefore does not show that those

representations are inadequate. It shows only that, just
like representations employing completely abstract and
arbitrary means of indicating scope, such as (Dx), they would
need to be supplemented with some general rules which, when
applied to the representations, generated the entailments.

It should be observed that Postal's argument (or
assumption) that the ambiguity of descriptive content should
be captured by deriving noun phrases from clauses conjoined
at different levels of embedding in underlying structures,
was one of his main arguments in support of the claim that
noun phrases must be derived from underlying conjoined
clauses. If the former argument does not hold, as I have
suggested, then it obviously cannot carry any weight as an
argument for the conjunctive analysis of relative clauses.
It seems, in fact, that there is virtually no positive
motivation for adopting such an analysis.

Section 5. The speaker's responsibility for the description.

The logical discussions focus mainly on the fact that
substitutivity of identicals is not a valid inference rule
within opaque contexts, that is, that one cannot move from
a sentence containing one description of something to a
sentence containing an alternative description of it. The
linguistic discussions focus mainly on the fact that
sentences containing opaque contexts are ambiguous and that

some account must be given of each of their readings and how the readings differ. These are, of course, opposite sides of the same coin, for it is some aspect of the opaque reading of these sentences, an aspect that it does not share with the transparent reading, that is responsible for the fact that substitutivity is invalid. In considering how this phenomenon should be handled in a grammar of English, linguists have assumed, and rightly I think, that the difference between the opaque and the transparent reading of a sentence is that the former expresses some relationship between the subject of the opaque verb and the descriptive content of the noun phrase in question. They also seem to have assumed that although on the transparent reading the usual relationship between a speaker and a description he uses holds, this is not so for the opaque reading; on the opaque reading the speaker is merely taking over a description from the subject of the opaque verb, saying what would count, in his opinion, as a description of the object in question from the point of view of that subject. This assumption, I shall argue, is incorrect.

The assumption that the source of the description, or the responsibility for it, is always <u>either</u> the speaker (on the transparent reading) <u>or</u> the subject of the opaque verb (on the opaque reading) is embodied in the proposed representations that we have been considering. The

difference between (16) and (17), or between (18) and (19)
above, is a matter of whether the descriptive content of
the noun phrase is represented as part of what the speaker
is asserting, or is represented as part of what he is
asserting that Mary realises, i.e. is ascribing to Mary.
I shall maintain that these two alternatives are not mutually
exclusive and that in fact the speaker is _always_ responsible
for the descriptions that he employs, even if he is also
attributing them to the person whose beliefs, hopes, etc.,
he is reporting. I shall maintain, that it to say, that
there is _no_ purely opaque reading of these sentences, of
the kind just outlined, but that every reading which is
opaque in this sense is also transparent. The contrast
between the two readings is not a matter of whether the
speaker _or_ the subject of the verb is responsible for the
description; the speaker is always responsible, and the
ambiguity is a matter of whehter or not he is _also_
ascribing responsibility to the subject of the opaque verb.

   To establish this will be a somewhat lengthy
business. Since it is a question of what sentences mean
on certain readings, it will require the examination of
examples. Since all the examples are ambiguous in other
ways, this will mean running through examples of each of
the various kinds, to make sure that my claim holds for
them all. The strategy will be the same in all cases,
however. If it assumed that the speaker and the subject

agree as to how the object in question may be described, there will be no way of telling who is supposed to be the source of the description. We must therefore consider the examples in relation to supposed situations in which the speaker and the subject disagree over what would be a correct description; we can then ask whose description may properly appear in a sentence reporting that situation.

Lakoff has observed (lectures, Illinois, Summer 1968), that in employing a noun phrase containing a demonstrative expression, the speaker is responsible for the description used. This can be illustrated by an example of Postal's.

(31)   Charley believes that this chicken soup is not
                              chicken soup.

We are concerned with the opaque reading of this sentence, the reading on which a contradictory belief is ascribed to Charley. (I have some doubts about such examples, since I have some doubts about what would count as grounds for holding that Charley believes something contradictory. I shall do my best to put these doubts aside, however, since examples with contradictory complement clauses make it very much easier to keep the difference between the opaque and transparent readings clear in one's mind.) Let us assume, as is most natural, that the speaker does not himself hold this contradictory view but believes that Charley has made a mistake. Now notice that what the speaker disagrees with must be Charley's opinion that the stuff in question is <u>not</u> chicken soup, not Charley's belief that it <u>is</u> chicken soup. To see this we have only to compare the two discourses:

(32) Charley believes that this chicken soup is not chicken soup. Silly old Charley. Of course it is chicken soup.

(33) !! Charley believes that this chicken soup is not chicken soup. Silly old Charley. Of course it isn't chicken soup.

I use the double shriek to indicate that a sentence or discourse, though not syntactically ill-formed, is one which no speaker in his rational moments would utter, that is, a sentence or discourse which commits the speaker to something which is quite patently logically inconsistent. I think it is clear that (33) deserves the double shriek and that (32) does not. A similar point can be made in respect of proper names, thus:

(34) Charley believes that Tom is not Tom. Silly old Charley. Of course he is Tom.

(35) !! Charley believes that Tom is not Tom. Silly old Charley. Of course he isn't Tom.

Before considering any further cases, I must introduce a word or caution. We are to contemplate situations in which Charley's views about something are in conflict with the speaker's, in order to decide whether, in such a situation, the speaker can take over a description from Charley and use it in reporting Charley's beliefs, hopes, etc., even if he, the speaker, believes the description to be incorrect. But when Charley's views are in conflict with our own, we may, for that very reason, be uncertain as to just what Charley does think, and what mistake it is that he is making. We may not know, for example, whether his mistake consists of thinking that something has a property which it does not in fact have, or whether it consists of thinking that something of a certain kind exists when in fact it does not. These two cases cannot even be clearly distinguished, for if, for example, Charley points to a red book and says something about 'that green book', then he is simultaneously indicating that he thinks that a certain book which is not green is green, and that he thinks there exists a green book in the place to which he is pointing even though there exists none. But we can certainly make a distinction in practice in many cases. If Charley points to a red book and calls it a green book, then, especially if the light is unusual, or if Charley is known to be colour-blind, it is reasonable to assume that he has mistaken the colour of the book. If he points into thin air and says something about 'that green book', then the most reasonable conclusion is that he is hallucinating a green book that is not there at all; to mistake thin air for a green book just is to hallucinate a green book. On the other hand, there may be a vast number of cases where Charley is not there, helpfully pointing at something or nothing. Then, unless we can question Charley further, and even if we can, his utterances and his other behavior may leave considerable room for doubt as to just what kind of mistake he is making, just where it is that we disagree with him. In these cases we may simply not know how to report Charley's beliefs for even what he said (see Davidson, 'On Saying That', Synthese 1968-69). Since we are concerned with what would count as a correct account of Charley's opinions, I shall try to avoid these cases of uncertainty in the discussion that follows, and consider only cases in which it is as clear as one could ever expect it to be, what Charley's views are, and exactly how they conflict with our own.

So far I have illustrated my claim about the nature of the opaque reading of descriptions with reference to proper names and demonstrative expressions. Demonstrative phrases might be considered suspect examples since they constitute a rather special case. For one thing, the demonstrative word itself is always interpreted transparently, in the sense that it is always interpreted relative to the speaker and not relative to anyone he is talking about

(except when it appears within a context of direct quotation).
In this respect it is like other 'token reflexive' expressions,
such as here, now, I, you, etc.. Whether because of this or
not, there also seems to be nothing like a referential/
attributive distinction for demonstrative noun phrases as
there is for other definite noun phrases; there seems to be
no difference between Charley's believing of that chicken
soup that such-and-such, and his believing that whatever is
that chicken soup is such-and-such. Furthermore, demonstrative noun phrases always apparently entail, or presuppose,
the existence of what they describe. Since by existence
we usually mean existence of things of a certain kind,
rather than just things in general with no properties at
all, that is, we mean existence under some description, it
might be thought that it is just this existence entailment
of demonstrative phrases that commits the speaker to the
descriptions they contain. We shall see shortly, however,
that this will not do as a general account of the commit-
ment.

I now turn to non-demonstrative definite noun phrases,
interpreted referentially. We can use another example of
Postal's:

(36)   Charley assumed that the book which was burned was

not burned.

Since we are to take the noun phrase referentially, we

must suppose that Charley had a particular book in mind and assumed of it that it was not burned. Since we are to take the sentence as opaque with respect to the descriptive content of the noun phrase, we must suppose that the speaker is attributing to Charley the description 'the book which was burned' as a description of that book. But now, just as for the demonstrative examples, for someone to say (36) is consistent only with his disagreeing with Charley over the assumption that the book was not burned. Thus:

(37) Charley assumed that the book which was burned was
not burned. Silly old Charley. Of course it was
burned.

The speaker cannot consistently disagree with Charley's view that the book was burned. Thus:

(38) !! Charley assumed that the book which was burned was
not burned. Silly old Charley. Of course it wasn't
burned.

There is, of course, nothing inconsistent about someone's thinking, like Charley, that the book was not burned. It is just that sentence (36) is not consistent with this belief. Someone who had that belief could perfectly well express it and Charley's views by means of a sentence with the complement of (36) reversed, thus:

(39) Charley assumed that the book which was not burned
was burned.

256

Whichever opinion as to the state of the book is expressed
by the content of the noun phrase is the one to which the
speaker is committed. He may be ascribing it to Charley,
but he is also, in using it in his report, endorsing it
himself. Notice that if the speaker has no opinion either
way about the book, then both (36) and (39) seem inappropriate, as witnessed by the inconsistency of both;

(40) !! Charley assumed that the book which was burned was
      not burned, but I don't know whether it was burned
      or not.

(41) !! Charley assumed that the book which was not burned
      was burned, but I don't know whether it was burned
      or not.

There seems, then, to be no possibility of taking over a
definite description from Charley, and using it referentially in a sentence, without thereby endorsing it oneself.

Indefinite noun phrases interpreted as specific have,
as we have seen, some affinities with definite noun phrases,
and they too cannot be used, even opaquely, without the
speaker being taken to assent to them. Thus:

(42) Charley thinks a certain book of mine belongs to him,
      but I can prove it is mine.

(43) !! Charley thinks that a certain book of mine belongs
      to him, and I can prove that it is his.

(44) !! Charley thinks that a certain book of mine belongs
      to him, but I don't know whose it is.

Plural specific indefinites, noun phrases with every, each, many, a few, etc., can also be substituted into frames such as these. If they are interpreted referentially, the same conclusions follow. I shall not go through these cases in detail.

One point remains to be made, however, before we can leave specific and referential noun phrases. We have observed (with some hesitation) in earlier chapters that, unlike demonstratives, specific and referential definite noun phrases are not inconsistent with the non-existence in the real world of the things that they describe. What is the status of the descriptive content of a noun phrase when what it 'describes' does not really exist? Since some people may boggle at the idea of either correct or incorrect descriptions of something that does not exist, I shall discuss this case in some detail.

If something does not exist, then we cannot go and look at it and see what properties it has to find out whether the way in which someone else would describe it is correct. We can know of its properties only by hearsay, on the report of the person who has imagined it or designed it or otherwise conceived of it, or else from a report based on his report. It may seem in this case that anything a person says about a non-existent object that he has in mind must be true of it, that his account of what it is that he is imagining must be regarded as authoritative. But

as a statement of the difference between the situation in
which the object described does exist and the situation in
which it does not, this is far too crude. For one thing,
many existent things are not available for inspection either,
and there may often be no way of checking on the properties
that someone ascribes to them. We very frequently rely on
other people's reports, even when the object concerned does
exist. We can, furthermore, often establish on the basis
of such reports that someone is in error about the supposed
properties of a thing, for his report may be internally
inconsistent, or it may conflict with things we are sure of,
such as that mice cannot fly. Questioning the person may,
though it also may not, establish the precise nature of
the error and allow us to determine what the real properties
of the object in question are. To some extent the same
applies to reports about non-existent things too. We may
be quite sure in some such cases that a person's description
of what he is imagining is incorrect and we may even be
sure about what would constitute a correct description.
However, since people can imagine or believe that there
are flying mice and even more extraordinary things than
that, the task of establishing that an error has been made
and what a correct description would be, is likely to be
much harder to succeed in in this case. Still, whether we
say that non-existent things have properties that can be

described correctly or incorrectly, or whether we say that one can give correct or incorrect descriptions of what would exist if what is imagined to exist did exist, it looks as if one of the main differences between the case of non-existent objects and existent ones is simply a matter of how easy it is to discover that a description is incorrect and what a correct description would be. And this has no bearing on the thesis that one cannot take over another person's description of something without thereby committing onself to its accuracy too. One's responsibility for the descriptions one uses could be just as great for non-existent things as for existent ones, even though harder to fulfill.

It might, however, be maintained that there is another, and more relevant, difference between the two cases, viz. that disagreements about merely imaginary objects must be terminological disagreements rather than factual disagreements. Suppose, for example, Charley tells me that he is off to catch an animal that he is convinced is eating the tulips and that he refers to this animal as a unicorn. In telling me about it, however, he gives me a perfect description of a griffin. I am not sure that it even makes any sense to suppose that a person can imagine a griffin and imagine that it is a unicorn in any sense other than thinking that griffins are called unicorns, but in any case it is this mistake that one would naturally suppose Charley to

have made -- apart, that is, from thinking that the animal
exists at all. But now if I describe Charley's plans in
the words of (45) rather than (46):

(45)   Charley wants to catch a certain griffin.

(46)   Charley wants to catch a certain unicorn.

this is not because I disagree with him about the particular
properties of his imaginary beast, but because I disagree
with him about whether 'unicorn' is the right word to use
of a beast with those properties. Charley still seems to
be the ultimate authority as to the nature of the beast
which he has imagined, even though I can correct him when
he calls it a unicorn. Whether or not my claim that factual
errors cannot be taken over by a speaker without his thereby being taken to endorse them is true, the speaker certainly does have a responsibility to correct terminological
errors that he detects, and I shall digress on this topic
briefly.

There is an important difference between verbs of
reported speech, such as <u>say</u>, <u>remark</u>, <u>announce,</u> etc., and
verbs which describe mental processes or states which are
not necessarily associated with any verbal behaviour, verbs
such as <u>believes</u>, <u>thinks</u>, <u>expects</u>, <u>hopes</u>, <u>wants</u>, <u>fears</u>, etc..
Suppose Charley utters the sentence:

(47)   Stephanie prevaricates so much that she is always late

for school.

I can certainly report:

(48)   Charley said that Stephanie prevaricates so much that
           she is always late for school.

but it would be very unfair and misleading of me to report:

(49)   Charley believes that Stephanie prevaricates so much
           that she is always late for school.

unless I honestly believe that Charley knows the difference
between the words 'prevaricate' and 'procrastinate', meant
to say 'prevaricate', and does believe that Stephanie tells
untruths and that this has some connection with her being
late for school. In the much more likely event that I
suspect Charley of having used the wrong word, that is, of
having used a word which does not, conventionally, mean
what he wished to express, then it would be more charitable
and less misleading of me to say:

(50)   Charley believes that Stephanie procrastinates so
           much that she is always late for school.

      The contrast between verbs of saying and verbs of
believing is seen very clearly in examples like:

(51)   Charley <u>says</u> that Stephanie prevaricates but he <u>means</u>
           that she procrastinates.

This kind of reformulation of Charley's propositional
attitudes does not involve a factual disagreement between
me and Charley. The situation we have imagined is one in
which both Charley and I are contemplating the proposition

that Stephanie dawles and not the proposition that she tells lies. The only disagreement between Charley and me is as to whether or not 'prevaricate' means to postpone doing something. It is a terminological disagreement. In reporting Charley's beliefs, hopes, etc., I clearly may, and in fact should, substitute my own terminology for Charley's when I believe his is incorrect, and this substitution is not restricted to noun phrases in a sentence but applies to every part of it. There will, of course, be cases in which I take Charley's remarks at their face value without it ever occurring to me to wonder whether he really said what he meant or meant what he said, and there will be other cases in which I suspect that he has misrepresented his views but I am not sure. But this does not affect the general principle that whenever I do realise that Charley has used an inappropriate word or expression to say what he meant to say, then I must change this to an appropriate word or expression when I report what he believes, hopes, etc., even though not when I report what he said.

While on the topic of the contrast between verbs of indirect speech and other verbs of propositional attitude, I should point out that for the former, the view held apparently by Postal, Lakoff and perhaps others, that on the opaque reading sentences with these verbs do not commit the speaker to the factual accuracy of the descriptions

he uses, does appear to have some truth in it. For verbs
of saying, that is, semantic representations like Postal's
do seem to do justice to the opaque as well as the transparent reading. There is one kind of use of verbs of saying
that quite obviously does not commit the speaker in any way
to the descriptions that appear in noun phrases in the
complement. This is when the complement consists of a direct quotation of Charley's words. In this case the speaker
should not correct even Charley's terminological errors,
yet alone his factual ones. On the other hand, one can put
Charley's remark into indirect speech, substituting third
person for first person, past tense for present tense, etc.,
wherever necessary. Already, in doing this, one is concentrating more on the content of what Charley said than on
the sounds that came out of his mouth. I go further in
this direction if I report what Charley said by using a
completely different but synonymous sentence, for example
if I report Charley's utterance of (52) in the words of (53).

(52) I am a bachelor.

(53) Charley said that he wasn't married.

There is yet another use of the verb say which takes me
even further from Charley's actual words, and is not even
necessarily connected with any particular act of saying
something on Charley's part. This is the repetitive sense
of the verb, as in 'Charley says that...' or 'Charley used

to say that...', the sense in which it means something like
'Charley tends to go around saying that...' or 'Charley once
said to someone, and if you ask him he will probably say
to you that...'. The correct use of say in this sense
perhaps does require that there was once an occasion on
which Charley uttered words expressing the proposition in
question, but apart from this, its meaning is very close
to that of thinks, believes, holds, etc.. After all, what
people say is one very important, if not infallible,
criterion for what they think, and so it is not surprising
that we often use say and think more or less interchangeably.
I suspect that closer observation of this end of the range
of uses of verbs like say would show them to be just like
other verbs of propositional attitude with respect to the
ambiguity of descriptive content. There is something clearly wrong, after all, in saying: .

(54) !! Charley said that this chicken soup was for me,

but actually it is cold tea.

Nevertheless at the other end of the scale, certainly for
direct quotation, these verbs do seem to require special
treatment in that they permit one to take over from Charley
all sorts of errors.

Now to pick up the threads of the discussion about
describing imaginary things which do not really exist, and
to return to the question whether only terminological

disagreement is possible in such a situation. First it should be observed that terminological disagreement is possible even over things that do exist. Thus if Charley points to a cat and calls it a rat, he may be making a factual error, but if he enumerates all its features and the features he enumerates are those characteristic of cats rather than of rats, then it is reasonable to suppose that his error is merely an error about the meaning of the word 'rat'. Secondly, even if terminological disagreement were the only possible kind of disagreement in the case of descriptions of non-existent objects, this would not contradict the claim that the speaker cannot take over factually incorrect descriptions from Charley without committing himself to them too, but would simply remove a certain set of examples from the domain of that claim. Thirdly, factual error _is_ possible in describing things that do not exist.

We observed in earlier chapters that to use a specific or referential noun phrase without any existential implications is most common and most acceptable either in talk about mythological or fictional creatures, or in talk involving the 'creative' verbs, i.e. in talk about situations in which it is being planned to create something, to bring it into existence even though it does not exist now. It is obvious that one can misdescribe Winnie the Pooh

266

or Santa Claus. It is also possible to misdescribe something whose existence is as yet only planned. Many of the properties of such a thing are determined before it is brought into existence, and even if it never is; it is just this which makes it possible to individuate such things and refer to them specifically even though they do not, and may never, actually exist. And, of course, Charley may be mistaken about these properties. Thus suppose a marble arch is to be built in memory of some eminent person, then it might be true that:

(55)   Charley thinks that the marble arch is to be made
                                    of granite.

or even perhaps that:

(56)   Charley thinks that the memorial arch is a bridge. Having finally hit upon a case where the descriptive phrase in question is being used of something that does not actually exist and is not being asserted to exist, and where it is nevertheless plausible to suppose that there is a factual, and not merely a terminological, disagreement, between the speaker and Charley, we must now see whether it would be consistent for the speaker to use such a sentence but to deny the correctness of the description that it contains. And it seems clear from the discourse:

(57)   !! Charley thinks that the marble arch is to be made
                of granite but in fact it is to be made of wood.

that this would not be consistent. These examples, then,
also conform to the principle that in taking over Charley's
description, the speaker commits himself to its accuracy
too.

The examination has so far covered all varieties of
noun phrases which are transparent with respect to specificity or referentiality, and they all conform to this principle.
This should really not be too surprising, since in these
cases the speaker is himself referring to something by means
of the noun phrase in question, just as he would be in using
a sentence that does not contain an opaque context. And
if one is to refer to something by means of a noun phrase
containing some descriptive content, then the description
had better be true of the thing one means to refer to.
It would in fact be surprising if this principle did not
hold for examples like:

(58)   Charley assumed that the book which was burned was

not burned.

where the phrase the book which was burned is interpreted
referentially, just at it does for examples like:

(59)   The book which was burned was mine.

where only a referential interpretation of the book which
was burned is possible. The story is not quite as simple
as this, for there certainly is a sense in which one can
quite properly take over someone else's description of

268

something, knowing it to be an incorrect description of the
object to which one means to refer. Donnellan's discussion
of this phenomenon is familiar to many linguists and I shall
therefore comment on it briefly with a view to showing that
it does not significantly affect the point at hand.

Donnellan illustrates the phenomenon as follows
(Reference and Definite Descriptions, pp. 290-1).
"Suppose the throne is occupied by a man I firmly believe
to be not the king but a usurper. Imagine also that his
followers as firmly believe that he is the king. Suppose
I wish to see this man. I might say to his minions 'Is
the king in his countinghouse?'. I succeed in referring
to the man I wish to refer to without myself believing
that he fits the description." The point is even stronger;
I succeed in referring to him even though I myself believe
him not to fit the description. The first point to be made
about this is that Donnellan's example is not an example of
an opaque context. The possibility of using an incorrect
description in referring to someone or something applies
to all referential noun phrases, and thus has no special
bearing on questions about opacity. Secondly the use of
an incorrect description in referring to something is only
acceptable in a limited kind of situation. It was in order
to communicate effectively with the usurper's minions, in
order to find out what he wanted to know, that Donnellan
employed the misdescription 'the king.', and the phenomenon

is in general characteristic of situations in which one is trying to get something across or to get something done. The misdescription is used for practical purposes, and not simply in order to state some truth about the world. Of course the assertion of a fact may often count as an instance of trying to do something, trying to get something across to someone else effectively, but this just brings us to a second constraint on the use of a misdescription for the purpose of referring. There is no point to it unless the person addressed believes the misdescription to be a correct description. In the case of noun phrases in opaque contexts, such as in sentence (58) above, we are concerned with whether or not Charley, the subject of the opaque verb, accepts the description employed. Since (48) is not the kind of sentence that characteristically would be addressed to Charley, the existence of the phenomenon that Donnellan describes would therefore not constitute adequate grounds for taking over from Charley the description the book which was burned if one believed that to be a misdescription of the object in question. Of course, a sentence like (58) might be addressed to a third person who, like Charley, apparently accepts the description the book which was burned, and in that case one would be justified in using (58) even if one believed that description to be an incorrect one. But this simply emphasises the fact that the phenomenon

has nothing to do with opaque contexts, and nothing to do
with ascribing a description to the subject of an opaque
verb. In particular, it does not save representations like
Postal's from the criticism that they imply, incorrectly,
that on the opaque reading only the beliefs of the subject
of the opaque verb are relevant to the appropriateness of
the description used. If one felt obliged to take account
of the phenomenon in formal semantic representations of
sentences, then not Postal's representations, but something
along the lines of:

(60)   You believe x is the king. Is x in x's countinghouse?
would be needed to do it justice. However, I suspect that
it is no more necessary or even desirable to set up such
representations to capture this way of using descriptive
phrases than it is to set up representations like:

(61)   I don't believe that p but p.
in order to capture the fact that any sentence that can be
used to assert something sincerely could also be used, in
other circumstances, to tell a lie.

I assume, therefore, that Donnellan's observations
can be set aside as having no bearing on the point with
which we are concerned here. The point has, however, only
been established so far with respect to referential and
specific noun phrases, and we must now consider attributive
and non-specific noun phrases. To imagine a case of

factual disagreement relevant to the descriptive content
of a non-specific noun phrase is not easy. This is in part
because such a noun phrase does not entail the existence of
anything falling under the description used, and these
examples are therefore subject to all the problems that we
observed earlier in connection with specific noun phrases
used non-existentially. But whereas in the latter case
the noun phrase is used to describe something in particular,
an individual, even if a non-existent one, in the case of
a non-specific noun phrase the subject need not even have
any particular object in mind at all. What, then, could
he possibly be said to be misdescribing? If Charley says
he wants to buy an astrakhan coat, he is not either describing or misdescribing any individual at all, real or
imaginary; he is stipulating some property that something
must never have if he is to be interested in buying it,
and how could he make a factual error in stipulating something? It is easy to see how he could make a terminological
error, but we already know that terminological errors have
to be corrected by the speaker.

For non-specific, and for attributive, noun phrases,
which are not used to refer to or describe any particular
individual, the question who is responsible for the correctness of the descriptive content of the noun phrase thus
appears to take on a different sense, to be a rather different

question from the one asked of noun phrases which do refer to individuals. Since there can be cases of non-specific wants, hopes, etc., which are based on factual errors, I shall discuss some examples and I hope to establish in the course of the discussion that in these cases it is acceptable for the speaker to take over from Charley a descriptive phrase which is based on Charley's error, but that the reason for this is not that the speaker has no responsibility for the correctness of the descriptions he uses, but rather that in such a case Charley's description of what he wants, hopes, etc., even if it is based on some error, must be regarded as a true description.

Suppose Charley mistakenly believes that astrakhan is sealskin, in the sense that he believes that the stuff, astrakhan, is what seals are covered in. And suppose that Charley, having reflected upon seals and how they keep warm in the arctic, decides that what he needs for the winter is a coat made out of the skin of seals. Now it seems proper to say:

(62) Charley wants to buy a sealskin coat.

But it also seems proper to say:

(63) Charley wants to buy an astrakhan coat.

since it is astrakhan that he has in mind whenever he thinks about seals. This should be contrasted with the situation in which Charley picks out a particular coat that he wants

273

to buy, thinking that it is a scalskin coat whereas in fact it is astrakhan. Here one could say:

(64) Charley wants to buy this astrakhan coat.

but not:

(65) Charley wants to buy this sealskin coat.

Sentences (62) and (63), on the other hand, are both true. (62) is true because what Charley really wants is to have a sealskin coat, and it can in fact be construed opaquely since a sealskin coat is also what Charley thinks he wants. (63) is also true, because for Charley, believing that sealskin is astrakhan, wanting to buy a sealskin coat just is wanting to buy an astrakhan coat; astrakhan is what he has in mind when he thinks about what he wants to buy. If Charley does not realise that the stuff that he thinks is sealskin is called astrakhan, then (63) will, however, be true only in its transparent interpretation. If there is any doubt about the fact that both (62) and (63) are true, one need only consider the criteria by which we characteristically determine what it is that someone wants, for these criteria pull apart in such situations; some of them provide justification for the truth of (62) and others for the truth of (63). Thus we can imagine Charley scanning advertisements for sealskin coats, seeking out shops reputed to carry sealskin coats, asking salesgirls if they have any sealskin coats in stock and so on, but also as picturing himself in an astrakhan coat, trying on astrakhan coats in shops, finding out what colours astrakhan comes in, and so on. Thus (63), unlike (65), contains not a description, based on a mistake, of what Charley wants to buy but a description of what Charley, due to a mistake, wants to buy.

The same is true of generic noun phrases. Suppose, for example, that Charley believes that Russian women are beautiful on the grounds that Brigitte Bardot, Jeanne Moreau and Francoise Hardy are beautiful, believing these women to be Russian. Though the source of his belief is a mistake it is nevertheless true that Charley believes that Russian women are beautiful if he is prepared to generalise from these three women to what he supposes to be their fellow-countrywomen. On the other hand, given his opinion of those three and his willingness to generalise about national types, we are also justified in saying that Charley believes that French women are beautiful. The latter claim must be taken transparently, the former may be taken opaquely, but both in their way are accurate statements of what Charley believes. To say that Charley believes that Russian women are beautiful, knowing that the belief is based on a mistake, is thus not to take over the mistake oneself, but to give an accurate statement of the con-sequences of Charley's mistake.

In examples of this kind, the speaker is not using

275

the noun phrase in question to describe any individual or
individuals at all, and to ask whether he may properly take
over the description from Charley is therefore not to the
point. If the speaker is describing anything, it is simply
Charley's belief or want or hope etc., and this is presumably something that he will try to get right; otherwise
his assertion that Charley believes it or hopes it etc.,
will just be false. If Charley is wrong about the meanings
of words and thus misstates his belief or hope, then the
speaker must correct this in his report. If Charley is
wrong about the facts of the case then this will actually
<u>affect</u> his beliefs, hopes, etc., but the speaker's task is
still just to describe these beliefs and hopes correctly.
There is still no question of his taking over from Charley
a false description of anything.

The idea that the speaker may be describing something,
referring to it under a certain description, and yet may
take over that description from Charley knowing it to be
incorrect, looks very much as if it derives from a confusion
of the two kinds of case, the referential case in which
the speaker <u>is</u> referring to something under a certain
description, and the attributive case in which what Charley
mistakenly believes <u>is</u> relevant to what he hopes, wants,
etc.. And this confusion in turn is due to the failure to
recognise that the ambiguity of descriptive content is

independent of specificity or referentiality, and thus
to see that it may take different forms depending on whether
a sentence is transparent or opaque in these other ways.

Section 6. Peculiarities of the scope of the description
operator.

The observations of the previous section mean that a
specific or referential noun phrase interpreted as opaque
with respect to its descriptive content has two functions
within the sentence. It is used to attribute acceptance of
that descriptive content to the subject of the opaque verb,
and it is also used to refer to something in the usual way.
A similar noun phrase interpreted as transparent with respect
to its descriptive content has only the latter function.
This suggests, and it appears to be true, that the opaque
reading of a sentence with respect to the descriptive
content of a noun phrase entails the transparent reading
of that sentence with respect to that noun phrase. It is
on the opaque reading that the sentence expresses the
stronger claim. This is exactly the reverse of the situation
for specificity and referentiality of noun phrases. We
saw in earlier chapters that for these ambiguities it is
the transparent reading, i.e. the specific or referential
reading, that expresses the stronger claim.

There is certainly a way of describing the difference
between the opaque and transparent readings of descriptive

content which makes it look as if the opaque is the weaker one. Opacity was, after all, originally defined in terms of the failure of an inference rule; the opaque reading does not permit inferences which are admissible on the transparent reading. But the reason for the failure of the substitutivity of identicals, unlike the failure of existential generalization, is, to put it roughly, that the opaque reading of a description says more than the transparent reading. The description has two functions in the sentence, and though any other true description would do as far as one function is concerned, this is not the case for the other.

I know of no special reason for supposing that an opaque reading should in general be weaker than the corresponding transparent reading, but this observation about the opacity of descriptions does have some rather strange consequences for the nature of the formal representations of meaning. The arguments given in Section 2 above to the effect that the phenomenon is a scope phenomenon are, I think, valid, but the idea that an operator like (Dx) can be used to indicate the scope of descriptions runs into some problems. By analogy with the representations of specificity and referentiality, we would represent the reading of (66) which is fully transparent

(66) Charley believes that Mary wants Jim's brother to win. with respect to the descriptive content of Jim's brother,

278

by means of a (Dx) operator at the far left of the representation, thus:

(67)   (Dx) Charley believes that Mary wants (Jim's brother)$_x$
to win.

But the sense that this representation is supposed to capture is that Jim's brother is such that Charley hopes of him, though not necessarily under the description 'Jim's brother', that Mary wants of him, though not necessarily under that description, that he will win. In other words, the descriptive content of the phrase Jim's brother is not part either of what Charley is said to believe, or of what Mary is believed by Charley to want. Thus the scope of the description should be shown not to extend over the Charley believes.. and Mary wants.. clauses. However if the (Dx) operator is regarded as anything like ordinary quantifiers, then by the usual conventions which define scope its scope does extend over these clauses.

Sentence (66) can also be read with the description opaque with respect to Charley's belief but transparent with respect to Mary's want. On this reading it means that Charley believes of Jim's brother, under the description 'Jim's brother' that Mary wants of him, though not necessarily under that description, that he should win. This reading, we might suppose, is to be represented as:

(68)   Charley believes that (Dx) Mary wants (Jim's brother)$_x$
to win.

279

But now, assuming that the scope of (Dx), as for quantifiers, extends to its right, this representation is also precisely the reverse of what it should be, for it suggests incorrectly that the description 'Jim's brother' is part of what Mary is believed by Charley to want, though not part of what Charley believes. The representation (68) would only be appropriate to the reading we are trying to capture if we could regard the (Dx) symbol as indicating the <u>end</u> of the scope of the description, that is, if we could regard the scope of the description as running backwards from the (Dx) symbol.

The third possible reading of (66) makes the same point. The sentence is to be read as saying that Charley believes of Jim's brother, under that description, that Mary wants of him, under that description, that he should win. This reading is thus fully opaque with respect to the description. Assuming that the opaque reading is to be represented with the scope operator <u>within</u> the scope of the opaque verbs, we shall have:

(69)   Charley believes that Mary wants (Dx) (Jim's brother)$_x$

to win.

But here again, by the usual conventions for scope, the scope of the description would be taken to be just the <u>Jim's brother win</u> clause, and not the higher clauses, whereas what we need is exactly the reverse. If the (Dx) operator

can be taken to mark the scope of the description at all,
its scope would have to be read leftwards over the representation rather than rightwards as is usual.

The (Dx) operator not only requires an odd convention
for specifying its scope, it also forces us to recognise the
possibility that an operator can have scope over a part of a
sentence which is not a constituent. This is not the case in
standard systems of logic. As a simple example, the formula:

(70) (p & (qvr)) $\supset$ s

contains the sub-formulae (constituents):

p, q, r, s, (q v r), (p & (q v r)), ((p & (q v r)) $\supset$ s).
Any one of these constituents could be negated, or placed
within the scope of a sentential operator such as the
necessity operator, or a quantifier. What is not possible
is to insert into the formula, for example, a negation sign
with scope over just the string of symbols p & (q for this
string is not a constituent. (Incidentally, the notion of
constituent negation does not conflict with this principle.
It departs from standard assumptions only in that, while
standardly only constituents which are 'sentential', in the
sense that they can stand alone as well-formed formulae,
may be placed within the scope of some logical operator, in
a system with constituent negation, predicates and terms
could also be negated. However, since predicates and terms
are constituents of formulae, this does not involve extending

scope over non-constituent strings of symbols.)

The (Dx) operator that we are considering, however, must be regarded as having scope over non-constituent strings of symbols if it is to be used in the way we have supposed in semantic representations. In (68) it is to have scope over <u>Charley believes</u> though not over <u>Mary wants</u>; in (69) it is to have scope over <u>Charley believes that Mary wants</u> but not over <u>Jim's brother wins</u>. But <u>Charley believes</u>, for example, is not a proper constituent of the sentence, in fact the smallest constituent of which both these words are part is the whole of the sentence and thus includes constituents over which we do not want the description to have scope.

These features of the (Dx) operator could presumably be incorporated into a formal grammatical system, even if not into anything resembling standard systems of logic. And there are other ways out if we do not wish to take this one. We might, for example, adopt an operator (NDx), with exactly the inverse of the meaning of (Dx), that is, something like 'but not necessarily under this description'. Then we could represent the possible readings of (66) as:

(71)   (NDx) Charley believes that Mary wants (Jim's brother)$_x$

to win.

(72)   Charley believes that (NDx) Mary wants (Jim's brother)$_x$

to win.

(73)   Charley believes that Mary wants (NDx) (Jim's brother)$_x$

to win.

282

Substitutivity of descriptions could then be set up to apply only within the scope of this operator. Notice, however, that it would be semantically quite odd, in this system, to identify the scope operator with a clause containing the descriptive content of the noun phrase, as Postal does.

I shall pursue this point in Section 9. Meanwhile I shall consider some further facts about the opacity of descriptive content which are relevant to semantic representations

Section 7. The substitutivity of non-nominal constituents.

The customary emphasis on the substitutivity of descriptions in opaque contexts tends to suggest that opacity affects only the noun phrases within an opaque context, and not the predicative constituents of a complement clause. It seems to be assumed that in reporting Charley's beliefs, hopes, wants, etc., I can if I wish substitute for a description of Charley's an alternative description on the basis of some identity known to me though not necessarily to Charley, but that I cannot make any such substitutions when it comes to predicative parts of the sentence. Thus if Charley wants to marry a certain chorus girl and thinks she is the most beautiful of them all, whereas to my mind she is quite the ugliest, I will report this as:

(74) Charley wants to marry the ugliest chorus girl.

not as:

(75) Charley wants to marry the most beautiful chorus girl.

But it would not be appropriate to substitute my opinion
for Charley's in the predicative part of the complement
clause. I cannot properly say:

(76) Charley thinks that the chorus girl he wants to marry
is the ugliest one.

but only:

(77) Charley thinks the chorus girl he wants to marry is
the most beautiful one.

The same point was made with respect to examples (36)
and (39) in Section 5 above.

This is not to say that in my reports I am bound to
the words that Charley himself would use. Even if I know
how he would express his belief or hope or want, then unless
I quote him directly, I shall almost certainly have to make
some changes in his words, such as interchanging I and you
and adjusting time and place expressions. Since Charley
may not have expressed his belief or hope in words at all,
or may have expressed it in some other language, it is
generally accepted that I can substitute for what I believe
Charley might himself have said, some synonymous expression.
Thus if Charley says 'Tom is a bachelor' it is reasonable
to report that Charley believes that Tom is unmarried. And
if Charley were to reject this as a report of his opinion,
for any reason other than simply not knowing what the words

mean, then this would not show that my report was faulty
but that there was something wrong with Charley.

It is arguable, however, that substitutions for non-
nominal constituents in opaque contexts are acceptable even
if they are based on factual identities and not simply
identities of meaning. Suppose, for example, that there is
a curfew in force, and that it takes effect at 6 p.m., though
Charley does not know what time it begins. And suppose that
Charley is afraid that his wife broke the curfew last night.
Then surely I can report:

(78)   Charley is afraid that his wife was out after 6 p.m.

last night.

This will only be true if it is interpreted transparently,
of course, for it is an account of what Charley fears that
he is in no position to provide himself and might even, in
his ignorance, positively disagree with. The importance
of (78) is that it is not the result of substituting one
noun phrase for another, but the result of substituting the
verb phrase was out after 6 p.m. last night for the verb
phrase broke the curfew last night. Other examples are not
hard to find. To have been convicted of a felony is to be
ineligible for the draft. Therefore if it is true that:

(79)   Charley proved that he had been convicted of a felony.

then it is also true that:

(80)   Charley proved that he was ineligible for the draft.

(even if Charley does not realise this, though it is only transparently true in that case). If Tom and I disagree utterly about something, so that to believe Tom is to disagree with me, then one can infer from:

(81) Charley expects that most people will believe Tom.

that:

(82) Charley expects that most people will disagree with me.

Such substitutions are very like substitutions in noun phrases which are not being used specifically or referentially. One is substituting not one description of an object for another, but one description of what Charley fears, or proved, or expects, for another description. The examples given so far have involved situations in which Charley is simply ignorant of some fact known to the speaker, but just as for non-referential noun phrases, substitutions are possible even where Charley and the speaker flatly disagree about some fact, and in these cases, just as for non-referential noun phrases, both accounts of what Charley believes, fears, etc., seem to be justified. Thus if Charley thinks the curfew takes effect at 7 p.m. rather than 6 p.m., and if he is afraid that his wife broke the curfew, then all three of the following are correct reports:

(83) Charley is afraid that his wife broke the curfew.

(84) Charley is afraid that his wife was out after 7 p.m.

(85) Charley is afraid that his wife was out after 6 p.m.

The reason why (76) is not a correct report of Charley's

opinion is not just that Charley and the speaker disagree about the chorus girl, but because there is no identity statement to the effect that to be the most beautiful chorus girl is to be the ugliest chorus girl, on which the substitution could be based. But because to break the curfew is to be out after 6 p.m., to have been convicted of a felony is to be ineligible for the draft, to believe Tom is to disagree with me, there can be substitutions based on these identities.

The impression that substitutions, other than merely terminological ones, can be made only for noun phrases in opaque contexts is, I think, due once again to the failure to distinguish the ambiguities of specificity and referentiality of noun phrases from the ambiguity of descriptive content. The former ambiguities do affect only noun phrases; an adjective cannot be non-specific, a verb phrase can only be non-specific insofar as it contains a noun phrase which is non-specific, and it does not make sense to talk of a referential verb phrase, for example. Because opacity of these kinds shows up only in noun phrases, it is easy to suppose that opacity with respect to the lexical content of constituents applies only to noun phrases too. But it seems that this is not the case, and that 'opacity of descriptions' is in fact a much more general phenomenon. It is worth observing that many examples of opacity in noun phrases actually affect only part of the phrase, thus:

(86) Charley thinks that this green book is a red book.

(87) Charley thinks that this green book is a green envelope.

(88) Charley thinks that the book which was burned was not

burned.

On the assumption that substitution involves substituting one noun phrase for another, the transparency of some part of a noun phrase has to be described in terms of the transparency of the whole phrase. If we recognise that any kind of constituent may be interpreted transparently and may be substituted for on the basis of a factual identity, then we can describe this situation in a much more natural and intuitive way, and simply say that it is an adjective, or a relative clause, etc., that is being substituted for.

There may, in some cases, be independent motivation for an analysis of a sentence on which the transparent constituent, though not superficially a noun phrase, is one in deep structure. For example, the sentence:

(89) Mary thinks that John is cleverer than he is.

appears to involve the transparency of a measure adverb modifying clever. But it has often been claimed that comparatives should be analysed in terms of a phrase like 'the degree to which...', and if this is correct then the transparent constituent can, after all, be regarded as a noun phrase. In many cases, however, this manoeuvre of analysing a sentence so that a noun phrase can be regarded as transparent would be motivated solely by the desire to preserve the principle that only noun phrases are substitutable, for it would lead to otherwise unnecessary complications in the syntactic component. Thus sentence (86), for example, might be rendered as:

(90) Charley thinks that this book which is of the colour
                     green is a book of the colour red.

with the adjectives expressed by noun phrases. In formal logic, such a move would constitute a move from a first order logical system to a second order (i.e. a much more powerful) system. It may turn out to be necessary to make this move, but it does not appear to be required by the facts under consideration, as long as we permit non-nominal constituents in opaque contexts to be represented as transparent.

Even if, in principle, any constituent in an opaque context may be interpreted as transparent, some may in practice be excluded because of the absence of any appropriate identity statement that could serve as the basis for the speaker's substituting his own words for those of the person whose belief, want, etc., he is reporting. For example, though a noun phrase governed by a preposition may be substituted for, and a prepositional phrase as a whole may be substituted for, on the basis of an identity such as:

(91) behind the aspidistra is next to the whatnot.

it is hard to imagine an identity statement that would serve as the basis for substituting one preposition for another. This will limit the number of possibilities to be captured formally to some extent, though not perhaps very much.

It is also obvious that if a certain constituent is interpreted as transparent with respect to its descriptive content, then all constituents in which it is included must also be regarded as transparent. For example, if we interpret the sentence:

(92) John thinks Smith's murderer is insane.

as transparent with respect to the description 'Smith', i.e. as not implying that John accepts this as a description of Smith (or anyone), then clearly the sentence must also be interpreted as transparent with respect to the description 'Smith's murderer', i.e. as not implying that John accepts this description either. Transparency of descriptive content is thus inherited from internal constituents to the constituents that contain them. It is interesting to contrast this with the case for specificity and referentiality, which can be indicated schematically in the following way:

(92) a ($\left\{ \begin{array}{l} \text{specific} \\ \text{non-specific} \end{array} \right\}$) friend of a (specific) actor

a ($\left\{ \begin{array}{l} \text{*specific} \\ \text{non-specific} \end{array} \right\}$) friend of a (non-specific) actor

the ($\left\{ \begin{array}{l} \text{referential} \\ \text{attributive} \end{array} \right\}$) best friend of a (specific) actor

the ($\left\{ \begin{array}{l} \text{*referential} \\ \text{attributive} \end{array} \right\}$) best friend of a (non-specific) actor

the ($\left\{ \begin{array}{l} \text{referential} \\ \text{attributive} \end{array} \right\}$) best friend of the (referential) bridegroom the $\left(\begin{Bmatrix}*\text{referential} \\ \text{attributive}\end{Bmatrix}\right)$ best friend of the (attributive) bridegroom

a $\left(\begin{Bmatrix}\text{specific} \\ \text{non-specific}\end{Bmatrix}\right)$ friend of the (referential) bridegroom

a $\left(\begin{Bmatrix}*\text{specific} \\ \text{non-specific}\end{Bmatrix}\right)$ friend of the (attributive) bridegroom

There is certainly more to be said than is contained in this informal chart (particularly in connection with phrases like the colour of a lemon, the insanity of Smith's murderer, etc.), but what the above examples illustrate is that for specificity and referentiality of noun phrases, it is opacity rather than transparency which is inherited by a constituent from the constituents that it contains. This contrast between specificity and referentiality on the one hand, and the opacity of descriptive content on the other, is related to the observations of Section 6 above about the logical relationships between the opaque and transparent readings.

Section 8.   Descriptive content and surface structure.

Chomsky has suggested, informally, that the opaque reading of a sentence should be represented by means of a pair consisting of a semantic representation of the usual kind, and a representation of the surface structure of the material within the opaque context.   The former will indicate what the sentence says is believed (hoped, wanted, etc.,) and by whom; the latter will provide the description under which it is believed (hoped, wanted, etc.).   For the transparent reading, since the actual descriptions employed are irrelevant to its truth value except in the usual way, a representation of surface structure will not be included as a part of the formal semantic representation.

This proposal, unlike Postal's, does not run into problems connected with reconciling the representation of specificity and referentiality of noun phrases with the representation of the opacity of descriptive content. The interpretation of the descriptive content of a phrase is not represented by variations in the position of that phrase in the semantic representation. The phrase can be left in its normal position, and the presence or absence of a surface structure representation will determine how it is to be read. Notice, incidentally, that specificity and referentiality cannot be treated in this fashion; a surface structure representation of the clause within an opaque context will not distinguish a specific reading from a non-specific one, or a referential reading from an attributive one.

However, this analysis in terms of surface structure is in fact appropriate only for a certain rather small subset of opaque constructions, for in the majority of cases surface structure is not relevant to the truth value of the sentence. It is relevant in the case of verbs that introduce direct quotations, and perhaps also (if some allowance is made for pronouns, demonstratives, and other 'token-reflexive' items) for verbs that introduce indirect speech (see Section 5). Conceivably it is also relevant in the case of a number of other verbs such as is aware or realises. For most verbs, however, though the truth value of the opaque reading of the sentence does depend on the descriptions employed, it is not sensitive to variations merely in surface structure -- it does not depend on the actual words that are employed. A sentence such as:

(93) John believes Smith's murderer is insane.

may after all be true, and true on an opaque reading, even if John has never uttered any sentence resembling the complement clause. People do often express their beliefs or their wants, hopes, etc., in words, but they also often do not, and we can know that someone has a certain belief, want, hope, etc., without knowing anything at all about what he has said. The strongest possible claim about the relationship between a sentence such as (93) and the surface structure of its complement clause is therefore that those words are the words that John would use if he were to express his belief in words. But even this conditional statement is too strong because of the fact that we can know and report someone's beliefs, wants, etc., and report them opaquely, even if that person only speaks languages other than the one in which we are doing the reporting. We can report John's belief by means of (93) even if John speaks only French and

Swahili. And, furthermore, we can report opaquely the beliefs and wants of people and animals that speak no language at all. The most we could claim, therefore, is that the words that appear in the opaque context are the words that the subject would use to report his own belief, want, etc., if he were able to report it in English. But it is clear that by now we are no longer talking of a relationship between the truth of a sentence and a particular form of words, a particular surface structure. We can pin down the way in which John's belief is expressed only within the bounds of a set of synonymous sentences.

It is widely accepted that the substitution, within an opaque context, of one expression for another with which it is synonymous does not affect the truth value of the sentence even on an opaque reading. The kind of substitution that differentiates opaque and transparent readings is the substitution of one expression for another that, as a matter of fact, is co-extensive with it, not the substitution of synonymous expressions. This observation leads to the same conclusion as in the previous paragraph. Surface structures are too particular a specification of the description under which someone believes, hopes, wants, etc., something. On the assumption that all and only expressions which are synonymous are assigned the same semantic representation, it is in fact the semantic representation of the material within the opaque context, not a representation of its surface structure, which is needed to indicate the description under which something is said to be believed, wanted, etc..

Now, however, the suggestion that the representation of the opaque reading consists of a semantic representation of the usual kind plus a representation of the descriptions which appear within the opaque context, turns out to be simply the suggestion that the representation is a semantic representation of the usual kind. There will therefore be nothing to distinguish the representation of an opaque reading of a sentence from a representation of a transparent reading. The distinction that was proposed, and that we have rejected, was a distinction between John's believing that a certain form of words expresses a true proposition, and John's simply believing that the proposition is true. The distinction that we actually need is a distinction between John's believing that a certain proposition corresponds to some state of affairs in the world and John's believing simply that that state of affairs does obtain. For example, if John believes (opaquely) that Smith's murderer is insane but does not know that Smith's murderer is Jones, then we cannot conclude that John believes the proposition that Jones is insane. But if Smith's murderer _is_ Jones, then the proposition that Jones is insane and the proposition that Smith's murderer is insane do in fact correspond to the same state of affairs, and from

the fact that John believes that the state of affairs corresponding to the proposition that Smith's murderer is insane
does obtain it follows that he believes that the state of affairs
corresponding to the proposition that Jones is insane does
obtain. The whole distinction has thus been shifted along the
scale. What we have now is not the contrast between the pair:

(94) John believes the proposition p in the words 'p'. (OPAQUE)

John believes the proposition p. (TRANSPARENT)

but, if I may be forgiven some imprecision in expressing it,
the contrast between the pair:

(95) John believes the state of affairs p in the proposition

p. (OPAQUE)

John believes the state of affairs p. (TRANSPARENT)

I shall not even attempt to formulate (95) more
precisely than this since, because of a number of observations
made in earlier sections of this chapter, it is not suitable as
even the basis for an adequate representational system. It is
important to bear in mind, however, that whatever representational system we do employ must not portray the difference
between opaque and transparent readings in terms of anything
as particular as surface structures. What is common between
the two readings is what I have loosely called the state of
affairs that is believed (wanted, hoped, etc.) to obtain.
What differentiates them is whether or not the subject of the
opaque verb is supposed to accept as an account of this state
of affairs some sentence which means the same as the
sentence which appears within the opaque context.

Section 9. Implications for semantic representation.

A number of observations have been made in this chapter which must be regarded as constraints on a formal system for the semantic representation of the opacity of descriptive content. The difference between the alternative readings of an ambiguous sentence is a difference in scope relationships (Section 2). Whatever operator is used to indicate these scope relationships must be independent of the operators used to represent specificity and referentiality of noun phrases (Section 3). Either the scope of this operator must be regarded as running in a backward direction, or else a semantic interpretation must be found for this operator which is designed to avoid this (Section 6). It is not only noun phrases but also other types of constituent within the opaque context that may be interpreted transparently (Section 7).

What is needed, therefore, is some formal device that can appear in any one of the clauses of the representation to indicate scope. It must be applicable to verb phrases, adjectives, etc., as well as to noun phrases. It must be interpreted to mean not something like 'under the description..' but something like 'not necessarily under the description..'. The representation of the ambiguous phrase itself should not be used positionally in the role of scope operator because of interactions with the specificity and referentiality operators. One formal system which fulfills these conditions can be illustrated by the following representations for the sentence: <u>Mary hopes that John believes that my brother is ineligible for the draft.</u>

(96)   Mary hopes that John believes that my brother is
                    ineligible for the draft.

(97)   Mary hopes (ND John believes that my brother is
        ineligible for the draft) that John believes that my
                    brother is ineligible for the draft.

(98)   Mary hopes that John believes (ND my brother is
        ineligible for the draft) that my brother is
                    ineligible for the draft.

(99)   Mary hopes (ND John, my brother) that John believes
        (ND ineligible for the draft) that my brother is
                    ineligible for the draft.

(100) Mary hopes (ND John) that John believes (ND my brother)
                    that my brother is ineligible for the draft.

This is just a selection from the set of possible readings that could be represented. Of these, (96) represents the fully opaque reading, and (97), since the (ND...) operator has scope over the embedded clause too, represents the fully transparent reading. In (98) the clause 'my brother is ineligible for the draft' is represented as opaque with respect to Mary's hope but transparent with respect to John's ·belief. In (99) the phrases 'John' and 'my brother' are represented as transparent with respect to Mary's want, the phrase 'my brother' is therefore also to be taken as transparent

298

with respect to John's belief, and in addition the phrase 'ineligible for the draft' is represented as transparent with respect to John's belief. In (100), the phrase 'John' is transparent with respect to Mary's hope, and the phrase 'my brother' is transparent with respect to John's belief.

The repitition, inside the (ND...) operator, of material that also appears elsewhere in the representation makes these representations look extremely redundant. The repeated material is, however, merely serving in the role of an indexing system; instead of duplicating the lexical material we could instead have used a set of subscripts on phrases to indicate which operator, if any, governs them. The two systems would be formally equivalent. Neither, obviously, is particularly elegant or simple, but this seems to be unavoidable. As long as we take seriously the idea that any constituent within an opaque context may be interpreted as transparent independently of the others, then we shall need a representational system that allows for a rather large number of distinct readings for all but the simplest of sentences. A proposal such as Chomsky's, discussed in the previous section, ascribes far fewer readings to sentences, for it treats clauses within opaque contexts as a whole as either opaque or transparent, and does not make distinctions among the internal constituents of these clauses. A very much less complex indexing system is obviously sufficient on such a theory.

The difference between these approaches is very like the difference between theories which recognise constituent negation, and those which permit only sentence negation. The decision between these types of theory also turns on intuitions as to when a sentence is ambiguous and when it is simply non-committal, i.e. when it has a number of distinct readings and when it has a single reading which is compatible with a number of distinguishable states of affairs. For negation there do exist some clear examples (e.g. sentences containing quantifiers) which have two or more distinct negations. For opaque constructions, however, it is less easy to find any hard facts to back up the claim that, for example, sentence (96) has the distinct readings represented above (and others too), and not simply the three readings that an analysis such as Chomsky's would assign to it. This claim therefore rests solely on the intuition that such a sentence is in fact many ways ambiguous, but this intuition might be questioned and I admit to being unable to shake off a lingering doubt about it myself.

Section 10. The meaning of 'under the description...'.

I have so far given more attention to the problem of providing distinct representations for the various readings of a phrase which is ambiguous with respect to descriptive content, than I have to the question of what precisely is

involved in each of these various readings. Finding natural
informal paraphrases of the readings is not easy. I have
expressed the opaque reading by saying that it entails that
the subject of the opaque verb 'accepts' the description expressed by the phrase in question, or alternatively that
the subject wants or hopes or thinks something 'under the
description' which the phrase expresses. But these explica-
tions explain nothing unless we can state what is meant by
them in their turn.

I shall take it for granted that, as argued in Section 8,
to ascribe acceptance of a description to someone is not to
ascribe to him the use, or even the potential use, of a
particular form of words. Setting this aside, there are still
at least two ways in which we might construe the claim that
the opaque reading of a sentence such as:

(101) John wants to buy a coat like Bill's.

entails that John 'accepts' the description 'a coat like Bill's',
or wants to buy something 'under the description "a coat like
Bill's"'. We might be claiming that John believes (or knows
or realises or is aware) that what he wants to buy is a coat
like Bill's. Alternatively we might be claiming that John
wants to buy such a coat inasmuch as it is a coat like Bill's.
Since this could hardly be the case unless John believed
(at least in some weak sense of 'believe') that such a coat
is a coat like Bill's, this second version of the claim is a
stronger one than the first. It is very like, though perhaps

not quite as strong as, the claim that John wants to buy something _because_ it is a coat like Bill's.

The difference between the two accounts becomes clear if we consider a situation in which they pull apart. Thus suppose John wants to buy a coat, knowing that it is like Bill's coat, but insofar as its being like Bill's coat affects him at all, he would prefer it not to be. He might, for example, be quite put out that Bill has caught on to the latest fashion before he himself has done so. Now is this situation compatible with the truth of the opaque reading of sentence (101) with respect to the descriptive content of the phrase _a coat like Bill's_, or is it compatible only with the truth of the transparent reading of that sentence? Should we, that is to say, take the opaque reading to require John's wanting to buy something inasmuch as it is a coat like Bill's, or should we take it to require only that John wants to buy something knowing it to be a coat like Bill's?

From the literature on opacity, it is not at all easy to determine what the answer to this kind of question is commonly supposed to be. Much has been written on the topic of 'wanting something under a certain description', and it appears that someone's merely knowing that a description is true of something that he wants is not generally regarded as counting as his wanting it under that description. For example,

302

the fact that I want to spend next week in Paris, knowing
that this would mean missing three lectures, is not usually
held to be sufficient grounds for the claim that I want to
miss three lectures.

On the other hand, Linsky, in discussing the familiar
example:

(102)   Oedipus wanted to marry his mother.

says ('Referring', pp. 74-5): "Understood transparently,
'Oedipus wanted to marry his mother' means something like,
'Oedipus wanted to marry a person who, in fact, was his
mother'. This last would naturally be understood not to
imply that Oedipus knew that the woman he wanted to marry
was, in fact, his mother. Understood opaquely, 'Oedipus
wanted to marry his mother' means something like 'Oedipus
desired to make true the proposition that the mother of
Oedipus is the wife of Oedipus'. This last paraphrase is
correct only if it would naturally be understood in such a
way that it would not be true unless Oedipus did know that
the woman he wanted to marry was his mother." The trouble
is that Linsky's paraphrase 'Oedipus desired to make true
the proposition that the mother of Oedipus is the wife of
Oedipus' does not distinguish between Oedipus wanting to
marry Jocasta despite the fact that she was his mother and
his wanting to marry her inasmuch as she was his mother.
Linsky's stress on the question whether Oedipus knew that the
woman he wanted to marry was his mother suggests that he
regards the opaque reading as consistent with Oedipus's wanting

to marry her despite her being his mother as well as with his wanting to marry her inasmuch as she was his mother, as long as, in both cases, we assume that he knew that she was his mother.

It is possible that the reason for this diversity, or even confusion, of opinion about what is involved in wanting something under a certain description is that philosophers have concentrated mostly on examples with verbs like know and believe rather than want, hope, fear, and so on. For know and believe and similar verbs, the difference between the two accounts more or less vanishes. If I know that Cicero denounced Catiline, knowing him to be Cicero, then surely I know that Cicero, under the description 'Cicero', denounced Catiline. There does not even seem to be any sense to the further condition that I should know that Cicero, inasmuch as he was Cicero, denounced Catiline. For examples with necessary and possible, which have also been studied in detail, it is by contrast only the 'inasmuch as' paraphrase that makes sense. Thus it is necessarily true that my mother, inasmuch as she is my mother, is related to me; it is not necessarily true that inasmuch as she is the chairman of the drama committee she is related to me. In these examples, of course, the verb has no subject and so there is no-one to whom knowledge of the description could be ascribed.

Sentences with verbs like want, hope, fear, and so on, seem to be under tension from the opposite pull of these two

304

kinds of paradigm. My intuition is that they can be, and are, taken in both ways. In fact there is an interesting correlation between the referential/attributive ambiguity and the way in which the opaque reading with respect to descriptive content is construed. The fact that these two different kinds of opacity are often confused probably also helps to explain the uncertainty about what is involved on the opaque reading of a description. Thus Linsky distinguishes only 'two readings of the sentence (102), and although his paraphrases do not make entirely clear what these two readings are supposed to consist of, it appears that the first is both referential and transparent with respect to descriptive content, and the second is both attributive and opaque with respect to descriptive content. If, however, we distinguish the two kinds of ambiguity, and thus recognise four readings of sentence (102), then an interesting point emerges.

On the attributive reading, no particular individual is referred to by the phrase his mother; rather, this phrase functions more as a criterion or condition than as a description. What Oedipus wants is that he should marry whatever person satisfies this condition. Thus for the attributive reading, the 'inasmuch as' account of wanting under a description, though not actually forced on us, will in fact be much more natural than the 'knowing who' account. For the referential interpretation of the phrase his mother, on the other hand, the sentence will be true only if there is some person

of whom Oedipus wants it to be the case that he should marry
her. In Chapter III we found it extremely difficult to state
the truth conditions on this kind of statement, but it was
clear that merely knowing one description which was true
of his mother would not count as sufficient for Oedipus'
wanting, in the referential sense, to marry his mother.
On the referential reading, therefore, we can assume that
Oedipus knows more than one description that is true of his
mother, and then it is an interesting question whether or not
he knows that the description 'Oedipus' mother' is true of
her. Thus the referential reading tends to favour (though,
once again, it does not force on us) the 'knowing who' account
of wanting under a description, at the expense of the 'inasmuch
as' account.

In addition to depending on the kind of opaque verb
in the sentence, therefore, the way in which the opaque reading of a description is construed also seems to depend upon
whether the phrase is interpreted as referential or attributive.
If I am right that in many cases it may be construed in either
of the ways I have described, then this doubles the number
of readings that must be recognised for the already many
ways ambiguous examples that have been discussed, and thus
puts an additional burden on a system of semantic representation.

306

Section 11. <u>Some further logical relationships between noun</u>

<u>phrases.</u>

In Chapter II it was argued that the specific
reading of a sentence with an indefinite noun phrase in
an opaque context does not, for many opaque verbs, entail
the non-specific reading. An analogous question can be asked
about the relationship between the referential and
attributive readings of definite noun phrases. I did not
discuss this question in Chapter III because the answer
to it involves matters concerning the opacity of descriptions.

The referential reading of a definite noun phrase,
as I have characterised it, is 'stronger' than the attributive
reading since it requires that the subject should know who
the definite noun phrase refers to. To determine whether
the referential reading actually entails the attributive
one, we must control for the effects of the ambiguity
of the descriptive content of the phrase. But this is in
fact extremely difficult to do. If we suppose the phrase
is opaque with respect to its descriptive content, then
we come up against the problems raised in Section 10,
viz. the uncertainty as to what is involved in the opaque
reading of a description, and the correlation between
what is usually taken to be involved and the referential/
attributive contrast. The referential reading of:

(103) John wants to meet the Lord Mayor.

may be true when the description 'the Lord Mayor' is taken

opaquely, in the sense that there is some person whom John knows to be the Lord Mayor whom he wants to meet. But the attributive reading which is opaque for descriptive content is only naturally taken in the 'inasmuch as' sense, i.e. John wants to meet whoever is the Lord Mayor because there is something about Lord Mayors that interests him. And read this way, the attributive reading of (103) certainly does not follow from the referential reading outlined above. It may, perhaps, be entailed by the referential reading if this too is taken in the 'inasmuch as' sense, but my own intuitions and those of many other English speakers become just too shaky here to be certain.

Since this variation in the construal of the opaque reading of a description is not found for epistemic verbs, we may consider instead an example such as:

(104)   John knows that the Lord Mayor has gout.

In this case the attributive reading does seem to follow from the referential one (at least, given a theory of immediate reference). It should be remembered, however, that epistemic verbs differ in a number of ways from non-epistemic opaque verbs (for example, the specific reading of an indefinite noun phrase entails the non-specific; the attributive reading of a definite noun phrase does not entail the specific reading of a related indefinite phrase). Thus this observation about the referential and attributive readings of (104) may not be generalizable.

If we try to determine the relationship between referential and attributive phrases when they are both read as transparent with respect to their descriptive content, we come up against the point made in Section 3, viz. that it is not clear that an attributive noun phrase does have a reading which is transparent with respect to descriptive content. In the light of the discussion of Section 5, some further, though tentative, comments can be made on this point. For indefinite noun phrases, the non-specific reading may be transparent with respect to descriptive content because, although no <u>particular</u> referent for the noun phrase is supposed, the speaker, knowing what <u>kind</u> of thing John wants to catch, hopes to buy, etc., can provide an alternative description of this <u>kind</u> of thing. If we try to extend this account to attributive definite noun phrases, the only sense that can be made of it is that the speaker may provide an alternative description which will always pick out the same person as John's own description, <u>regardless of which particular person fits either description</u>. The kind of contingent identity statement that would mediate a substitution for attributive noun phrases is thus not one that is tied to a particular individual but one which is true in general, for example:

(105)   The Commander in Chief of the Armed Forces is the
President.

(106) The man I shall marry will be the first man who asks
me.

There are obviously fewer contingent identity statements
of this kind than of the usual kind.

And the condition may be even stronger than this.
Since the function of an attributive noun phrase is
apparently to provide a criterion rather than a description
in the usual sense, it may be that attributive phrases
are subject to substitution only on the basis of an
identity between the properties expressed by the two
phrases in question. Thus instead of (105), we might
require:

(107) To be the Commander in Chief of the Armed Forces is
to be the President.

which, though true in a sense, is not true in the stronger
sense in which (108) is true:

(108) To be out after 6 p.m. is to break the curfew.

given that there is a curfew that takes effect at 6 p.m..
But if this is what is involved in the transparency of
descriptive content of an attributive definite noun phrase,
then the phrase the man who broke the curfew in the sentence:

(109) John wants to meet the man who broke the curfew.

is still functioning as a criterion rather than as a
straightforward description, even if it is taken as
transparent (i.e. as one that John would not necessarily
be able to provide himself). And so once again the 'inasmuch

as' implication of the attributive reading tends to obscure the nature of the connection between referential and attributive noun phrases.

All of these comments a 'e very tentative and imprecise, but in view of the uncertainty of intuitions in this area, any hard and fast conclusions are more or less bound to be incorrect. I shall therefore leave this question and turn to another point about the relationship between referential and attributive noun phrases. This is that the inference from an attributive reading of a definite noun phrase to its referential reading can be mediated by an identity statement; therefore the referential/attributive distinction appears to be very like the opacity of descriptive content (which concerns the substitutivity of identicals). Since I have taken pains to keep these two kinds of opacity distinct, some comment is in order.

If, as I have maintained, the referential reading of a definite noun phrase requires that the subject knows who (what) the referent of the noun phrase is, then the referential reading of a sentence should follow from the attributive reading together with the premise that the subject knows to whom the attributive phrase applies. For example the referential reading of:

(110) John wants to meet the Lord Mayor.

should follow from the attributive reading together with:

(111) John knows who the Lord Mayor is/who is the Lord
Mayor.

But (111) is true if John knows the truth of an identity statement concerning the Lord Mayor. It is therefore important to observe that the descriptions involved may be held constant in this identity statement, so that this is not a case of substituting a phrase expressing one description for a phrase expressing another which happens to be co-extensive with it. A sufficient condition for the truth of (111) is the truth of:

(112) John knows that the Lord Mayor is the Lord Mayor.

This distinguishes the relationship between referential and attributive readings from the opacity of the descriptive content of noun phrases. But another point now arises. Sentence (112) seems to express an almost trivial claim. Since (112) mediates the inference of the referential reading of (110) from the attributive reading, this inference will be just as trivial as the truth conditions on (112). It is true that sentence (112) can be taken in a way which makes it almost trivial. If both of the noun phrases in (112) are taken as attributive, then the sentence will be true just as long as John knows that there is a Lord Mayor --- since John surely does not doubt that everyone is identical with himself, then as long as he knows that someone is the Lord Mayor, he could hardly doubt that whoever that

person is, he is identical with himself, i.e. with the
Lord Mayor. Similarly, if both of the noun phrases in (112)
are taken as referential, then as long as John is acquainted
with the person who is, in fact, the Lord Mayor, i.e. is
in a position to know anything of the Lord Mayor in the
referential sense, then he could hardly fail to know that
that person is identical with himself. These two readings
of (112) can be rendered roughly as respectively:

(113)   John knows that it is true that whoever is the Lord

Mayor is identical with whoever is the Lord Mayor.

(114)   The Lord Mayor and the Lord Mayor are such that John

knows that they are identical.

However, it was pointed out in Section 6 that if the noun
phrases in a sentence such as (112) are both interpreted
referentially or are both interpreted attributively, then
the sentence does <u>not</u> constitute grounds for the <u>John</u>
<u>knows who...</u> statement (111). If the truth of (112) is
to mediate the inference from the attributive reading of (110)
to the referential reading, then one of the noun phrases
in (112) must be taken referentially and the other
attributively. And then (112) is no longer trivial. (Hintikka
makes much the same point as this in <u>Knowledge and Belief</u>,
Chapter Six, in his discussion of Quine's views on opacity.)

313

CHAPTER V. THE SYNTAX OF OPAQUE CONSTRUCTIONS.

Section 1. Introduction.

In the previous chapters I have attempted to establish the nature of the semantic representations that must be assigned to sentences containing complement clauses. The semantic relationships between the constituents of such sentences are not congruent with the syntactic relationships between them. Therefore the semantic representations must either contain representations of the same constituents as in surface structure but in a different configuration, or else they must contain operators of some kind that 'bind' these constituents and mark their semantic relationships (scope) with respect to other constituents. For a complete account of opaque constructions, we must specify the rules of the grammar that correlate surface structures with semantic structures of this kind.

The general properties of this body of rules is a subject of some disagreement at present. There are differences of opinion as to the answers to such questions as whether the semantic component should be interpretive or generative, whether there is a semantic component distinct from the syntactic component at all, whether recognition of a level of deep syntactic structure simplifies or obstructs grammatical derivations, whether surface structures should be semantically interpreted, and so on. It would be absurd

314

to pretend that my observations about opaque constructions
determine the answers to these questions. It is widely agreed
that all of the current linguistic theories are too powerful,
that they do not impose sufficient constraints upon the range
of possible grammars. While there is no shortage of facts
that we cannot account for at all, for most observations there
are too many, rather than too few, possible ways of handling
them formally. It should therefore not be too surprising to
find that the facts about opaque constructions are compatible
with more than one answer to the kinds of question just raised.
It is possible, however, to make certain negative points, to
show that as far as opaque constructions are concerned,
certain powers are not required of the grammar and certain
possible treatments are excluded. Since opaque constructions
are syntactically complex and are not, by any standards,
semantically impoverished, these observations may perhaps
turn out to have some significance in the determination of
the constraints that can be imposed upon grammars.

I shall present arguments in this chapter to the effect
that surface structures do not contain sufficient information
to serve as the input to an interpretive semantic component,
that deep structures as standardly defined (e.g. by Chomsky,
in Aspects of the Theory of Syntax, 1965) are adequate as input
to such a component, that the specific and non-specific
readings of ambiguous sentences are not distinguished at this

level of deep structure, and that the facts about opacity
do not, as has been claimed, show that this level of
representation should be abandoned.

Section 2. Surface structures and semantic interpretation.

If a grammar contains an interpretive semantic component,
the representations of sentences which serve as input to this
component must determine the set of possible readings that
any sentence has. It is not required, though it may be the
case, that each of the possible readings of a sentence has a
different structural representation at the input level. All
that is required is that it should be possible to state (and
the more general the statement the better, of course) which
structures at this level are open to multiple interpretation,
and how many and which readings they have. Distinct representations for each of these readings could then be constructed
by the rules of the semantic component which operate on the
input structures.

It is obvious, just from the fact that English sentences
containing complement clauses are systematically ambiguous,
that the level of surface structure does not provide distinct
representations for each of the readings of opaque constructions. It might nevertheless be possible to state a generalization over surface structures about which noun phrases (and
perhaps other constituents in the case of the opacity of

descriptive content) are ambiguous, and what readings they
may have. It can be shown, however, that even if this is
possible, it is very far from optimal.

With some exceptions on either side, all and only
those noun phrases which appear in complement clauses are
ambiguous with respect to opacity, and any grammar that failed
to capture this generalization would be defective to that
extent. However, a noun phrase which is in a complement
clause in deep structure but is moved out of that clause
during the transformational derivation, is still ambiguous.
Sentence (1) is ambiguous with respect to specificity in the
same way as sentence (2):

(1)   Mary believes one of the eggs to be broken.

(2)   Mary believes that one of the eggs is broken.

even though there may be, for some speakers, a difference as
to which of the possible readings is the 'preferred' one in
each case. Similarly, sentence (3) is ambiguous with respect
to the referential/attributive distinction in the same way as
sentence (4):

(3)   John proved Smith's murderer to be insane.

(4)   John proved that Smith's murderer was insane.

Assuming that the pairs (1) and (2), (3) and (4), are indeed
transformationally related (by the subject-raising rule),
then this suggests at the very least that a more general
statement about which noun phrases may be interpreted opaquely
could be defined over a level prior to the application of

317

the subject-raising transformation.

An even stronger point can be made, however. There is, as far as I know, no reason to assume that the surface structure of sentences like (1) and (3) differs in relevant respects from that of a sentence such as:

(5) Mary persuaded one of her friends to sing.

but the noun phrase one of her friends in (5), unlike one of the eggs in (1), does not have a non-specific interpretation. If the range of readings of a noun phrase is determined prior to subject-raising, there is an obvious explanation of this fact. The noun phrase in (5) is in the main clause prior to subject-raising, the noun phrase in (1) is in the complement clause prior to subject-raising; the difference between (5) and (1) is therefore in accord with, rather than an exception to, the generalization about noun phrases in complement clauses. Since subject-raising applies within the transformational cycle, this argument applies not only to the level of surface structure but equally to any other post-cyclic level of representation, for example the level of 'shallow structure' which has recently been proposed.

If the opacity of noun phrases were to be read off some post-cyclic level of representation rather than a level prior to subject-raising, the class of opaque noun phrases could not be structurally defined. Reference would be needed to the particular verb present in a sentence, and the class of verbs which would have to be mentioned

318

would be precisely those which already have to be categorized
for the subject-raising rule. An even greater loss of
generality would be involved, however, for to state which
noun phrases not in complement clauses may be read opaquely
would require a further subdivision of this class of verbs,
and this subdivision will mirror precisely the subdivision
between verbs which take subject complements and those which
take object complements. Thus in the sentence:

(6)   Someone seems to have taken my coat.

the subject noun phrase someone may be specific or non-
specific. In sentences (1) and (3), it is the object noun
phrase which is ambiguous, and the subjects of those sentences
are unambiguous. Given that there is a subject-raising rule,
the difference between (6) and (1) or (3) is obviously that
the verb seem takes a subject complement, and subject-raising
affects its subject position, while believe and prove take
object complements and subject-raising affects their object
positions.

It is in fact obvious in general that if the class of
noun phrases that may be read opaquely were to be defined
over surface structures, this would involve, in effect, the
unpicking of the operations of the transformational component.
For example, the contrast between:

(7)   Someone is thought to have taken my coat.

in which the subject noun phrase may be specific or non-
specific, and:

319

(8)   Someone was persuaded to sing.

in which the subject noun phrase has no non-specific reading,
is a result of subject-raising together with passivization,
and it obviously should not be recorded as an independent fact
about the verbs think and persuade. We may conclude, therefore, that deep structures rather than surface structures
should constitute the input to the semantic component.

Section 3.   Opacity and the level of deep structure.

Bach (Nouns and Noun Phrases, 1968) has argued in a
fashion somewhat similar to the preceding section that
the level of deep structure as traditionally conceived
(for example in Chomsky, Aspects of the Theory of Syntax,
1965) should be rejected. Bach claims that the distribution
of opaque noun phrases can be defined most simply and generally
over a level of representation 'deeper' (more abstract) than
the traditional level of deep structure, and that recognition
of the traditional deep structure level actually obstructs
the statement of the generalization in question. The argument
concerns opacity in sentences which do not contain complement
structure. Since I have ignored these cases in preceding
chapters, I shall now consider their implications for the
linguistic description of opacity before discussing Bach's
argument in detail.

There are a number of different types of example of
non-complement constructions which are opaque, for example:

(9) One of the burglars may be hiding in the cellar.

(10) Bill has apparently proposed to a friend of mine.

(11) John wants a yacht.

(12) I am looking for a pencil.

It was pointed out in Chapter I that not only do complement constructions constitute much the widest class of opaque contexts, but there also seems to be some inherent connection between these structures and the possibility of opaque interpretations. The ambiguities we have been concerned with appear to be ambiguities of the scope relationships between a noun phrase and the clausal units of the sentence in which it occurs, but this account of the nature of opacity only makes sense of the ambiguities if there is more than one clausal unit in the sentence. Any representational system which is based on the intuition that there is some inherent connection of this kind, and employs complement structure essentially in making formal distinctions between transparent and opaque readings, will have to make special allowance for examples like those above. It is not just that they are exceptions to the most obvious generalization about the distribution of opaquely interpreted noun phrases; even if we solve the problem of <u>predicting</u> that there are opaque readings of such examples, it is still not clear in what form these readings should be represented unless the semantic representations contain something like complement structure.

321

It may be possible to devise some king of formal representational machinery which does not essentially employ complement structure in distinguishing opaque and transparent readings. One would then have to decide whether to allow the semantic representations of sentences like those above to be quite different from the representations of sentences which are superficially complement constructions. This would, in effect, be to employ two different kinds of representational device for one and the same phenomenon. On the other hand one might decide that this other representational system cannot be employed in the case of complement constructions without the loss of some significant insight. In fact the tendency, both in philosophy and linguistics, has been to make the opposite move, that is to assume complement-like structure in the semantic representations of all sentences that have opaque interpretations even if their superficial syntax does not exhibit such structure. This move permits the essential connection between complement structure and opacity, if it really exists, to be captured. It is reinforced by the fact that non-complement constructions which have opaque readings can be paraphrased by complement constructions, but the reverse is not generally true. Thus the meaning of the sentence:

(13) I want an icecream.

can reasonably be expressed as:

(14) I want to $\begin{Bmatrix} \text{have} \\ \text{eat} \end{Bmatrix}$ an icecream.

but the meaning of:

(15)   I want to borrow a hammer.

cannot be expressed, without extreme unnaturalness, in a
sentence which does not contain complement structure (even
if disguised by means of anaphora). Whether this is universally the case I do not know; it certainly is so in all the
languages with which I am familiar. There even seems to be
some absurdity about the idea that it might not be so.

I shall simply assume, therefore, in what follows,
that in the semantic component there are no essential
differences between the representations of opaque contexts
which are superficially complement constructions and those
which are not. It still remains to be asked how the mapping
between the semantic representations and surface structures
is effected, and at what point in the grammar the two kinds
of example are differentiated. In particular, is it necessary
to assign examples like (9) - (12) syntactic representations
containing complement structure?

Any sentence containing a modal verb in its main clause
has an opaque interpretation, for example:

(16)   I shall bring a friend.

(17)   Someone should fix that traffic light.

(18)   A burglar might get in through one of those windows.

Generally, any noun phrase in the sentence may be interpreted
opaquely or transparently, even the subject noun phrase, which

323

precedes the modal verb in surface structure. Thus if what
we are dealing with is a scope phenomenon, the surface structure
appears not to display the scope relationships accurately.
There are some exceptions to this generalization, however.
In the sentence:

(19) One of the boys can do it.

if the can is a can of permission, then there is a specific
reading of the subject noun phrase and a non-specific reading.
The sentence can mean either:

(20) It is permitted that one of the boys should do it.

or:

(21) One of the boys is such that he is permitted to do it.

If, however, the can is a can of ability, then it appears
that there is only a specific reading, something like:

(22) One of the boys is such that he is able to do it.

and there is no non-specific reading any more than there is
a sentence:

(23) *It is able that one of the boys (should) do it.

For the adjective able, the fact that its subject
noun phrase has no non-specific interpretation can be
explained if we conclude from the ungrammaticality of (23)
that able takes an object complement rather than a subject
complement, and thus that the structure of the sentence:

(24) One of the boys is able to do it.

is something like:

324

(25)   One of the boys is able $_S$[he do it].

rather than:

(26) $_S$[one of the boys do it] is able.

Thus the subject noun phrase of (24) appears in the matrix clause in deep structure, which explains why it has no opaque interpretation. Any other noun phrase in such a sentence may be interpreted opaquely, however, for these will be in the complement clause in deep structure. For example, the noun phrase <u>one ball</u> is ambiguous in the sentence:

(27)   John is able to balance one ball on his nose.

This would be predicted from the deep structure:

(28)   John is able $_S$[John balance one ball on his nose].

Notice that exactly the same ambiguity exists in the corresponding sentence with <u>can</u>, thus:

(29)   John can balance one ball on his nose.

Either there is a particular ball such that John can balance <u>it</u> on his nose, or else John can balance any one ball on his nose at a time.

If it is assumed that sentences containing modals are like sentences containing complement structure not only at the semantic level but at the level of deep syntactic structure also, that is, that modals are not introduced into deep structures within an <u>Aux</u> constituent but are introduced as main verbs taking complements, then the generalization that noun phrases in complement structures have an opaque interpretation will cover sentences with modals too; one large class of exceptions to the partial generalization that <u>only</u> noun phrases in complements have an opaque interpretation will have been removed. Treating <u>can</u> on its two readings as structurally different, one taking a subject complement, and one taking an object complement like <u>is able</u>, will automatically explain the observations above about the distribution of opaque noun phrases in sentences with <u>can</u>. These advantages have an associated cost, of course, for something will have to be added to the transformational component, and also to the selection restrictions, in order to generate the proper class of surface structures. But Ross has put forward quite independent arguments for the analysis of modals as verbs taking complements (Auxiliaries as Main Verbs, 1968), and if those arguments are accepted, then the generalization of the statement of distribution of opaque noun phrases falls out as an automatic bonus. It will simplify the semantic component, since this component will not now need to contain a special rule mapping sentences containing modals onto semantic representations. The same rule can be used for sentences with modals as is already needed for sentences with complement structure.

A further move in the same direction would bring some of the other apparently exceptional cases under the same generalization about the distribution of opaque noun phrases. Adverbs such as <u>probably</u>, <u>perhaps</u>, <u>apparently</u>, <u>obviously</u>, <u>conceivably</u>, etc., create opaque contexts in the same way as explicit clauses like <u>It is probable that...</u>, <u>It may be</u>

326

the case that..., It is apparent that..., and so on. Thus
the sentence:

(30) Bill has apparently proposed to a friend of mine.

has the two interpretations:

(31) There is apparently a friend of mine that Bill has
                          proposed to.

(32) There is a friend of mine that Bill has apparently
                          proposed to.

These are very similar to the two interpretations:

(33) It is apparent that there is a friend of mine that Bill
                          has proposed to.

(34) There is a friend of mine whom it is apparent that Bill
                          has proposed to.

of the sentence:

(35) It is apparent that Bill has proposed to a friend of
                          mine.

Just as for the modals, we could assume that sentences (30)
and (35), and similar pairs, have different deep structures
but much the same semantic representations. In this case,
sentences like (30) would be exceptions to the generalization
that all and only noun phrases which are in a complement clause
in deep structure have an opaque interpretation, and the
semantic component would need a special rule for mapping
these sentences onto semantic representations. Alternatively,
it could be assumed that the deep structures of sentences (30)
and (35) are essentailly identical and are both complement

327

constructions. This would bring (30) under the generalization about opaque noun phrases, would permit one and the same semantic rule to be employed in both cases, but would require some rule(s) to be added to the transformational component to convert certain adjectives into adverbs and reduce the clausal structure. Independent arguments have, I believe, been put forward for this analysis too.

Another class of examples is the following:

(36) John wants a yacht.

(37) Bill is hoping for a birthday present.

(38) I am expecting a letter.

with verbs which do take complements but can also take simple object noun phrases. Unlike many of the examples with modals, or the examples with sentential adverbs, in these cases the subject of the opaque verb is not ambiguous; it is only the object noun phrase and other phrases which follow the verb, if any, as in:

(39) I am expecting him one Monday.

that are open to an opaque interpretation. Exactly the same is true of the most natural paraphrases with complement structure, thus:

(40) John wants to have (own, get) a yacht.

(41) Bill is hoping to receive a birthday present.

(42) I am expecting a letter to arrive (come).

(43) I am expecting him to arrive (come) one Monday.

The verbs which appear in the complements of these paraphrases
are to a large extent predictable; sentence (36), for example,
can be paraphrased as (40) but not as:

(44)   John wants to $\left\{\begin{array}{l}\text{sail}\\ \text{be on}\\ \text{eat}\\ \text{etc.}\end{array}\right\}$ a yacht.

It is therefore conceivable that the simple sentences should
be derived from the same deep structures as their paraphrases
containing complements, and thus brought under the generalization about opaque interpretation and complement clauses in
deep structure.   In this case, however, the transformational
rule which provides the correct surface structure for a
sentence such as (36) will not just be a governed rule, as
it will for the case of the sentential adverbs, but will
actually delete a different verb from the complement depending
on the verb in the matrix clause.   The cost of preserving
the generalization about the distribution of opaque noun phrases
would therefore be rather severe.   However, independent
arguments have been put forward for this analysis too (Ross,
A Note on <u>Have</u> Deletion, 1969, unpublished), and if these
arguments are accepted, then once again the generalization
about opacity falls out at no extra cost.

At the extreme end of the scale, we have examples like:

(45)   I am looking for a hammer.

(46)   Ernest is hunting lions.

Here too, only noun phrases following the verb are open to an
opaque interpretation and this is also true of the most

329

natural paraphrases, e.g:

(47) I am trying to find a hammer.

(48) Ernest is trying to catch lions.

There are very few examples of this kind in English, but the paraphrases seem to be idiosyncratic and not reducible to a general rule. Furthermore, they do not contain the verb that actually appears in the simple sentences. To derive the simple sentences from their paraphrases with complement structure would therefore involve not merely deletion, but either the mapping of some lexical items into others, or else the postponement of lexical insertion until after the operation of the relevant transformation which reduces the clausal structure of the deep structure.

It is for this very abstract conception of deep structure that Bach is arguing. However, although there are independent arguments for a syntactic analysis in terms of complement structure for the other types of example we have considered, there are none, as far as I know, in the case of examples like (45) and (46). What Bach assumes is that the preservation of the generalization about the distribution of opaque noun phrases is itself an argument for this analysis, but in fact the alternatives that we have to choose between seem to be as evenly balanced as it is possible to imagine. One alternative is, as Bach proposes, to assign to these examples deep structures containing a complement clause, and employ a very powerful system of rules for mapping

these deep structures onto surface structures. This move
will simplify the semantic component, since now all of the
sentences which have opaque readings will constitute a well-
defined class at the level of deep structure, and, furthermore,
their deep structures will be very close, if not identical,
to the semantic structures that have to be assigned. The
other alternative is to save in the transformational
component, by assuming that the deep structure of a sentence
like (45) contains only one clause, just like its surface
structure, and to adopt a special rule in the semantic component to map such a deep structure onto a semantic representation similar to that for the sentence (47). In the
absence of any further evidence, the choice between these
two treatments seems to me to be utterly undetermined;
simplicity measures are simply not refined enough to decide
between them.

The persuasiveness that Bach's argument has comes
from the parallel that he draws between his own argument and
Halle's argument against recognising the taxonomic phonemic
level. Bach maintains that opacity, like the devoicing of
obstruents in Russian, is a phenomenon that bridges a putative
level of linguistic representation, in this case the traditional
level of deep structure (at which (45) and (47) would have
distinct representations). He concludes that this level,
like the taxonomic phonemic level, is therefore an encumbrance
rather than an advantage in linguistic descriptions and should

331

not be recognised. But the analogy with Halle's argument is incomplete. In Halle's case, only the criteria of complementary distribution and contrast divide the class of obstruents which undergo devoicing in a given context into two distinct sub-classes, and it is only this which, in turn, requires the existence of two distinct devoicing rules in a grammar containing a taxonomic phonemic level. In all other respects the segments which undergo voicing are alike. Therefore jettisoning the taxonomic phonemic level permits a single obstruent devoicing rule with no loss of descriptive adequacy. But where is the rule that applies both to the object noun phrase of look for and to a noun phrase in a complement clause? Bach does not cite any, and it is for this reason that his argument is incomplete, for if there is no such rule, then there is no rule which would have to be duplicated, or even complicated, if the traditional level of deep structure is recognised in the grammar.

Since all that Bach discusses is the meanings of these sentences, it may be that what he had in mind was the saving of a rule of the semantic component, since assigning look for a deep structure with a complement would permit just one and the same rule to be used for mapping deep structures onto semantic representations of opaque readings. But, as pointed out above, this gain in the semantic component would have to be paid for in the form of complicating the transformational component. The reason for this difference between the case

332

of opacity and that of obstruent devoicing in Russian is
that look for and try to find are not exactly similar constructions. They are similar in meaning but obviously different
in their superficial syntactic structure. They could con-
sequently never be assigned completely identical derivations,
as can the obstruents which undergo devoicing in Russian.
The obstruents all begin and end their derivation as similar;
look for and try to find are similar at only one end of their
derivations, the semantic end, and their derivations therefore cannot be made exactly similar throughout by the dropping
of any level of representation, or indeed by any other
manoeuvre.

The question at what level (or if not at a level
then at what point) the derivations of sentences with
look for and sentences with try to find converge (or
diverge, if looked at the other way) still remains to be
answered. The only kind of fact that would force one
to assign them identical deep syntactic structures would
be the existence of some syntactic reflex of the opaque
reading of a noun phrase such that the proper set of
surface structures could be generated only if opaquely
interpreted noun phrases were recognised as a syntactic
class, that is to say, the existence of some rule applying
to the objects of look for and try to find, but not, for
example, to the object of catch or find or hit. There are
in fact very few syntactic phenomena specially associated

with the opaque readings of noun phrases. Although phrases like whichever... or some...or other are often used in paraphrasing opaque readings informally, these items do also occur freely in transparent contexts. Thus the existence of sentences such as:

(49) He is looking for whichever boy failed the exam.

(50) He is looking for some pencil or other.

like:

(51) He is trying to find whichever boy failed the exam.

(52) He is trying to find some pencil or other.

do not show that look for and try to find must be represented identically at the stage at which distributional constraints are imposed, because of transparent examples such as:

(53) He hit whichever boy failed the exam.

(54) He hit some boy or other.

In many cases, a non-specific noun phrase can be distinctively paraphrased by means of a there is internal to the sentence, as in:

(55) Mary thinks there is someone in the cellar.

as contrasted with the specific:

(56) There is someone that Mary thinks is in the cellar.

With look for, however, there can be no such internal there is marking the non-specific reading -- one cannot even imagine where to try to insert one, thus:

(57) **He is looking there is for a pencil.

(58) **He is looking for there is a pencil.

334

Also in some cases a distinctive kind of noun phrase is used
in referring back to a non-specific antecedent. Thus with a
non-specifically interpreted antecedent we have the discourse:
(59) John wants to catch a fish. The fish he catches...
while with a specifically interpreted antecedent we have the
discourse:
(60) John wants to catch a fish. The fish he wants to catch...
(See Dean, Non-specific Noun Phrases in English, 1968, for
further discussion.) But for look for, despite its possible
opaque interpretation, there is no such syntactic contrast
in cross-referring noun phrases, but only:
(61) John is looking for a fish. The fish he is looking for...
which must be taken as specific, just as for any fully
transparent verb, e.g.:
(62) John caught a fish. The fish he caught...
Similarly with pronouns coreferential with the object of
look for. The discourse:
(63) John is looking for a fish. It is in the bath.
is not ungrammatical with the it interpreted as coreferential
with a fish, though it is acceptable only on a specific
interpretation.

      There therefore appear to be no distinctive surface
structures to be generated for look for which would require
it to have a deep structure like try to find and different
from that of any transparent verb. Though this is not ruled

out, of course, the opacity of <u>look for</u> could quite well be handled by appropriate rules of interpretation.

There are in fact remarkably few syntactic phenomena which distinguish the opaque and transparent readings for any opaque verb. Most examples are systematically ambiguous, and there seems to be no motivation for assigning the readings distinct deep structure representations rather than deriving them from a single deep structure and distinguishing them only in the semantic component. The most striking facts relevant to this question are the distinctive <u>there is</u>... paraphrases for specific and non-specific noun phrases and I shall discuss these in detail in the next section. I mention here briefly one or two other cases where a deep structure difference between specific and non-specific readings of ambiguous surface structures might appear to be required.

The correlation between <u>which</u>-questions and specificity has already been noted. The question:

(64) Which fish does John want to catch?

presupposes that John wants to catch a particular fish, i.e. it presupposes the specific, and not merely the non-specific, reading of the sentence:

(65) John wants to catch a fish.

It is not obvious that presuppositions should be treated syntactically rather than in the semantic component, but

in this case it does look at first sight as though the facts
could be explained by a structural condition on the question
formation rules. It looks, that is, as if the question-word
preposing transformation is constrained not to move a noun
phrase out of the scope of its specificity operator. This
would explain why the question (64), with preposed noun phrase,
could correspond only to the specific reading of (65), for
which the specificity operator is already at the far left
of the structure, but not to the non-specific reading of (65),
for which the specificity operator is internal to the complement.

This would be interesting if true, especially as it
would suggest a relationship between which-questions and
relative clauses. It has already been mentioned that a
noun phrase which is 'relativised' is always interpreted as
specific with respect to the whole of sentence which underlies
the relative clause, and that the sentence as a whole therefore presupposes the specific reading, and not merely the non-
specific, of the relative clause sentence. Relative pronoun
preposing and question-word preposing might therefore be
supposed to be the same rule, or at least subject to the
same interesting structural constraint, viz. that they must
preserve the underlying scope relationships in the sentence.
It was observed in Section 2 that the subject-raising
transformation is not constrained in this way, so this
cannot be a general constraint on the operation of

337

transformations. And, in fact, it can be shown not even to be a constraint on the preposing of question words, for what-questions are not restricted to specific noun phrases. The question:

(66)　What does John want to catch?

although it contains a preposed noun phrase, does not presuppose the specific reading of the sentence:

(67)　John wants to catch something.

It does presuppose that John has decided what **kind** of thing he wants to catch, but not that he has decided on any thing in particular. Either reading of the sentence:

(68)　John wants to catch a fish.

therefore counts as an adequate answer to the question. It should also be noted that **which**-questions which have **not** undergone preposing are restricted to specific noun phrases just like those in which the noun phrase has been preposed. Thus the question:

(69)　John wants to catch which fish?

has the same presupposition as the question (64). It therefore cannot be the preposing of the noun phrase in (64) which accounts for the specificity of its presupposition.

The connection between **which** and specificity thus appears not to be a structural one and not, therefore, to require a structural difference between specific and non-specific sentences in the syntactic component. The observations above could be handled by means of interpretive rules. Notice,

338

incidentally, that if the which/what contrast is treated
as a definite/indefinite contrast as is sometimes proposed
(though it has also been regarded instead as a noun/pronoun
contrast, for example), then the semantic differences between
which- and what-questions just observed would tie up with the
observations of Chapter II, Section 5, about the relationship
between definite noun phrases and specific indefinite ones.
It should also be pointed out that the observations about
what- and which-questions above apply also to embedded questions
such as:

(70)   I wonder which fish John wants to catch.

(71)   I wonder what John wants to catch.

and also to cleft and pseudo-cleft sentences which, despite
the surface structure position of the noun phrases they
contain, are not unambiguously specific in meaning, for example:

(72)   What John wants to catch is a fish.

(73)   A fish is what John wants to catch.

and even:

(74)   It is a fish that John wants to catch.

These facts suggest, incidentally, that cleft sentences are
related to questions rather than to relative clauses, if
indeed to either.

Section 4.   Specificity and deep structures.   'There is...'
            constructions.

We have been considering two questions, (a) what

level of representation determines which noun phrases in
sentences are ambiguous with respect to opacity? i.e. how
'deep' must the level input to the semantic component be?
(b) at what level are the different readings of opaque noun
phrases assigned different representations? In Section 2
it was shown that surface structures are not 'deep' enough
to be the optimal input to the semantic component. In
Section 3 it was maintained that there is no positive
motivation, as far as the facts about opacity are concerned,
to assume a syntactic level much 'deeper' than the traditional
level of deep structure to serve as input to the semantic
component. It was also pointed out that a number of facts
which might suggest that specific and non-specific readings
of ambiguous sentences have distinct deep structures do not
in fact require this. I shall now consider the relationship
between there is... sentences and specificity with a view
to showing first that deep structures do not need to be
supplemented by information from surface structures as
input to the semantic component, and secondly that even though
the specificity of unambiguous examples is indicated
in their deep structures, it does not follow that ambiguous
sentences have multiple derivations from unambiguous deep
structures.

Although it has been shown that a pre-cyclic level
of representation permits a more general statement of the
distribution of opaque noun phrases than a post-cyclic

level, it does not follow that there is some pre-cyclic
level at which all the information relevant to opacity
of noun phrases is represented. Although characteristically
opaque constructions are systematically ambiguous, there
are sentences containing there is... which are unambiguous
with respect to specificity. If there is nothing in the deep
structures of these sentences from which their readings could
be predicted, then deep structures alone would not be sufficient
input to the semantic component, and the effect of a there is
on the meaning of a sentence would require the input of
some more superficial level of representation to the semantic
component.

The sentence:

(75)   Mary thinks a man is in the cellar.

is ambiguous with respect to the specificity of a man.   The
sentence:

(76)   There is a man that Mary thinks is in the cellar.

is unambiguously specific with respect to this phrase, however,
and for many speakers the sentence:

(77)   Mary thinks that there is a man in the cellar.

is unambiguously non-specific.   If, therefore, there are no
syntactic grounds for deriving (76) and (77) from distinct
deep structures, then the level of deep structure will not be
sufficiently informative to serve as the input to the semantic
component.   We should consider, therefore, the possibility
that both (76) and (77) are derived from the same deep

structure as (75), by means of a transformation that freely
introduces there is in the relevant contexts. I shall argue
that, on purely syntactic grounds, this analysis of (76)
and (77) is not optimal, that the simplest and most general
analysis of there is... constructions does in fact assign
distinct deep structures to these two sentences, and, furthermore, that the nature of these deep structures actually explains
why they have the particular readings that they do.

How to analyse sentences containing there is has
always been a rather murky question, and one on which
curiously little has been written. This may in part be
due to the fact that many of syntactically simplest examples
hover on the borders of acceptability, for example:

(78)   There is a boy.

(79)   There are elephants.

and even:

(80)   There are nine thousand and seventy three elephants.

(81)   There is someone that I saw.

It is not immediately apparent what distinguishes these
examples from the more acceptable:

(82)   There is a God.

(83)   There are purple elephants.

(84)   There are five continents.

(85)   There is someone that I have to see.

(I note in passing that the observation of Section 5 of
Chapter II, that there is... is not, or not necessarily,

to be interpreted as existential, helps to make some sense of these differences in acceptability. If the there is... sentence is taken to mean not that things of the kind described really exist but simply that individual ones have been conceived of, characterised in stories, imagined to exist, and so on, then a sentence like (79) is bound to be odd, because we could hardly have the word elephant in the language unless elephants had been conceived of. Hence the greater acceptability of (83). The non-existential reading of there is... will also be more natural when there is some other function for the there is... to serve, as in (85), where it distinguishes the specific reading of I have to see someone from the non-specific reading. Hence the greater acceptability of (85) as compared with (81), where there is no specific/non-specific distinction to be made.)

The most natural examples of there is... constructions are those with locative or time modifiers, such as:

(86) There is a cat on that roof.

(87) There was a protest meeting on Sunday.

and those with relative clauses on the noun following the there is, such as:

(88) There are elephants which are small enough to hold in
your hand.

In order to provide a uniform analysis of at least these two types of example, it might be proposed that the modifiers

343

in (86) and (87) should be derived from relative clauses by the usual relative clause reduction rule. Thus to bring these sentences into line with (88), they might be derived from:

(89) There is a cat which is on that roof.

(90) There was a protest meeting which was on Sunday.

All three sentences would thus consist of just a noun phrase following there is. Stephen Anderson has pointed out in support of this proposal (in 'What There Is', forthcoming) that the constraints on the modifiers that may appear in sentences like (86) and (87) parallel to a striking degree the constraints on relative clause reduction. For example, relative clauses with predicate nominals do not reduce. The sentence:

(91) I know a man who is a taxidermist.

has no corresponding reduced form:

(92) *I know a man a taxidermist.

In conformity with this, the sentence:

(93) There is a man who is a taxidermist.

even if not entirely acceptable, is at least considerably more so than:

(94) *There is a man a taxidermist.

Even if, for these reasons, sentences (86) and (87) are to be assigned a derivation from structures like (89) and (90), there are also grounds for deriving them from simply:

344

(95) A cat is on that roof.

(96) A protest meeting was on Sunday.

The modifiers in (86) and (87) are mobile, thus we have:

(97) On that roof there is a cat.

(98) On Sunday there was a protest meeting.

It is true that relative clauses can be moved around in sentences to some extent; they can be extraposed, as in:

(99) The books have not yet arrived which were ordered
last week.

but this is possible only if they have <u>not</u> been reduced, witness:

(100) *The books have not yet arrived ordered last week.

and in any case they cannot be preposed:

(101) *(Which were) ordered last week the books have not
yet arrived.

The relative clause derivation of (86) and (87) therefore does not account for the variants (97) and (98). The derivation from (95) and (96) does, since we also have:

(102) On that roof is a cat.

(103) ? On Sunday was a protest meeting.

The importance of the derivation of these sentences from sources like (95) and (96) is that the verb <u>is</u> of the <u>there is</u> is already present in (95) and (96). Only <u>there</u> has to be inserted transformationally. It takes the place of the subject noun phrase, which is repositioned after the verb <u>is</u>. The claim that it is only <u>there</u>, and not there is, that is introduced by transformation is strongly supported by the existence of sentences with there but a verb other than is, for example:

(104)   In the corner there stood a whatnot.

(105)   In the crib there lay a tiny baby.

There is no way of deriving such sentences by means of a transformation that introduces there is, (and because of selection restrictions, if nothing else, we should not want there stood and there lay to be introduced transformationally).   The transformation just outlined which introduces there and repositions the subject noun phrase could, however, be quite simply broadened to apply to certain intransitive verbs other than is, and (104) and (105) would therefore be derivable from:

(106)   A whatnot stood in the corner.

(107)   A tiny baby lay in the crib.

In other cases too, the is of there is must be regarded as present in the underlying structure rather than as introduced transformationally.   Thus the tense of the verb to be in the sentence:

(108)   There was a new theatre opened in Boston today.

suggests that this verb is in fact the passive auxiliary, and that (108) is derived from:

(109)   A new theatre was opened in Boston today.

rather than by reduction of the relative clause construction:

346

(110)   There was (?) a new theatre which was opened in Boston

today.

If we return now to the examples which have overt

relative clause structure, such as:

(111)   There is someone whom I have to see.

the transformation which is required for the other cases

will be adequate for these relative clause constructions

too, if we suppose that their underlying structure is of the

form:

(112) $_{NP}$[Someone whom I have to see] $_{VP}$[is].

To derive a sentence such as (111) from the simple sentential

source:

(113)   I have to see someone.

would require a transformation quite different from that

needed for other there is... constructions. Furthermore,

this transformation would be considerably more complex than

the one that has been proposed; it would have to introduce

a verb to be as well as there, the there would have to be

able to substitute for noun phrases other than the subject

noun phrase, and the rest of the sentence would somehow

have to be converted into a relative clause modifying

this noun phrase. By comparison, the only complication

involved in the derivation of (111) from (112) is that

the there introduction rule is obligatory when the verb

to be is clause-final.

Our original interest was in pairs of sentences such as:

347

(114) There is a man that Mary thinks is in the cellar.

(115) Mary thinks that there is a man in the cellar.

Although the analysis of there is... sentences was not developed
in connection with these examples, and in particular was not
based on a desire to ensure different deep structure
sources for such non-synonymous pairs, this is in fact
just what the analysis provides. Even if we assume
that the there of (114) and (115) is transformationally
introduced, these two sentences do not have identical
deep structures because the verb is must be assumed to
be present in their underlying forms, and it will be in
a different position in the two cases. The sources will
be respectively:

(116) $_{NP}$[A man $_S$[Mary thinks $_S$[a man is in the cellar]]]

$_{VP}$[is].

(117) Mary thinks $_S$[$_{NP}$[a man] $_{VP}$[is in the cellar]].

If sentence (115) can also be regarded as a reduction of:

(118) Mary thinks there is a man who is in the cellar.

then it will also have the source:

(119) Mary thinks $_S$[$_{NP}$[a man $_S$[a man is in the cellar]]

$_{VP}$[is]].

It appears, therefore, that it is not necessary
to input surface structures to the semantic component in
order that distinct semantic representations should be

assigned to pairs of sentences such as (114) and (115) which
differ with respect to specificity, for these sentences
will have distinct deep structures. It is a strong point
in favour of the proposed analysis that the difference between
the deep structures that have been assigned actually explains
why the presence of there is in a sentence disambiguates it
with respect to specificity. It was observed in Chapter III
that noun phrases containing relative clauses presuppose
the truth of the specific reading of the sentence which
underlies the relative clause. For example, the phrase:

(120)   The fish that John wants to catch

presupposes the truth of the specific reading of the
sentence:

(121)   John wants to catch a fish.

and the phrase has no referent if this sentence is false
or if it is true only on its non-specific reading, i.e. if
there is no particular fish that John wants to catch. It
therefore appears that any noun phrase which is 'relativised'
must be fully specific with respect to the relative clause
sentence (see Dean, Non-specific Noun Phrases in English,
 or further comment on this point). This means that in
the structure (116) the noun phrase a man inside the relative
clause must be interpreted as specific with respect to the
relative clause sentence:

122)   Mary thinks a man is in the cellar.

349

This explains why sentence (114), which is derived from (116), has the same meaning as the specific reading of (122), and has no reading corresponding to the non-specific reading of (122). On the other hand, sentence (115) is either to be derived from (117), which has no relative clause, or is to be derived from (119), in which the relative clause sentence is:

(123) A man is in the cellar.

The phrase a man in (115) must therefore be interpreted as specific with respect to (123), but this is consistent with its being non-specific with respect to the larger context (122).

The deep structure position of the is of there is serves to determine specificity and non-specificity in the examples we have considered. It might therefore be proposed that the scope operator for specificity simply is this is. Furthermore it looks as if this is can be assumed to be present in the deep structures, and not simply the semantic representations, of ambiguous sentences such as (122), without our needing to complicate the syntactic component in any way. If the grammar contained a rule which deleted the is, and the associated clausal structure, from structures of the kind that underlie there is... sentences, then the ambiguous sentence (122) would be derivable both from the structure that underlies the unambiguously specific sentence (114) and also from the structure that underlies the unambiguously non-specific sentence (115). The ambiguity of (122) would thus be accounted for. The rule that is needed is, however, very like the rule of quantifier lowering that Lakoff and others have proposed. Thus Lakoff (On Derivational Constraints, 1969) argues that the sentence:

(124) Many men read few books.

should be derived from an underlying structure of the form:

(125)

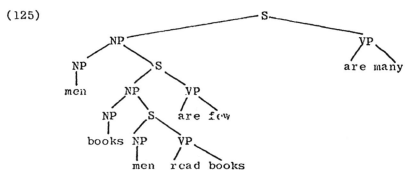

This structure is also supposed to underlie the surface structure:

(126) The men who read few books are many. (Many are the men who read few books.)

The rule of quantifier lowering, applied to <u>are few</u>, will produce (126). If applied twice, i.e. to <u>are many</u> as well as to <u>are few</u>, the result is (124). Now, comparing (125) with (116) above, it is clear that the rule that lowers <u>few</u> or <u>many</u> in (125) and gets rid of the <u>are</u> and the associated structure, will also serve to get rid of the <u>is</u> and the associated structure from (116). In fact, to bring the analysis of specificity even more closely into line with a general account of quantifiers, we might propose that the structure underlying (114) is not (116) but rather:

(127)
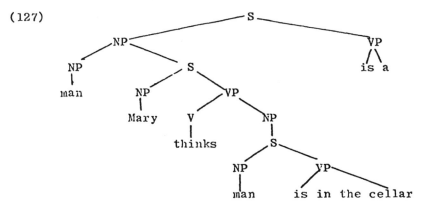

with the indefinite article _a_ (or _some_ in the plural) as part of the verb phrase, rather than simply the intransitive verb _is_. This article, just like the _few_ and _many_ of (125), would be lowered by the quantifier lowering rule. If, optionally, the quantifier lowering rule were not applied to (127), the _there is..._ construction (114) would be produced instead by the _there-insertion_ rule. Notice, incidentally, that because of the observations of Section 5 of Chapter II, the _is_ of _there is_ must not be taken to be synonymous with _exists_ but must be interpreted in terms of individuation. The analysis (127), in which the _is_ simply serves to introduce a quantifier, is therefore intuitively appropriate.

The proposal just outlined is that systematically

352

ambiguous sentences like (122) should be assigned two distinct deep structures, one identical with that of (114) and one identical with that of (115). This will account for the ambiguity of (122), and require no extra formal machinery in the grammar since the quantifier lowering rule will reduce the structures underlying (114) and (115) to the surface structure (122). I shall now show that this account of the ambiguity of a sentence like (122) suffers from a serious disadvantage. There are differences between sentences with <u>there is...</u> and the corresponding ambiguous sentences without <u>there is...</u> which it will be difficult, if not impossible, to capture if identical deep structure sources are assigned to both.

In many cases, a <u>there is...</u> paraphrase of the non-specific reading of a sentence is far from natural. Although (115) is a reasonable paraphrase of the non-specific reading of (122), the paraphrase:

(128)   John wants there to be a fish that he catches/will catch.

for the non-specific reading of:

(129)   John wants to catch a fish.

is far from elegant. There are, however, acceptable sentences with <u>there is...</u> in the complement of <u>want</u>, for example:

(130)   John wants there to be a fish in the pool.

and it may be only that tenses and modalities make for awkwardness in infinitival complement constructions.

What is important is that there are some verbs

353

which cannot have there is... in their complements at all.
Noun phrases in the complements of these verbs are nevertheless ambiguous with respect to specificity. In these cases,
therefore, there is no there is... paraphrase for the
non-specific reading. For example, the sentence:

(131) John forced Mary to say something.

is ambiguous with respect to the specificity of something.
Either there was something in particular that John forced
Mary to say, or else John just forced Mary to say something
or other, to break her silence. The specific reading can be
paraphrased as:

(132) There is something that John forced Mary to say.

but there is no acceptable paraphrase with there is...
for the non-specific reading, thus:

(133) *John forced Mary that there was something that she
said/say/should say.

(134) *John forced Mary into there being something that she
said.

This is not peculiar to the verb force, but is true of a
number of other verbs too, for example the verb try. The
sentence:

(135) John was trying to catch a fish.

is ambiguous. It can be taken to mean that John's efforts
were directed towards the capture of some particular fish, in
which case it can be paraphrased as:

354

(136) There was a fish that John was trying to catch.
But (135) can also be taken to mean simply that John was
endeavouring not to go home fishless, and for this (non-
specific) reading, there is no paraphrase with there is....
(137) *John was trying that there was a fish that he caught/
catch/should catch.

The absence of a surface structure with there is...
corresponding to the non-specific reading of the ambiguous
sentence does not, of course, automatically prove that
there is no deep structure source for this reading. There
might, after all, be a deep structure of the appropriate
kind but no there is... surface structure derivable from
it because of facts about the distribution of complementizers,
or the selective operation of certain transformations. However, there is already available a different but quite adequate
explanation to the ungrammaticality of (133), (134) and (137),
an explanation which does lead to the conclusion that there
are no deep structures of the kind that would underlie these
ungrammatical strings. The complement of the verb force
must have, in deep structure, a subject noun phrase
identical to the direct object of the verb force, and the
verb of the complement must be non-stative. The complement
of the verb try must have, in deep structure, a subject
identical to the subject of try, and the verb of the
complement must be non-stative. It is no wonder, then, that
the complements of these verbs cannot be there is...

355

constructions. The underlying subject of a <u>there is...</u>
construction is a noun phrase containing a relative clause,
and its main verb is the verb <u>to be</u>. The deep structures:

(138)   John forced Mary $_S[$ $_{NP}[$something $_S[$Mary say something$]]$
$_{VP}[$is$]]$.

(139)   John was trying $_S[$ $_{NP}[$a fish $_S[$John catch a fish$]]$
$_{VP}[$is$]]$.

would be ruled out by the constraints on the complements
of <u>force</u> and <u>try</u>.

I am assuming here that these constraints come into
force before the application of transformations. If this
is so, then the hypothesis that ambiguous examples are to
be derived from the same structures as underlie the
corresponding unambiguous sentences with <u>there is...</u>
must be rejected, for there will be no deep structure
source for the non-specific reading of sentences like (131)
and (135). If generated at all, these deep structures will
be filtered out by the selection constraints before the
quantifier lowering transformation that deletes the verb
<u>to be</u> is applied. Thus although all unambiguous
examples have deep structure sources from which their readings
can be predicted, the ambiguous examples cannot be assumed
to have a number of distinct deep structure sources which
predict their full range of possible readings, for then

it would be impossible to explain the existence of a non-specific reading of a sentence for which there is no unambiguously non-specific paraphrase with <u>there is</u>....
Only a grammar in which the selection constraints on verbs like <u>force</u> and <u>try</u> to operate <u>after</u> the quantifier lowering transformation would be able to account for these facts, that is, a grammar in which the selection constraints operate within the transformational cycle, or at some post-cyclic level. Unless this assumption about ordering is made, it must be concluded that sentence (122), for example, cannot be derived from a structure like (117) or (119). There would then be no advantage to providing it with a derivation from a structure like (116) either. Unless, therefore, there is some syntactic motivation for providing it with two distinct deep structures of a <u>different</u> kind, i.e. identifying the specificity operator with some element in deep structure <u>other</u> than the <u>is</u> of <u>there is</u>, it must be assumed that (122) has a single deep structure source (presumably roughly along the lines of Rosenbaum's analysis in The Grammar of English Predicate Complement Constructions, 1967), and that its two readings are distinguished only in the semantic component.

The conclusion that opaque and transparent readings of opaque constructions are not distinguished at the level of deep structure is in fact a welcome one, since the direct generation of structures in which the scope differences

357

concerned in opacity are explicitly marked is no simple matter. If, for example, the scope of a noun phrase which in surface structure is the object of the verb in a complement clause were marked, for one reading of the sentence, by letting this noun phrase appear in the matrix clause in the underlying structure, then the statement of selection restrictions over these structures would be extremely complex. For example, the range of noun phrases that can appear in the context:

(140)   John wants to catch _____.

is determined by the verb <u>catch</u>, that is, by the verb of which the noun phrase is a direct object. If, however, the specific reading of a sentence such as:

(141)   John wants to catch a fish.

is supposed to be represented in some such fashion as:

(142)   (A fish)$_x$ John wants to catch x.

in order to indicate the scope of this noun phrase, then the indexing system must be invoked in order to determine which noun phrase is the direct object of the verb <u>catch</u>, and to ensure that the selection restrictions between the verb and its object are not violated. Since there is in principle no limit to the number of complement clauses that may be embedded within each other, the noun phrase may be indefinitely far away from its verb in the underlying structure.

Furthermore, it is clear that structures such as:

(143)   (A fish)$_x$ (a tiger)$_y$ John wants to catch x.

358

(144)   (A fish)$_x$ John wants to catch y.

(145)   (A fish)$_x$ John wants to go home.

and perhaps also:

(146)   (A fish)$_x$ John wants y to catch x.

correspond to no possible surface structures. There must be
no more and no less of these re-positioned constituents than
there are positions that they could fill. This point holds
also for semantic representations which employ not representations of the constituents themselves, but operators
binding these constituents, in order to mark the semantic
relationships. The statement of strict subcategorization and
selectional constraints for structures of this kind will
clearly be considerably more complex than for structures
such as Rosenbaum, for example, proposed as the deep structures
for complement constructions and in which the scope relationships relevant to opacity are not marked. If, for these reasons,
it is structures of the latter kind which are directly
generated by the base component, then the proper set of well-
formed structures containing scope markings can be derived
from these base structures by rules of transformational power
in the semantic component.

BIBLIOGRAPHY

Anderson, Stephen R., "On What There Is." Forthcoming.

Bach, Emmon, "Nouns and Noun Phrases." In Bach, Emmon, and
Harms, Robert (eds.), Universals in Linguistic Theory,
1968.

Baker, C. Leroy, "Definiteness and Indefiniteness in English."
Unpublished M.A. thesis, University of Illinois, 1966.

Chomsky, Noam, Aspects of the Theory of Syntax, M.I.T. Press,
1965.

Davidson, Donald, "On Saying That." Synthese 19, 1968-69,
pp. 130-146.

Dean, Janet P., "Nonspecific Noun Phrases in English." In
Harvard Computation Center Report No. 18, 1968.

Donnellan, Keith S., "Reference and Definite Descriptions."
Phil. Review, Vol. 75, 1966, pp. 281-304.

Geach, P.T., "On Intentional Identity." J. of Phil., Vol. LXIV,
No. 20, 1967, pp. 627-632.

Hintikka, Jaakko, Knowledge and Belief, Cornell Univ. Press,
1962.

Hughes, G. E. and Cresswell, M. J., An Introduction to Modal
Logic, Methuen, 1968.

Katz, Jerrold J. and Fodor, Jerry A., "The Structure of a
Semantic Theory." In Fodor and Katz (eds.), The
Structure of Language, Prentice-Hall, 1964.

Klima, Edward S., "Negation in English." In Fodor and Katz
(eds.), The Structure of Language, Prentice-Hall, 1964.

Lakoff, George, "Counterparts, or The Problem of Reference in
Transformational Grammar." Unpublished paper presented
at summer meeting of L.S.A., Illinois, 1968.

Lakoff, George, "On Derivational Constraints." In Papers from
the Fifth Regional Meeting, Chicago Linguistic Society,
1969.

Linsky, Leonard, "Reference and Referents." In Caton, Charles
E. (ed.), Philosophy and Ordinary Language, Univ. of
Illinois Press, 1963.

Linsky, Leonard, _Referring_, Humanities Press, 1967.

Postal, Paul M., "Restrictive Relatives and Other Matters..." Unpublished mimeograph, 1967.

Quine, Willard van Orman, "Quantifiers and Propositional Attitudes." _J. of Phil._, Vol. LIIJ, No. 5, March 1956.

Quine, Willard van Orman, _Word and Object_, M.I.T. Press, 1960.

Rosenbaum, Peter S., _The Grammar of English Predicate Complement Constructions_, M.I.T. Press, 1967.

Ross, John Robert, "Auxiliaries as Main Verbs." In Todd, William (ed.), _Studies in Philosophical Linguistics_, Series I, Great Expectations Press, Illinois, 1968.

Ross, John Robert, "A Note on _Have Deletion_." Unpublished mimeograph, 1969.

Russell, Bertrand, "On Denoting." _Mind_, Vol. 14, 1905, pp. 479-493.

Strawson, P. F., "On Referring." _Mind_, Vol. LIX, 1950, pp. 320-344. Also in Caton, Charles E. (ed.), _Philosophy and Ordinary Language_, Univ. of Illinois Press, 1963.

Strawson, P. F., _Introduction to Logical Theory_, Methuen, 1952.

CPSIA information can be obtained
at www.ICGtesting.com
Printed in the USA
JSHW011437221219
3113JS00001B/40